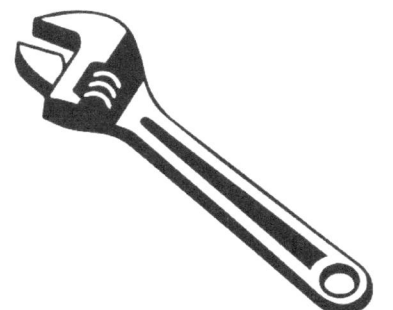
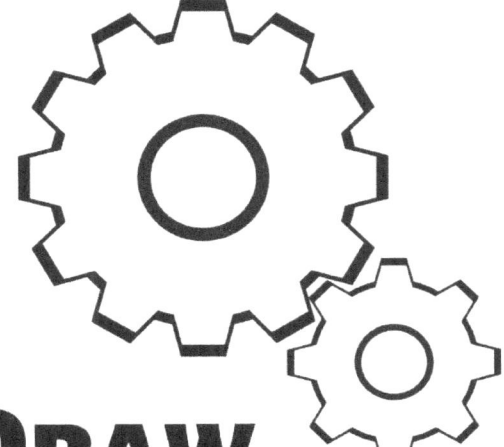

How to Draw Robots for Kids

Easy Step by Step Drawing Tutorial

Book 1

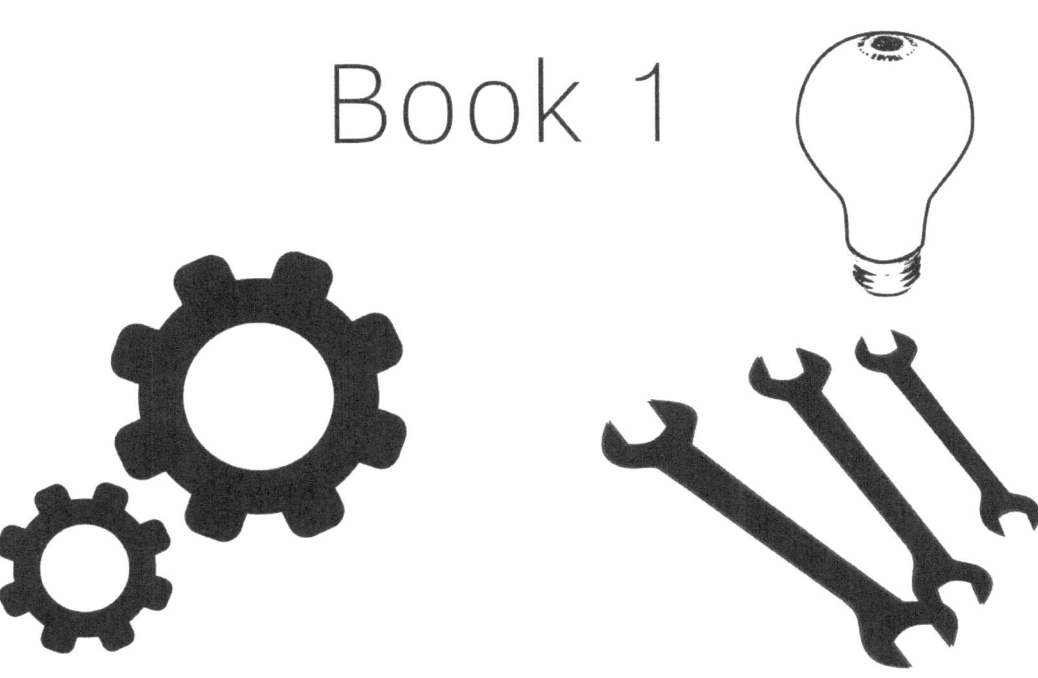

How to Draw Robots for Kids
Easy Step by Step Drawing Tutorial
Robby Bishop
ISBN-13: 979-8635542088

2020

How to Use a Book

Draw step-by-step, following the graphic instructions. Periodically look a few steps ahead to understand what exactly you are drawing now (which part of the character), and how it'll look in the finished version. If you didn't succeed the first time, don't be discouraged! Think about the mistakes you made and try drawing again. Even professional artists don't always manage to draw the drawings they have in mind the first time.

You Need

Blank sheet of paper. Even notebooks or journals will do.
A pencil. Make sure that you have many pencils.
Pencil sharpener. Pencils should always be sharpened to make good lines.
Good-quality eraser. The erasers on the pencil wear out very quickly, so use a separate rubber eraser.
Colored markers or pencils. You can trace the outline of your drawing with a thin felt-tip pen and then color in.

Drawing Tips for Newbies

Draw on different surfaces. Don't always use just plain A4 paper. Draw on notebook sheets, on the sidewalk, or in a small notebook. This will help you focus on what is important: when you have a small space for drawing, you need to develop imagination, and in order to fill a large space correctly, you should arrange everything so that it doesn't seem empty.

Periodically look at your drawing through a mirror. Thus, you can see your drawing as if with different eyes and notice the flaws. This tip helps a lot when painting portraits.

Use different materials: pencils of different thicknesses and hardness, pens (plain and helium), felt-tip pens, colored pencils, charcoal, and so on. This will help you get a feel for the peculiarities of working with this or that instrument. And choose your favorite.

Table of Contents

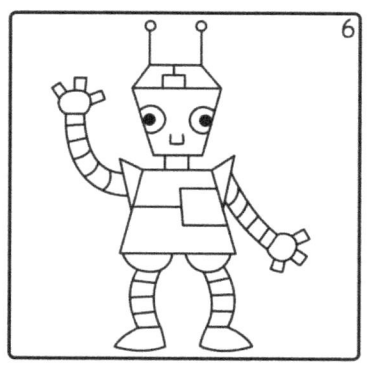 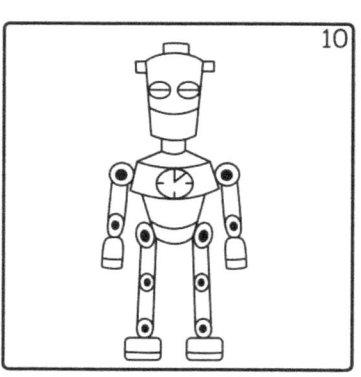 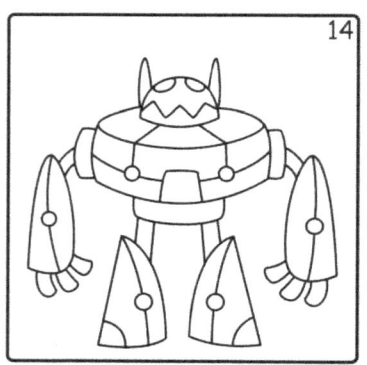
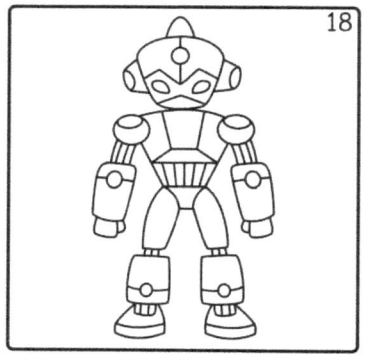 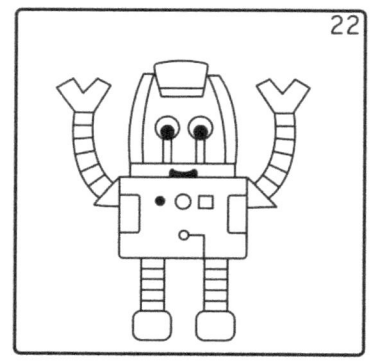 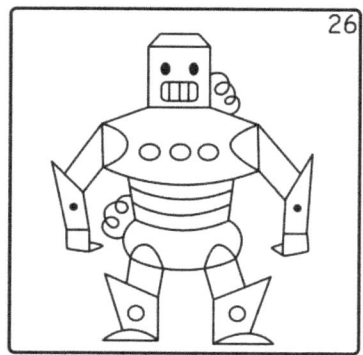
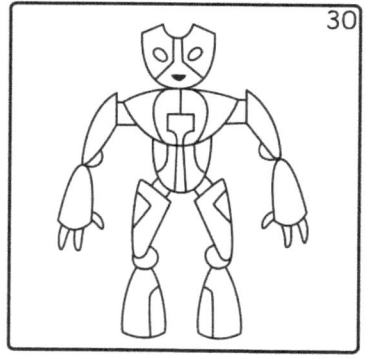 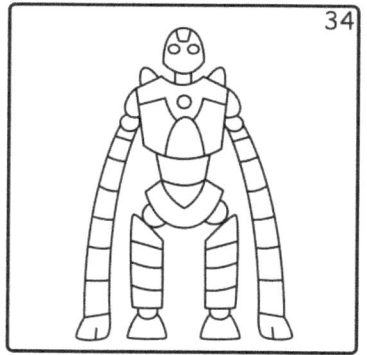 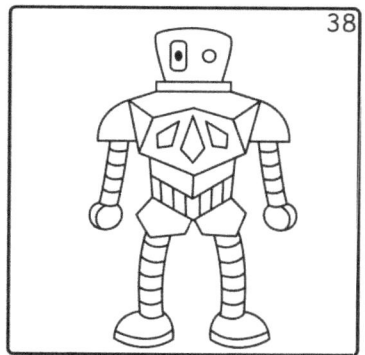
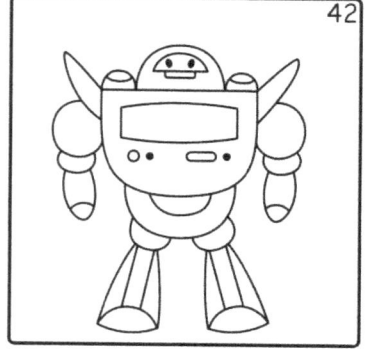 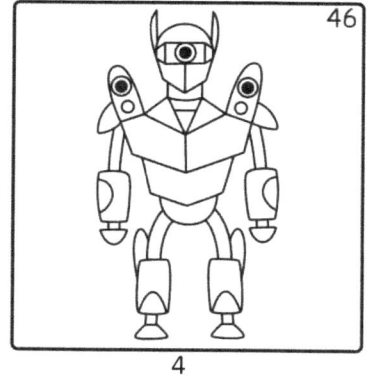 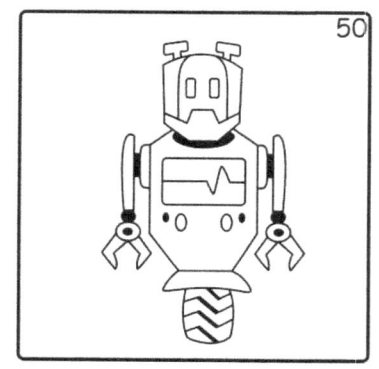

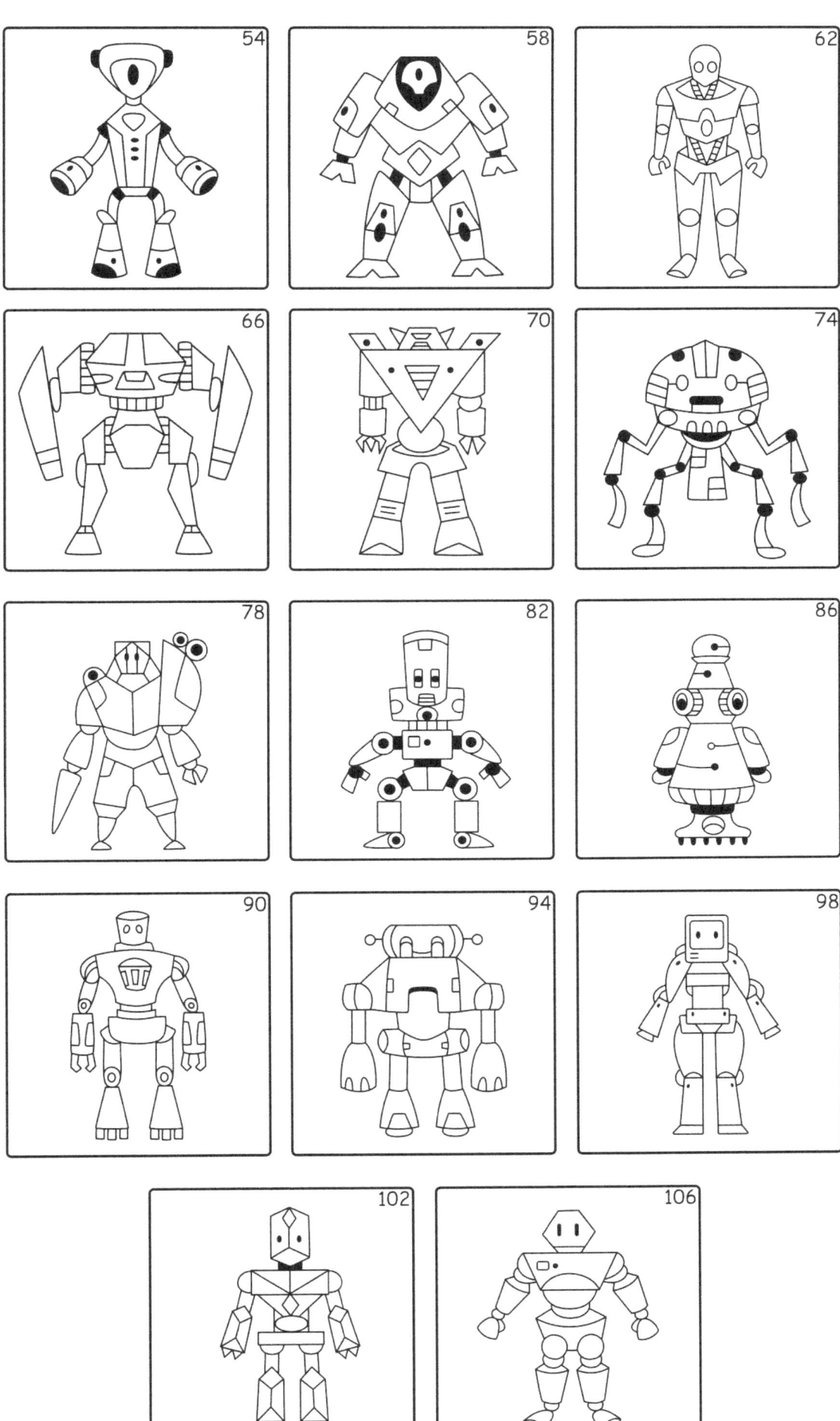

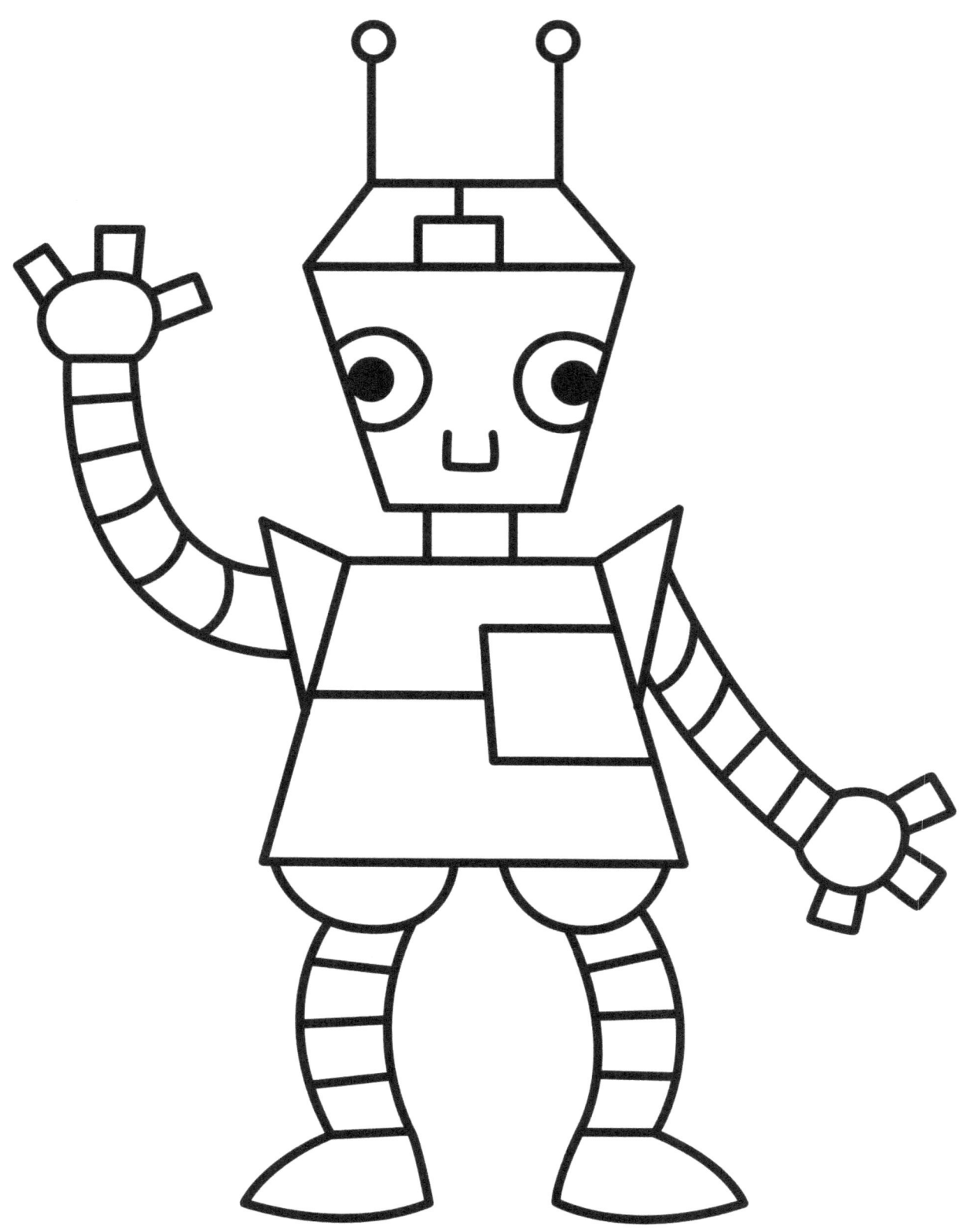

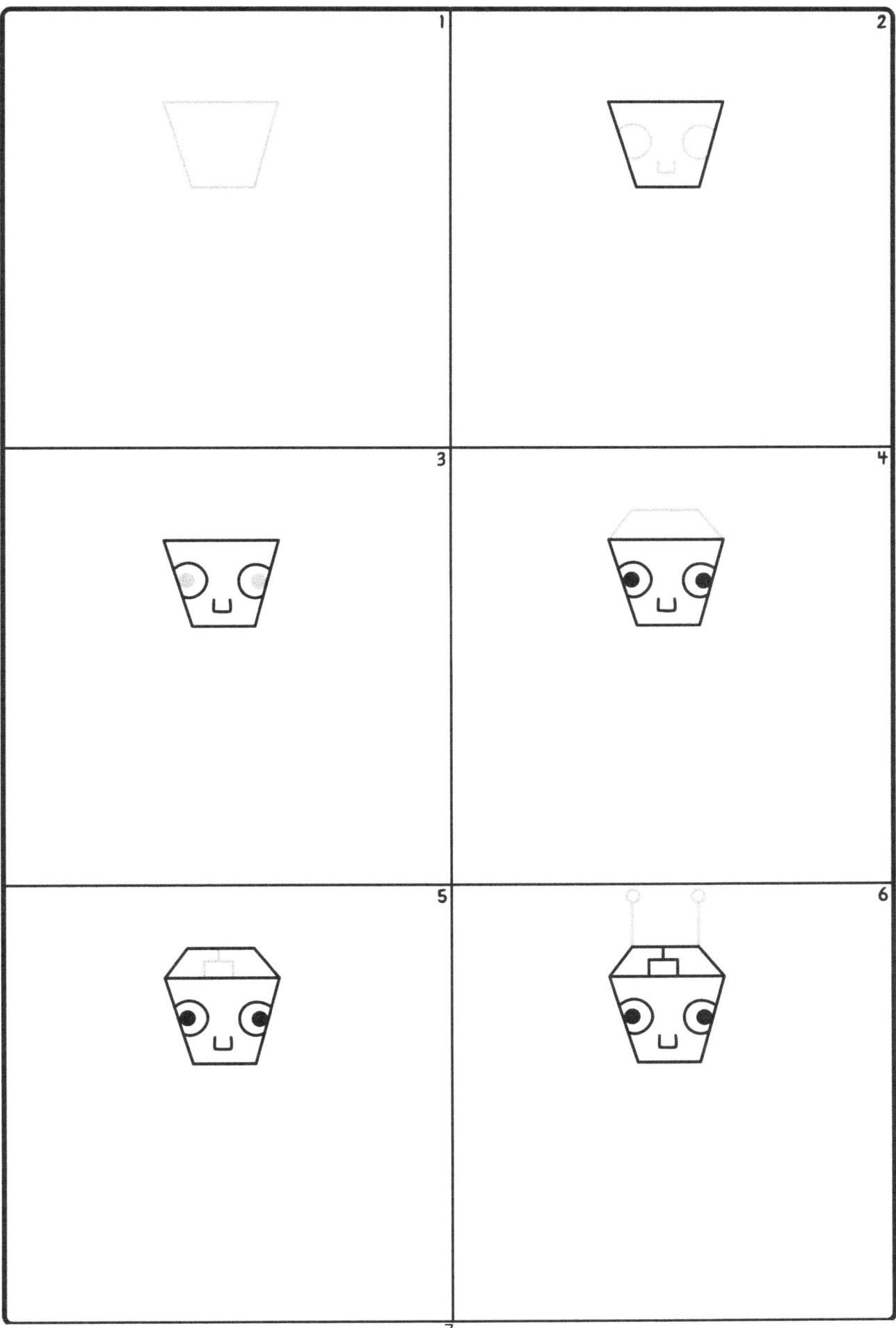

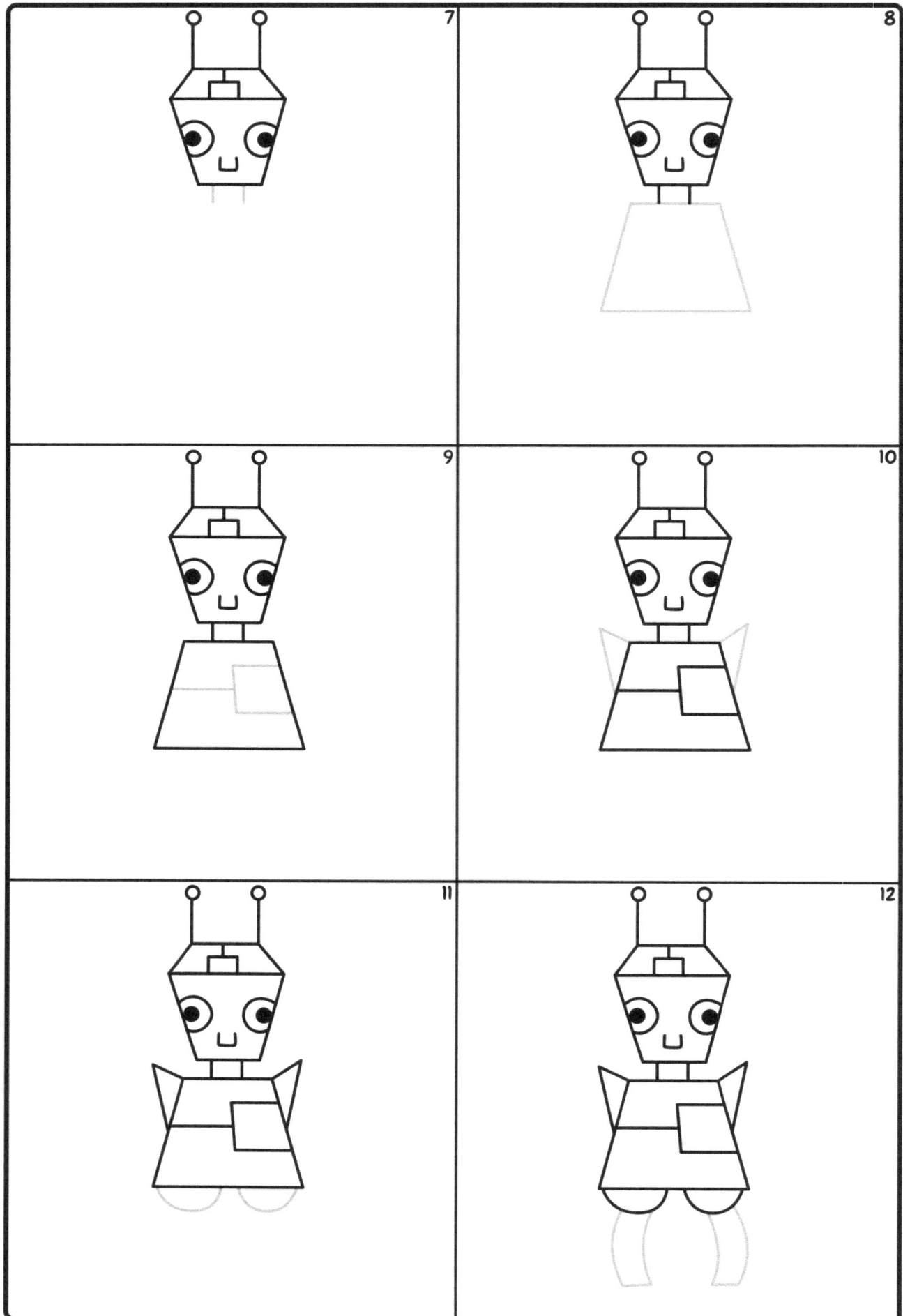

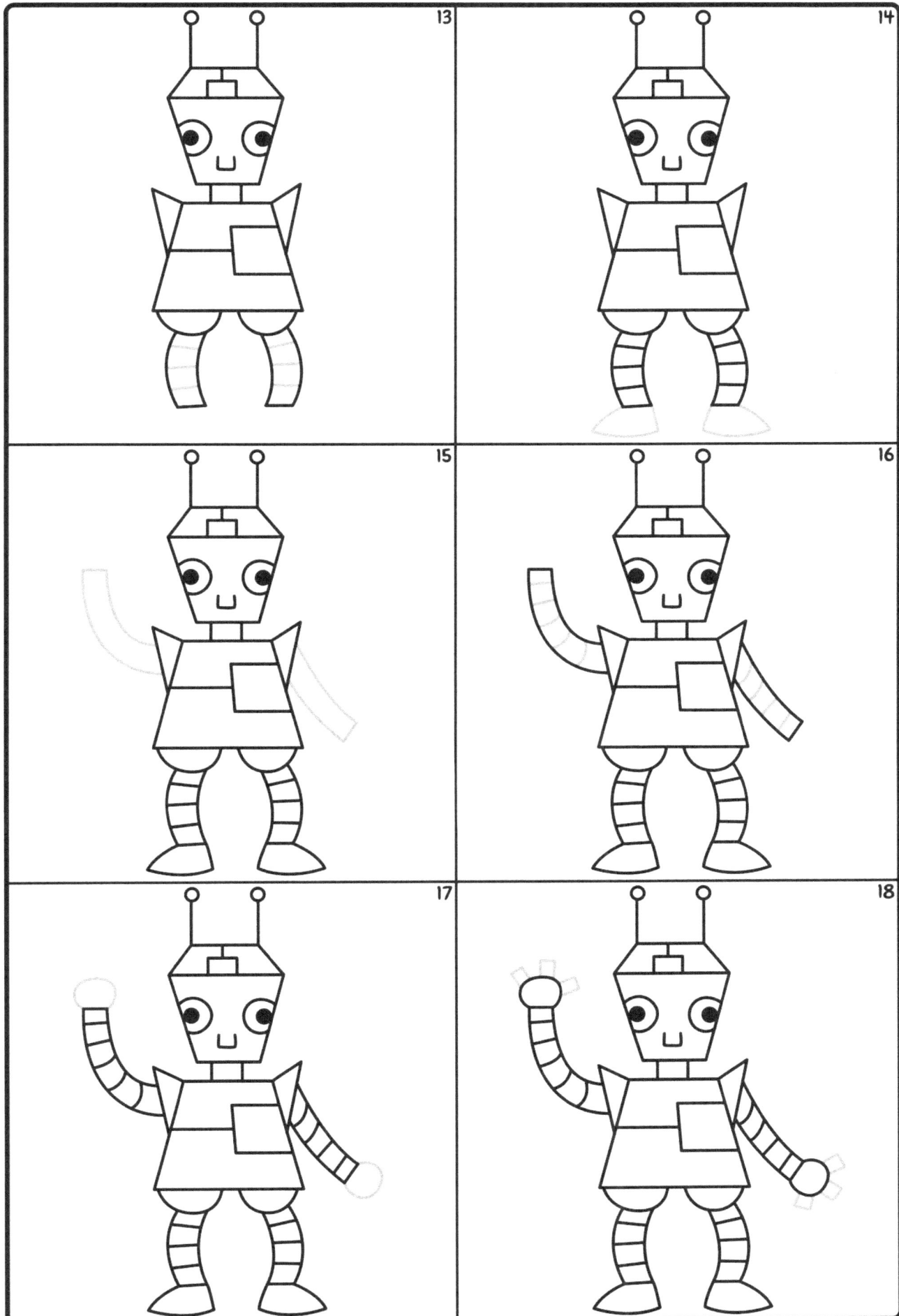

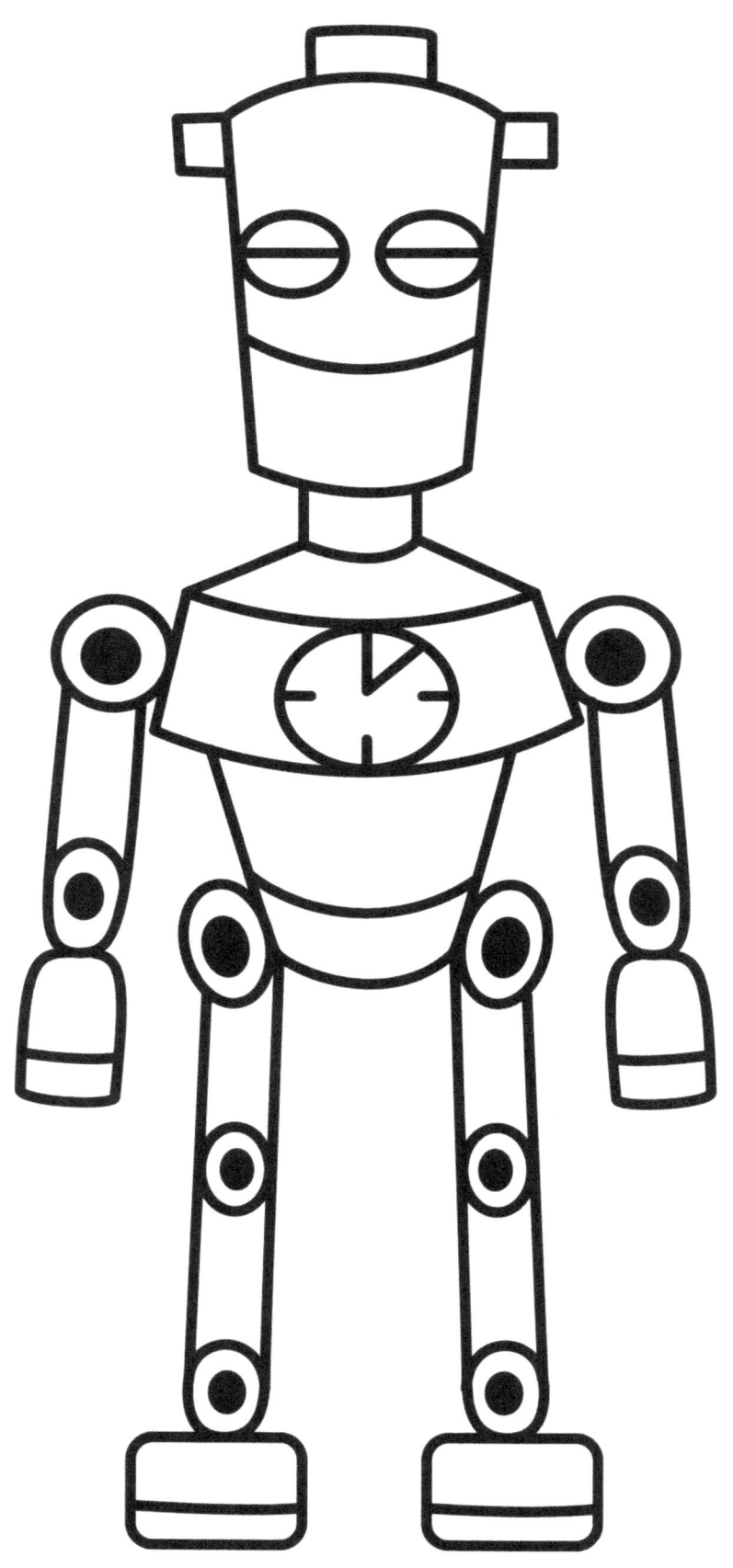

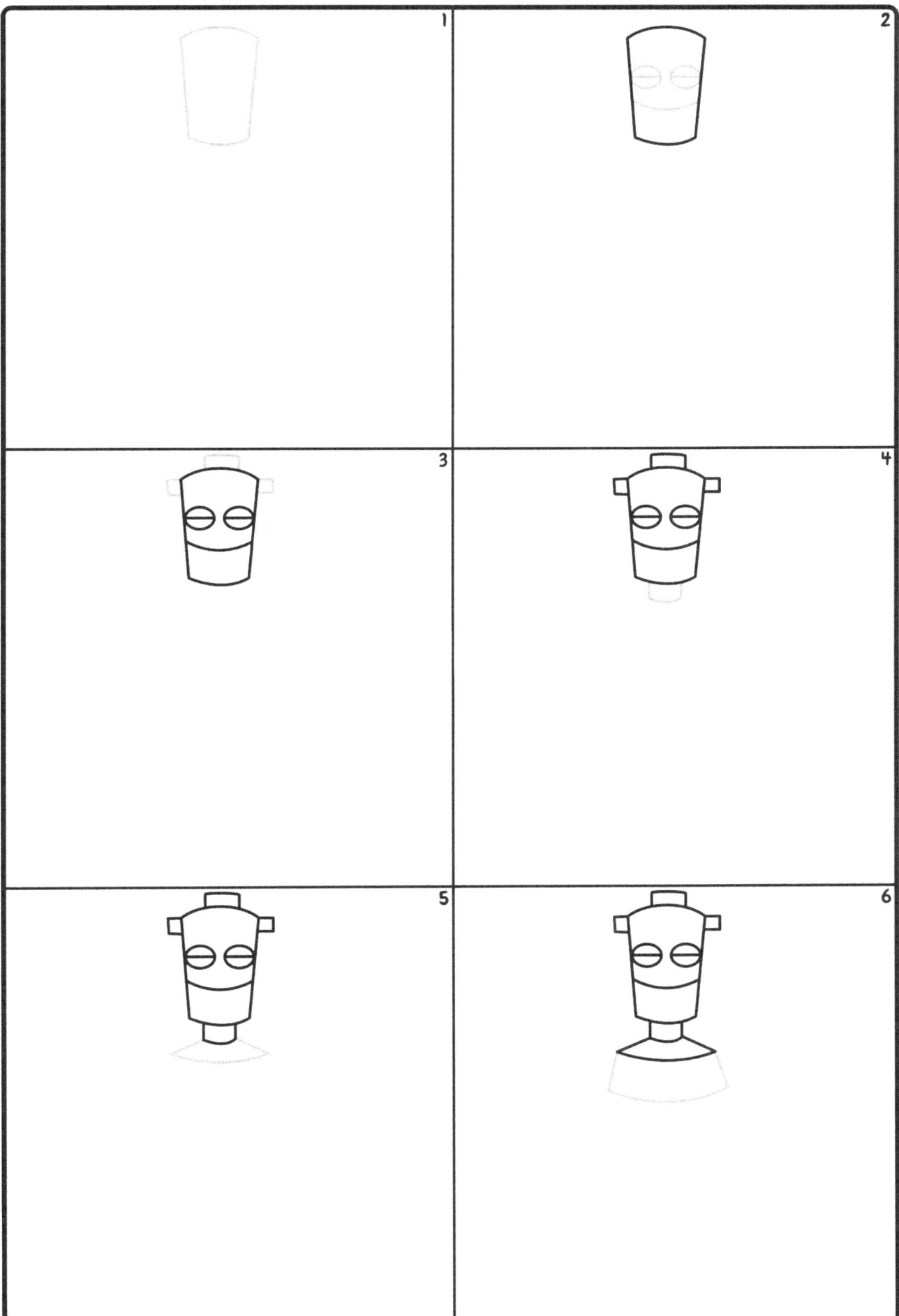

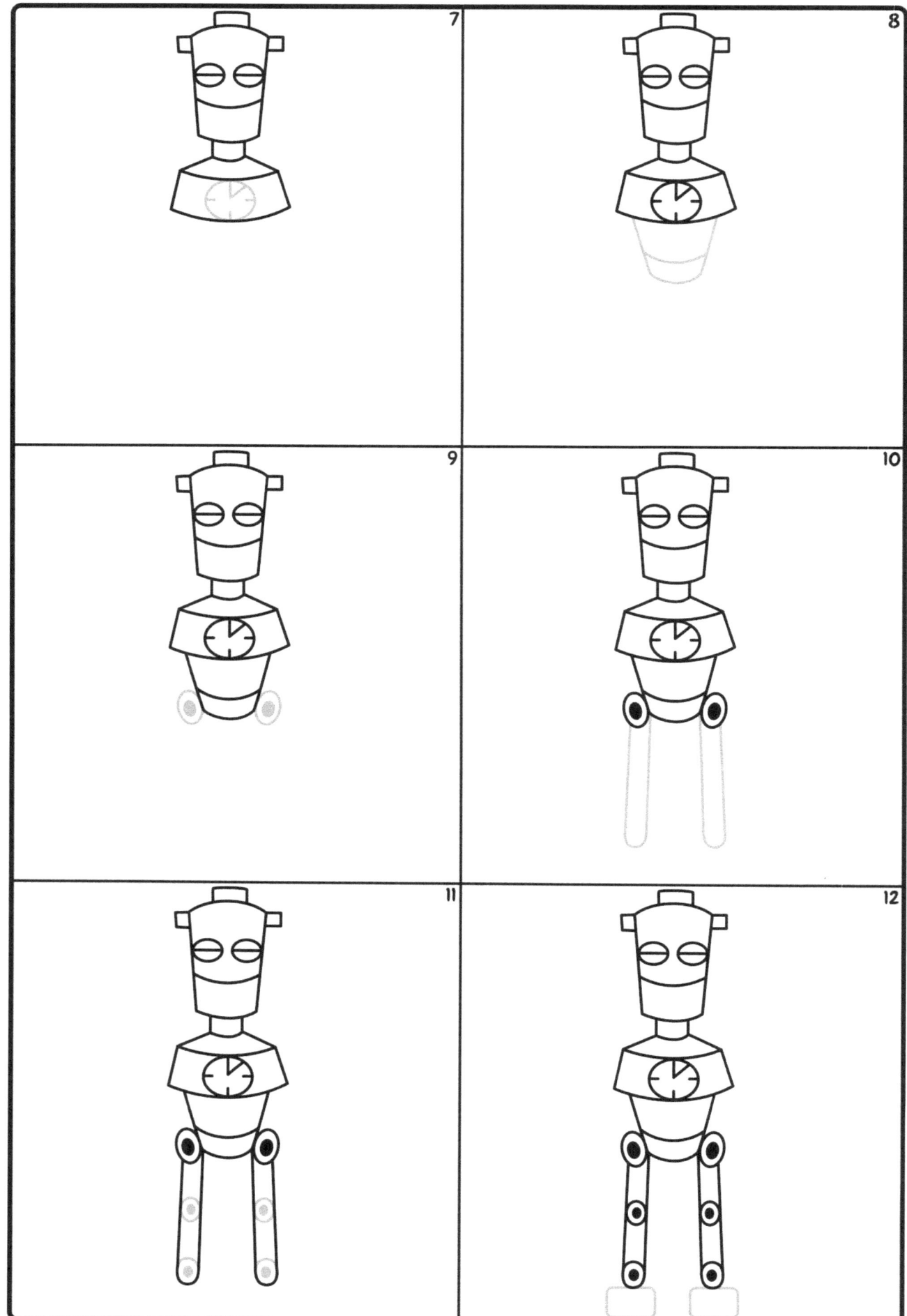

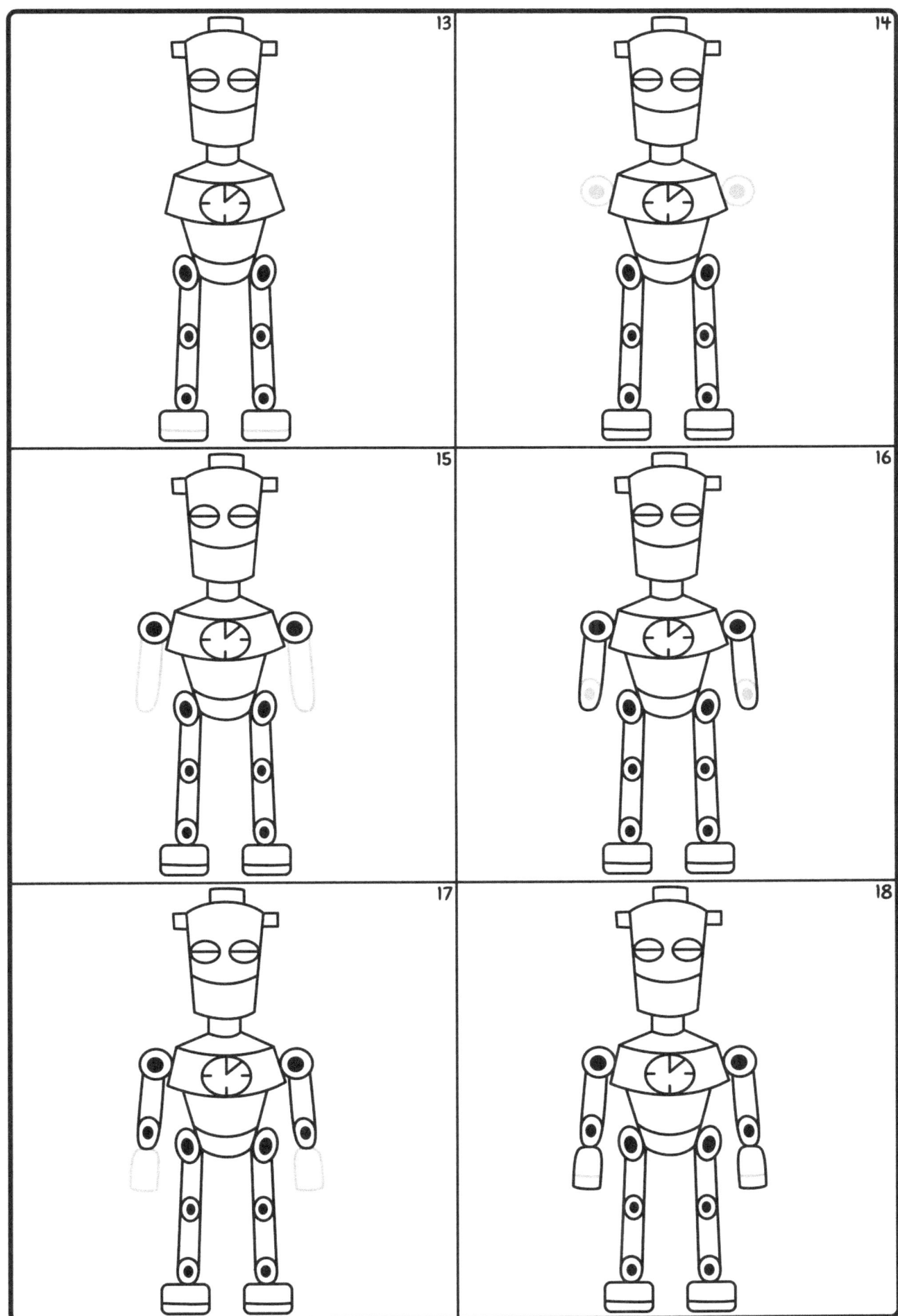

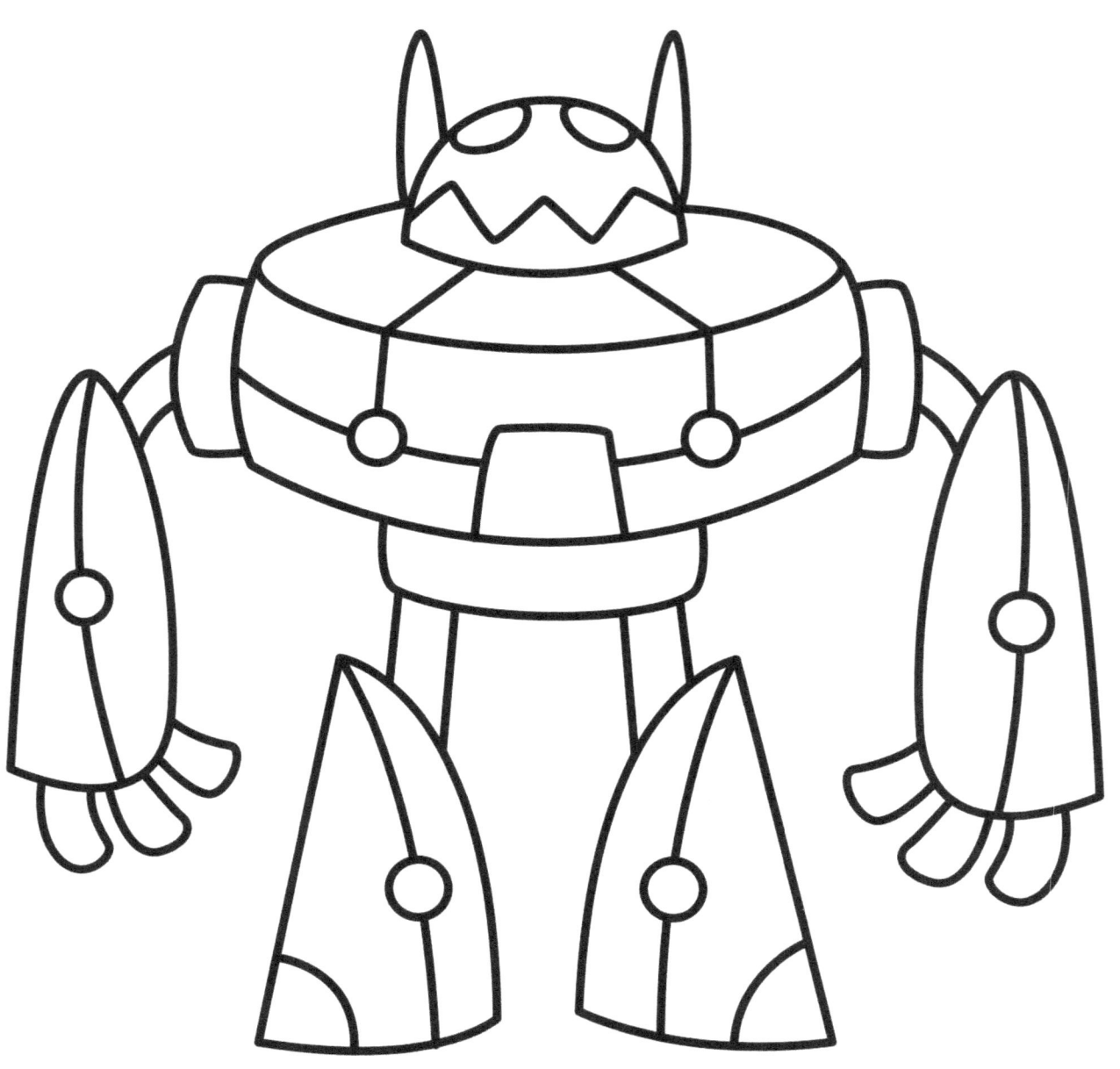

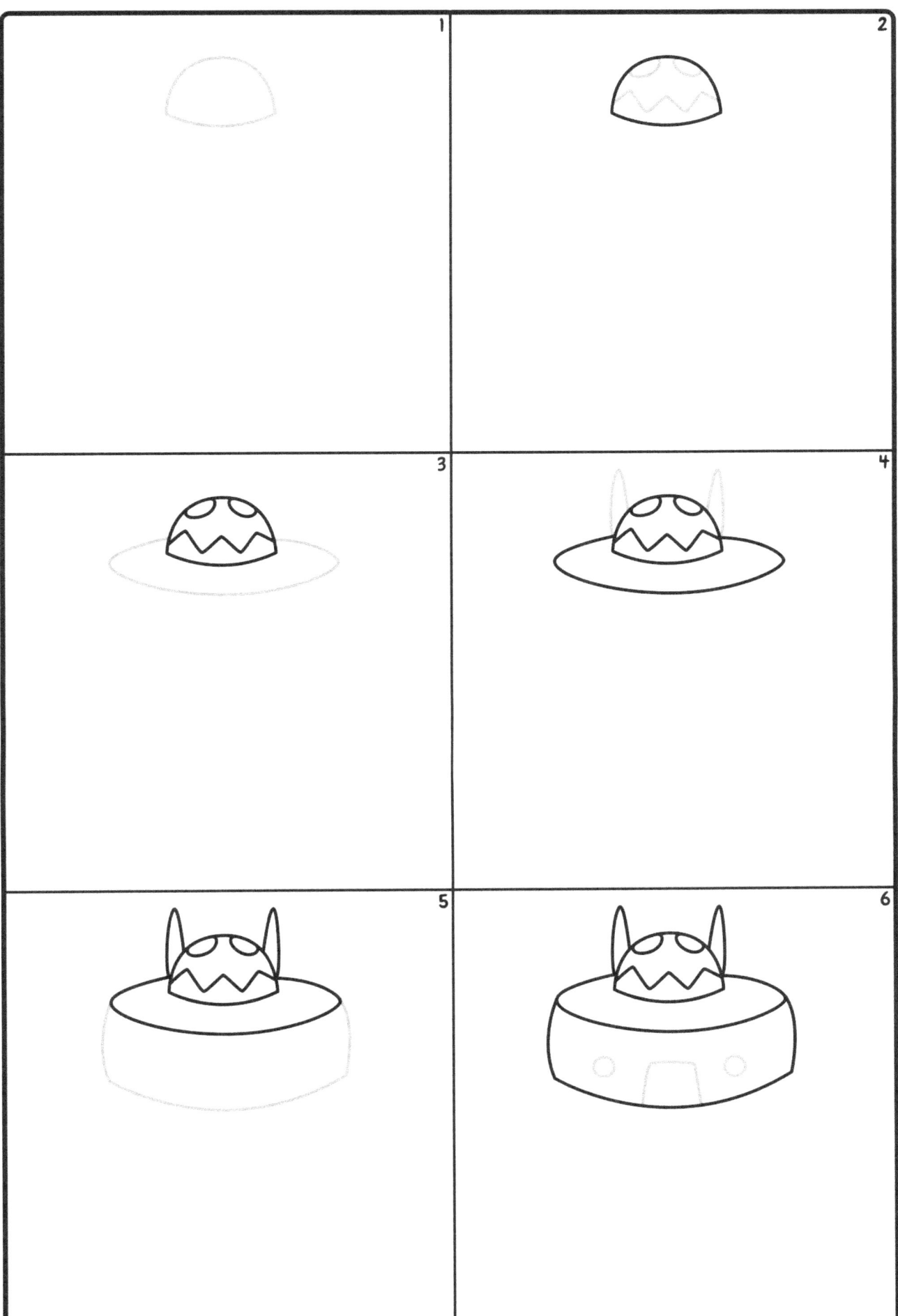

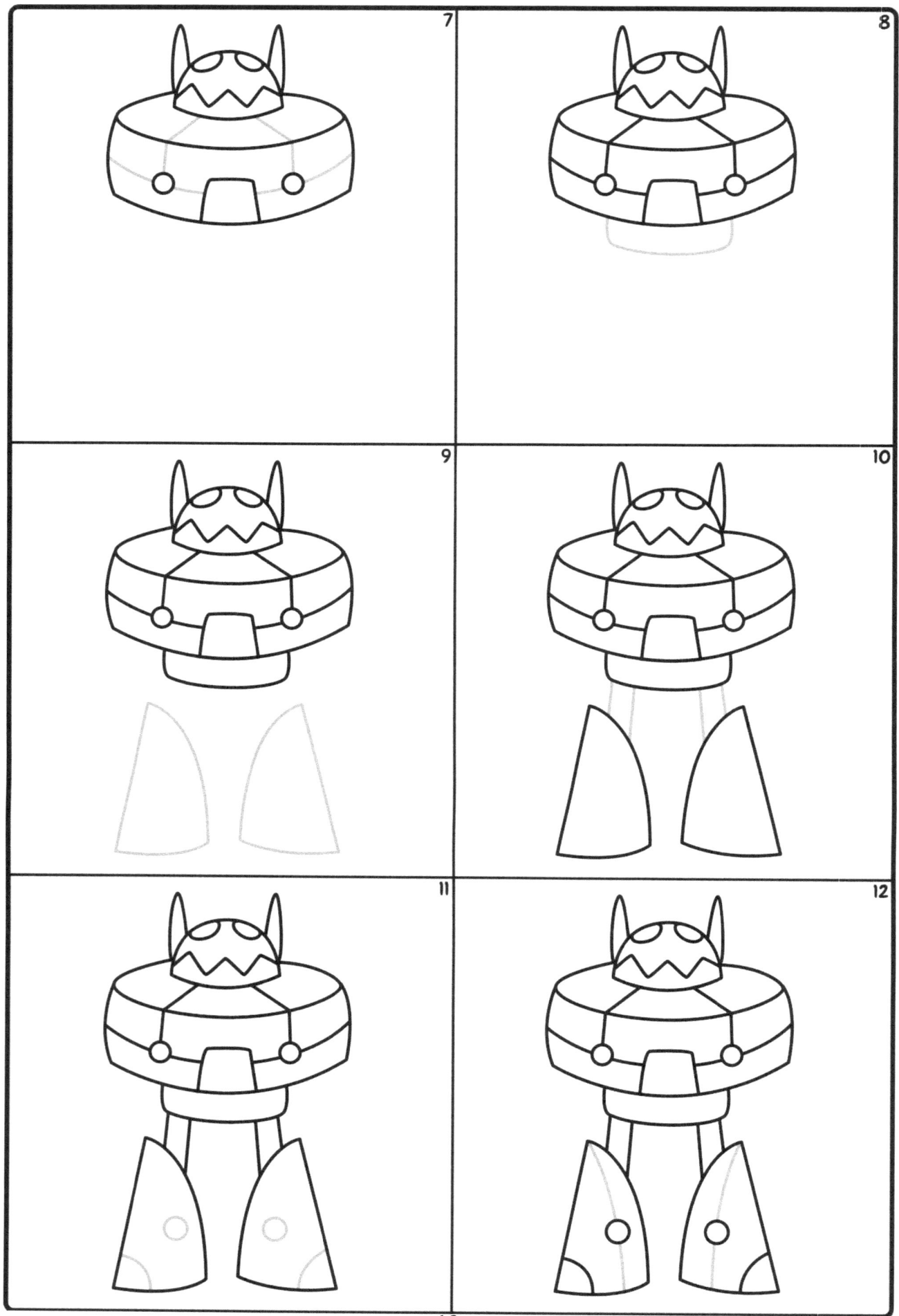

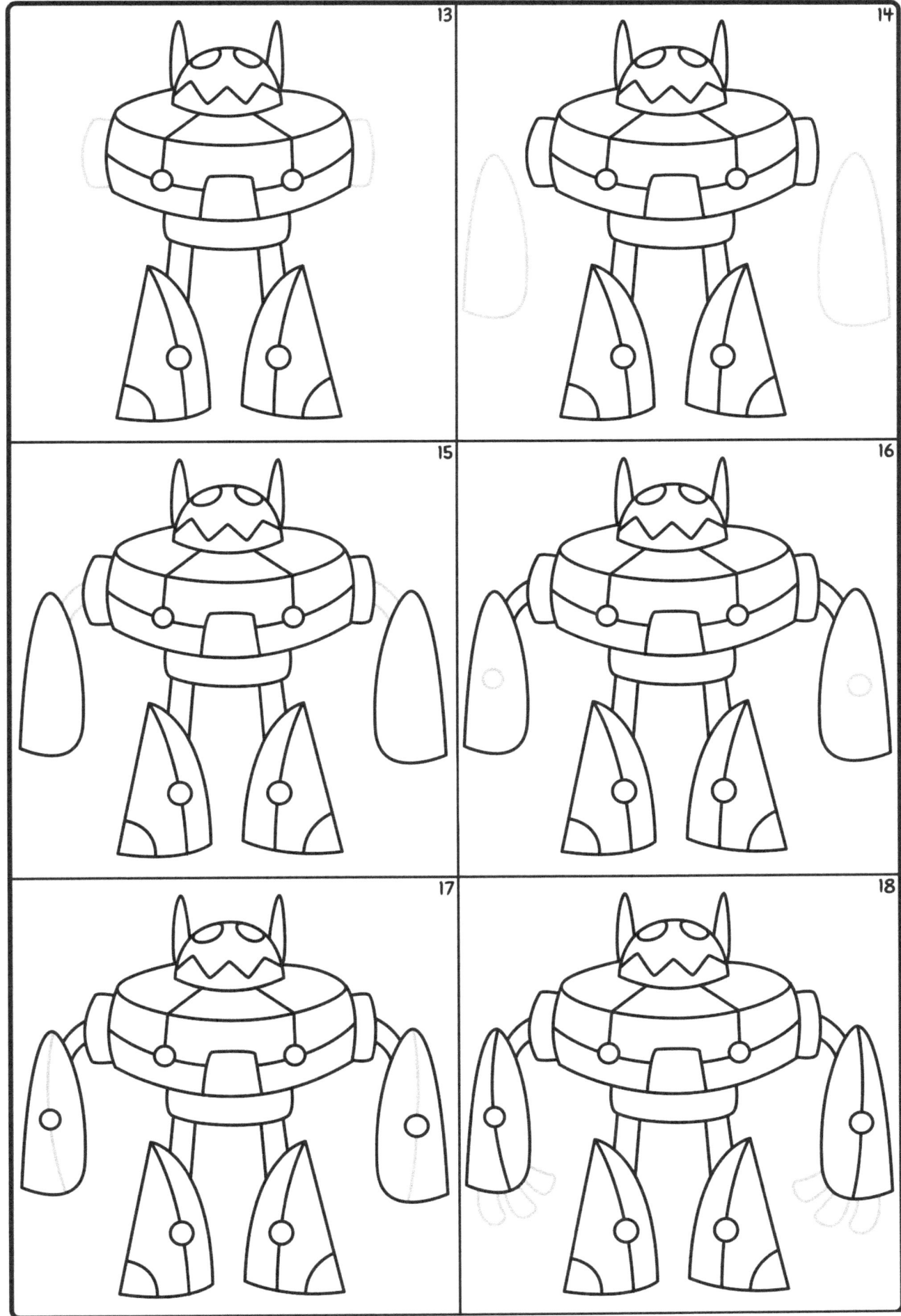

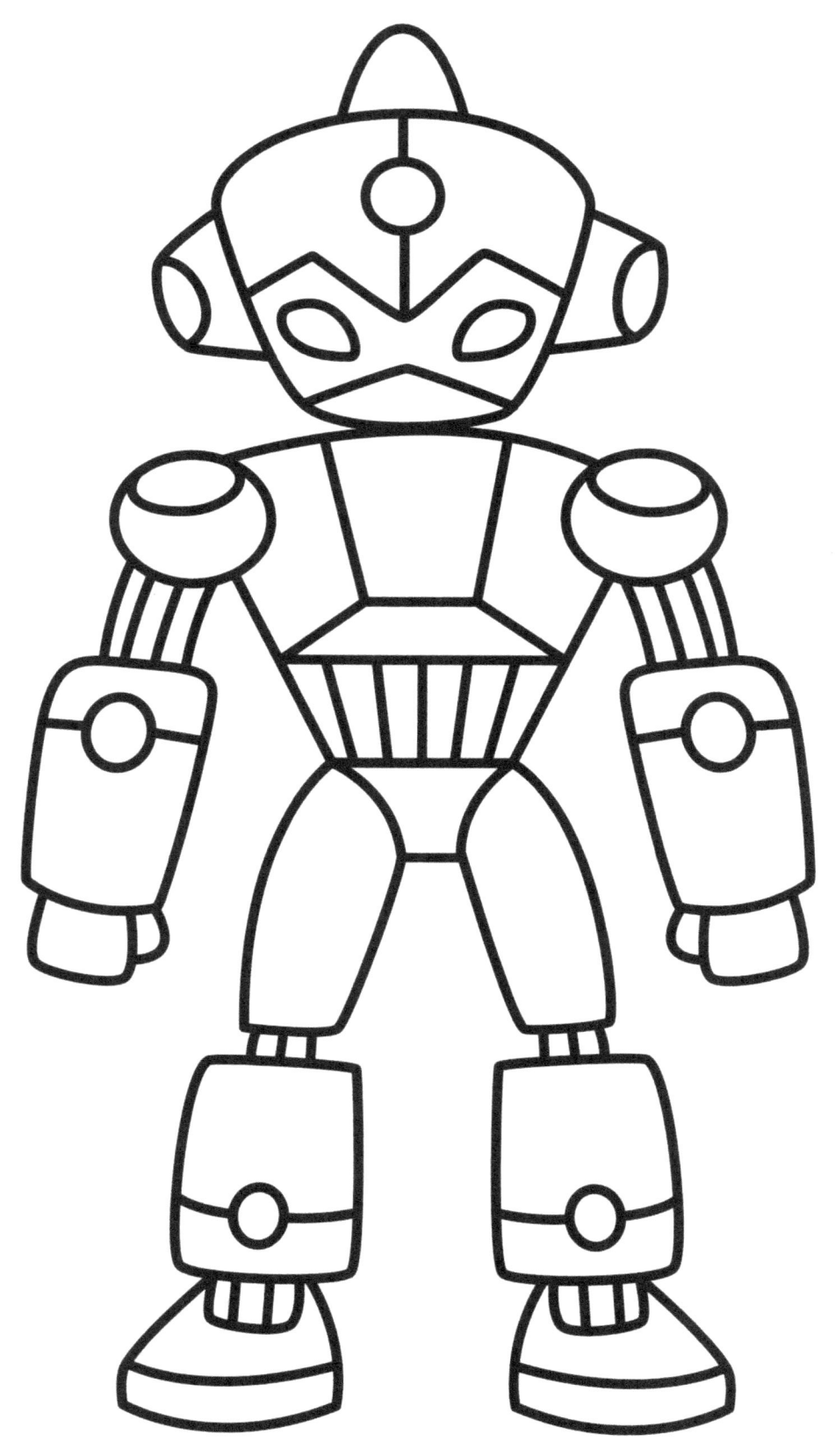

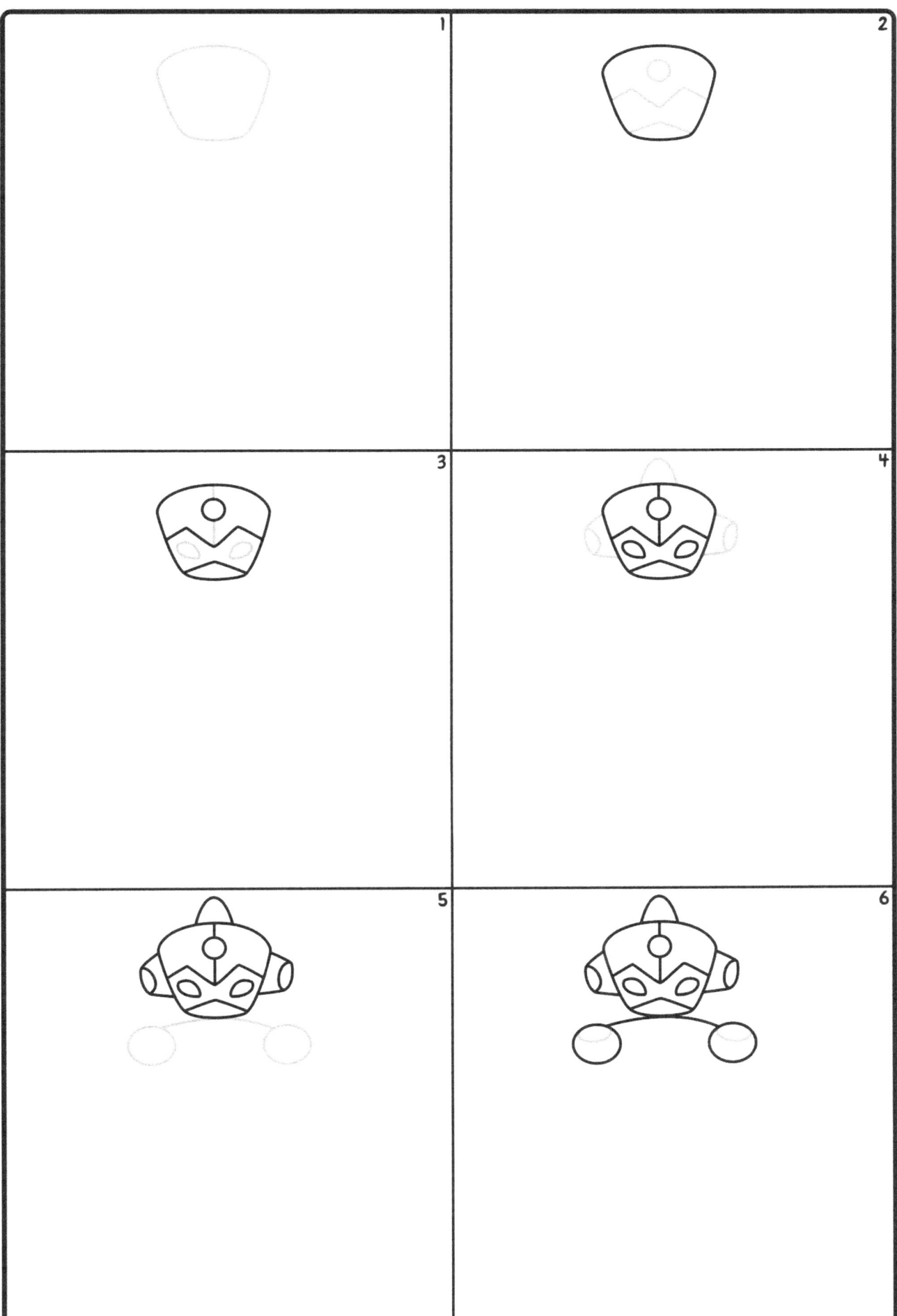

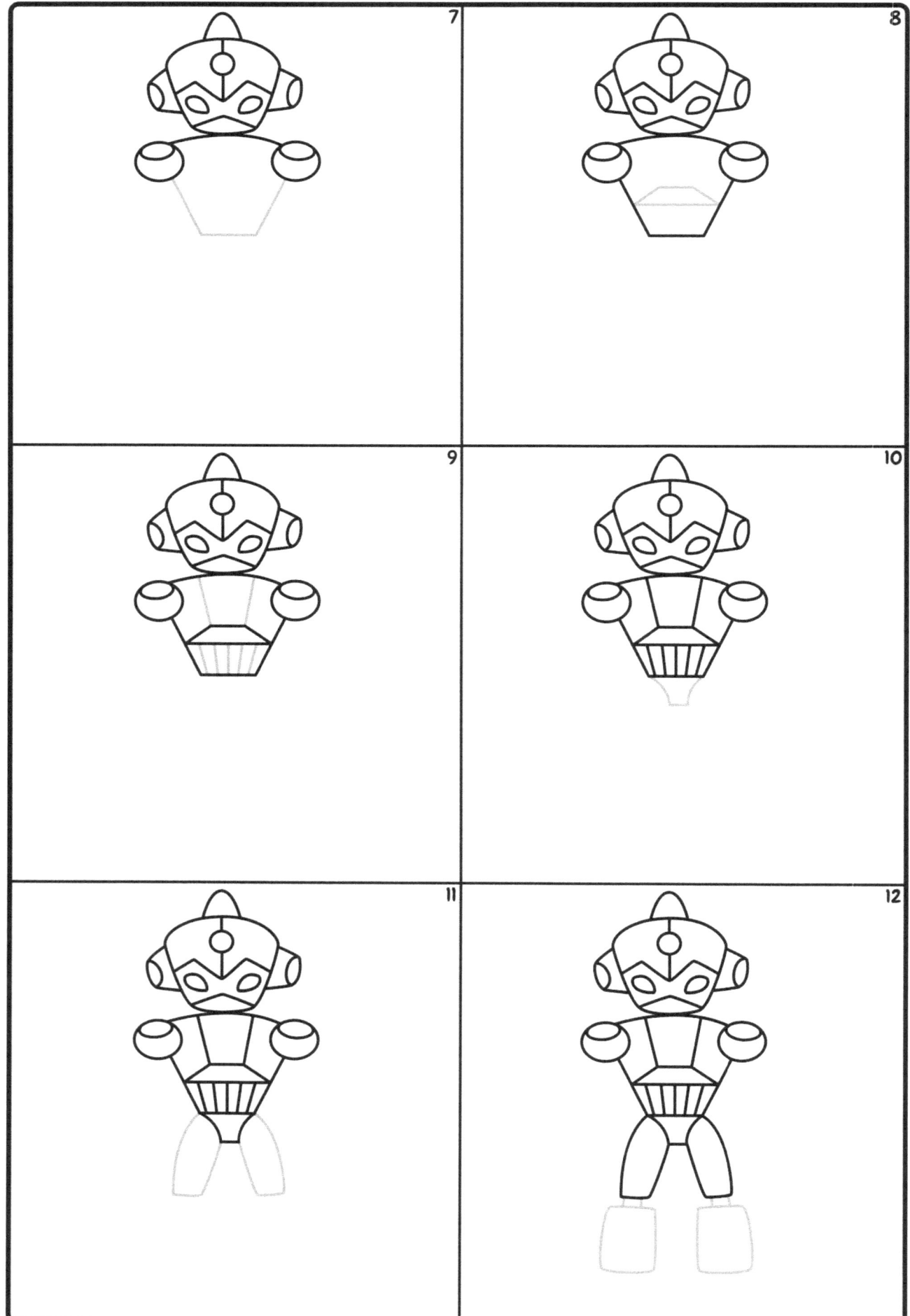

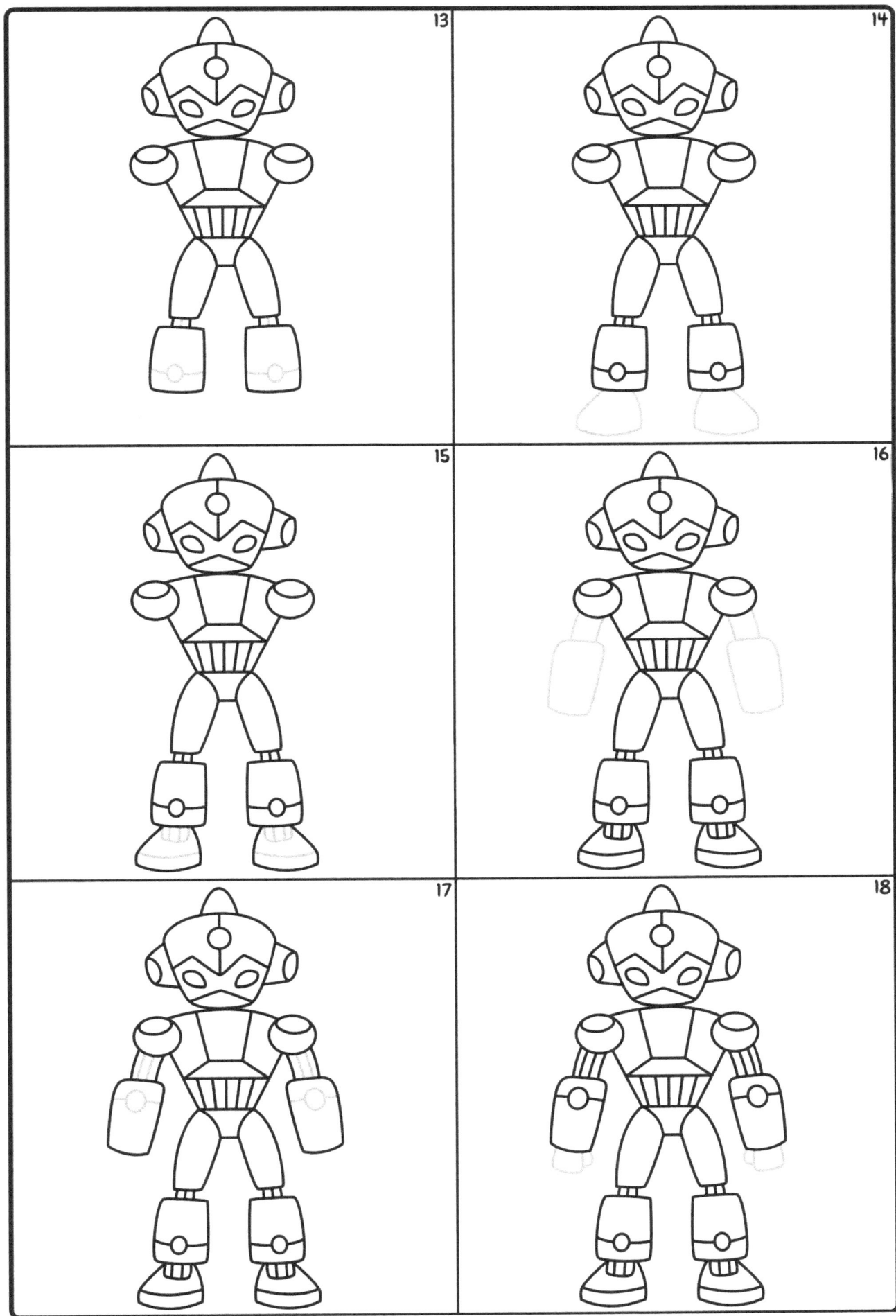

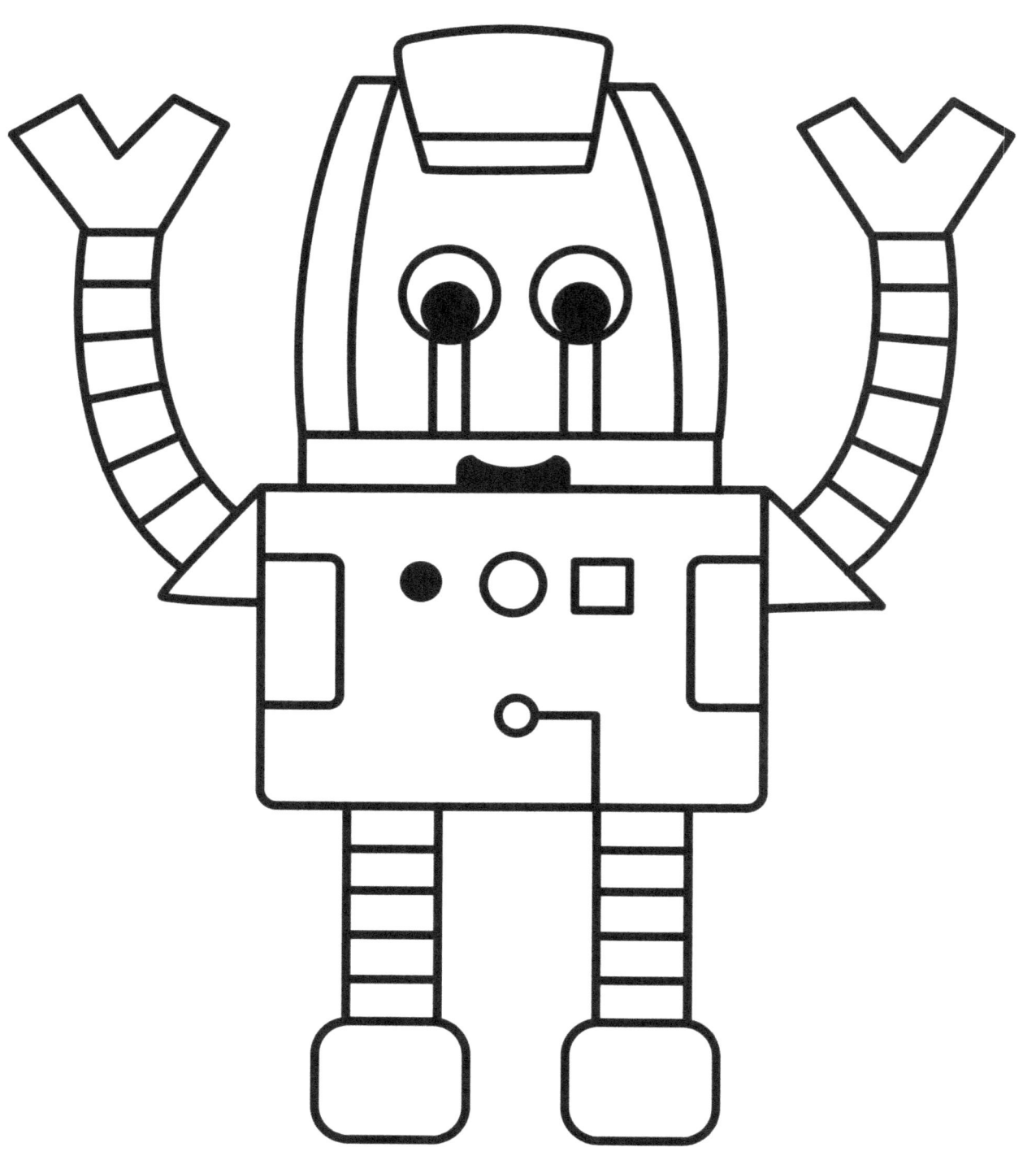

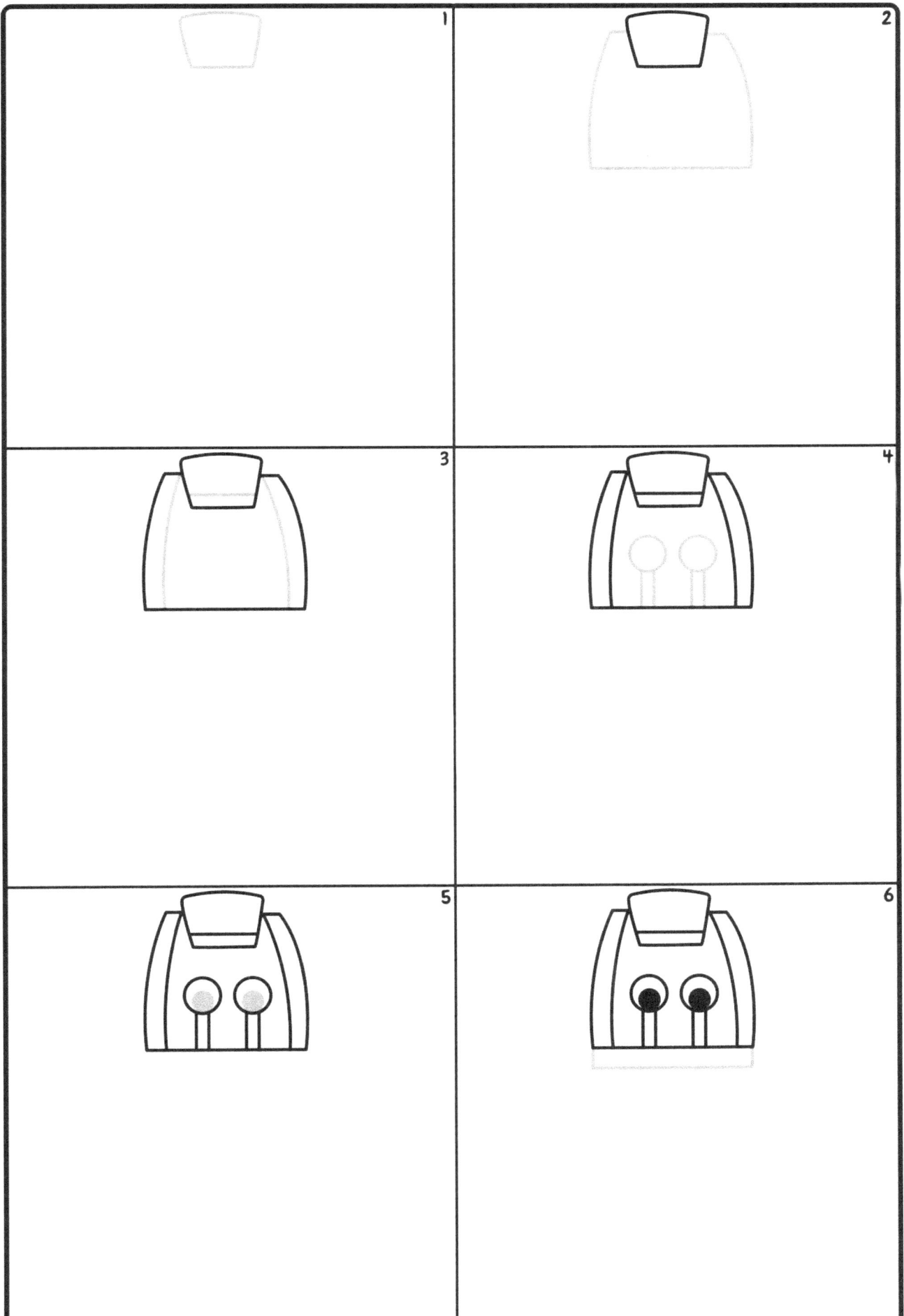

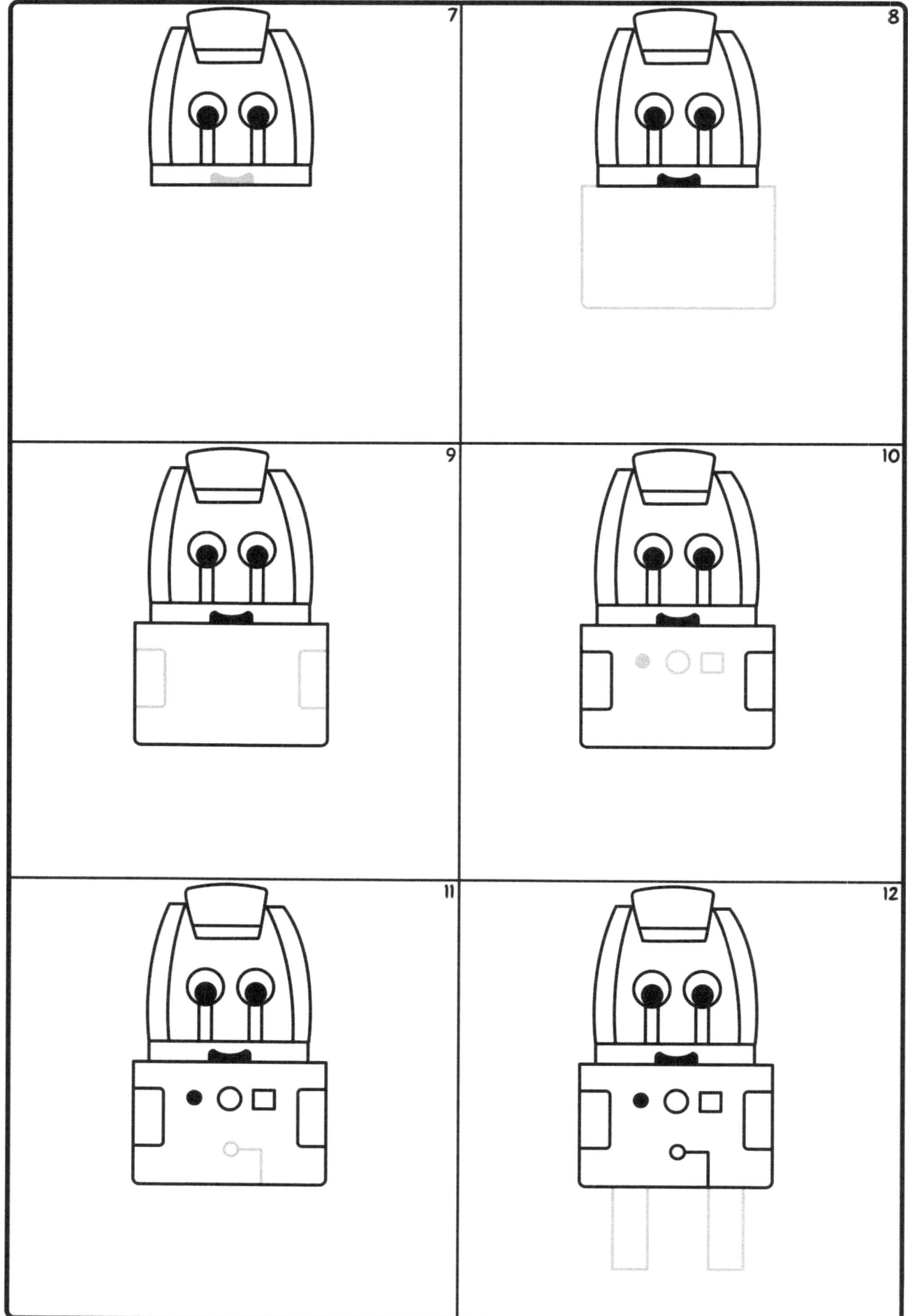

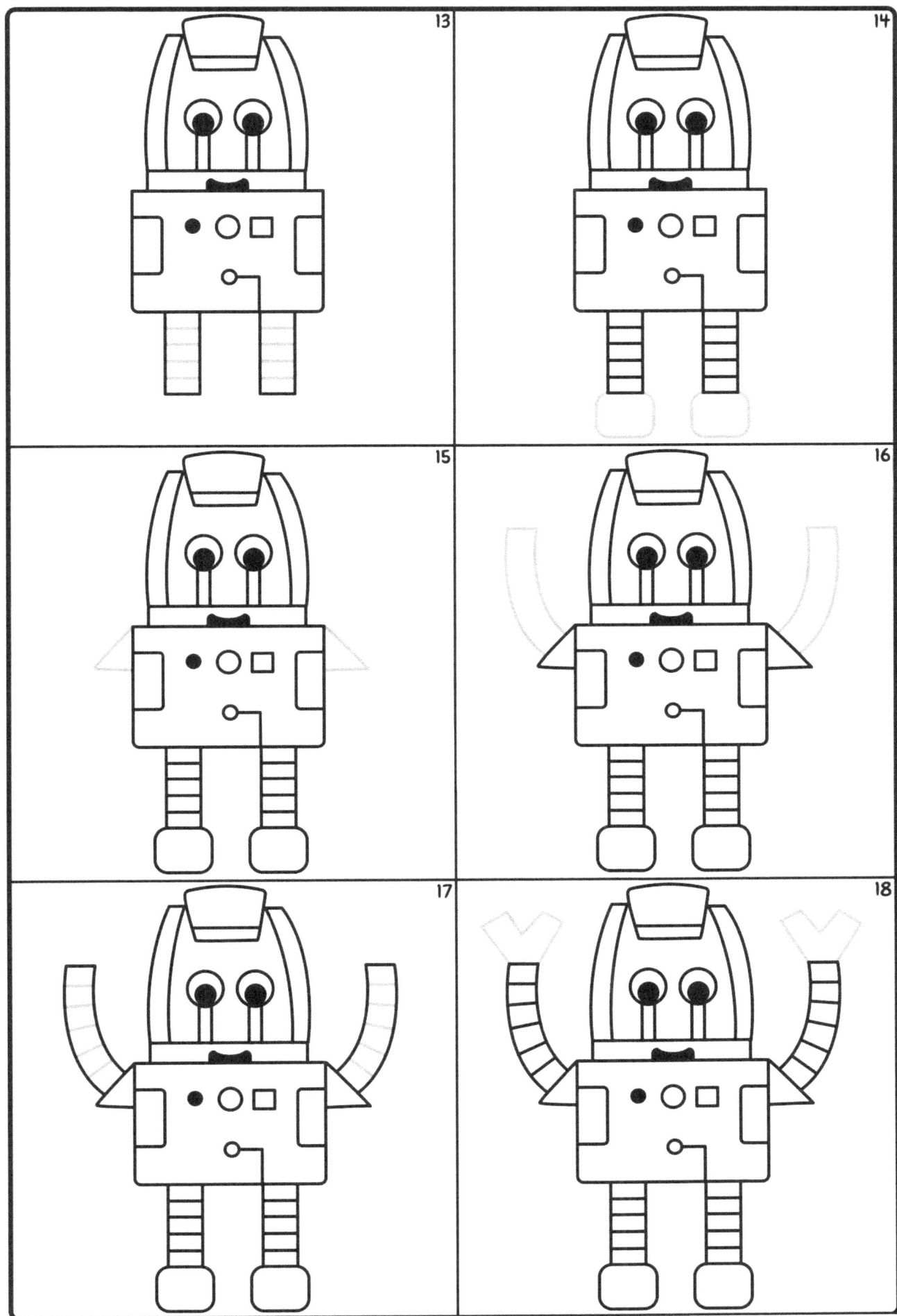

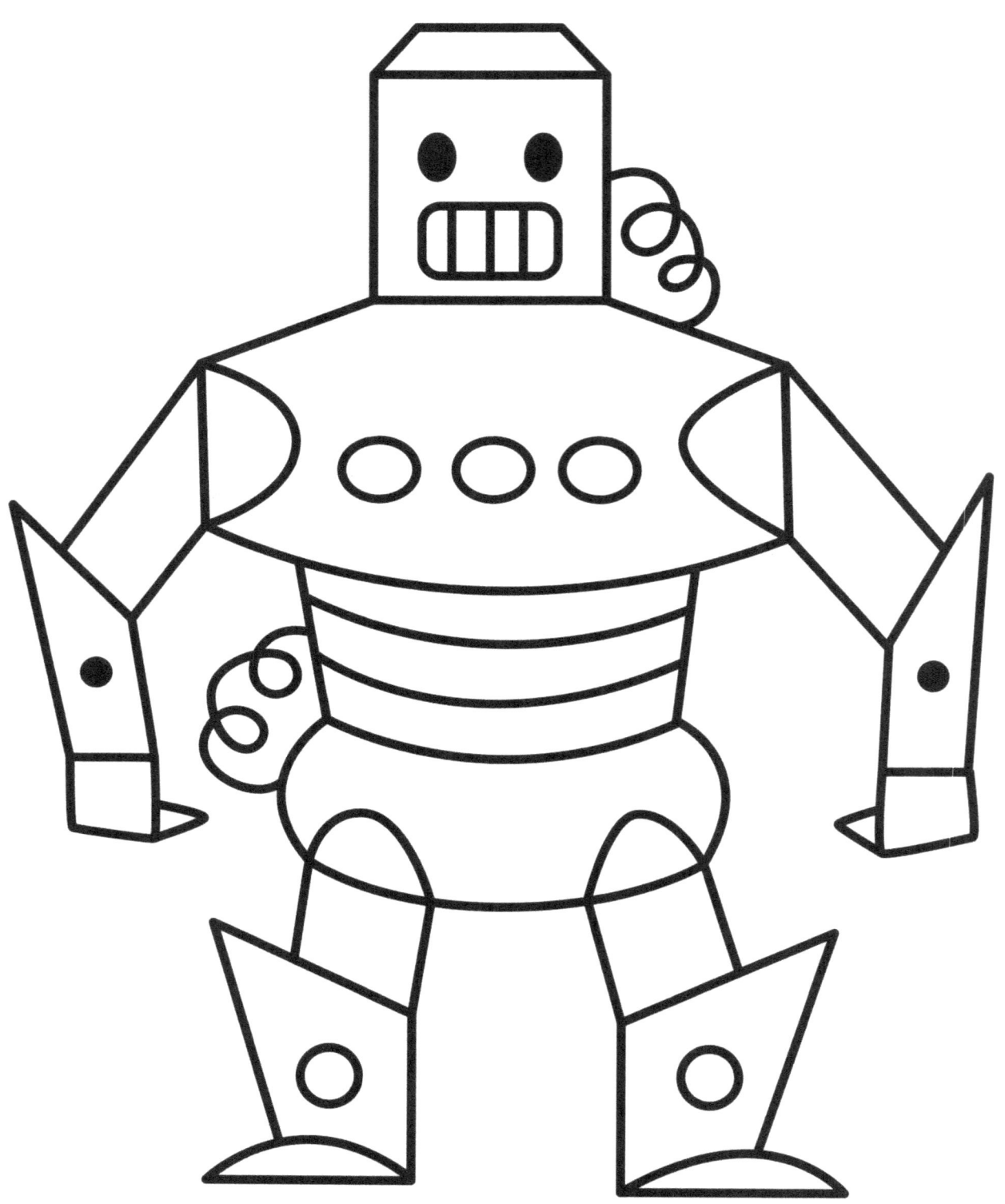

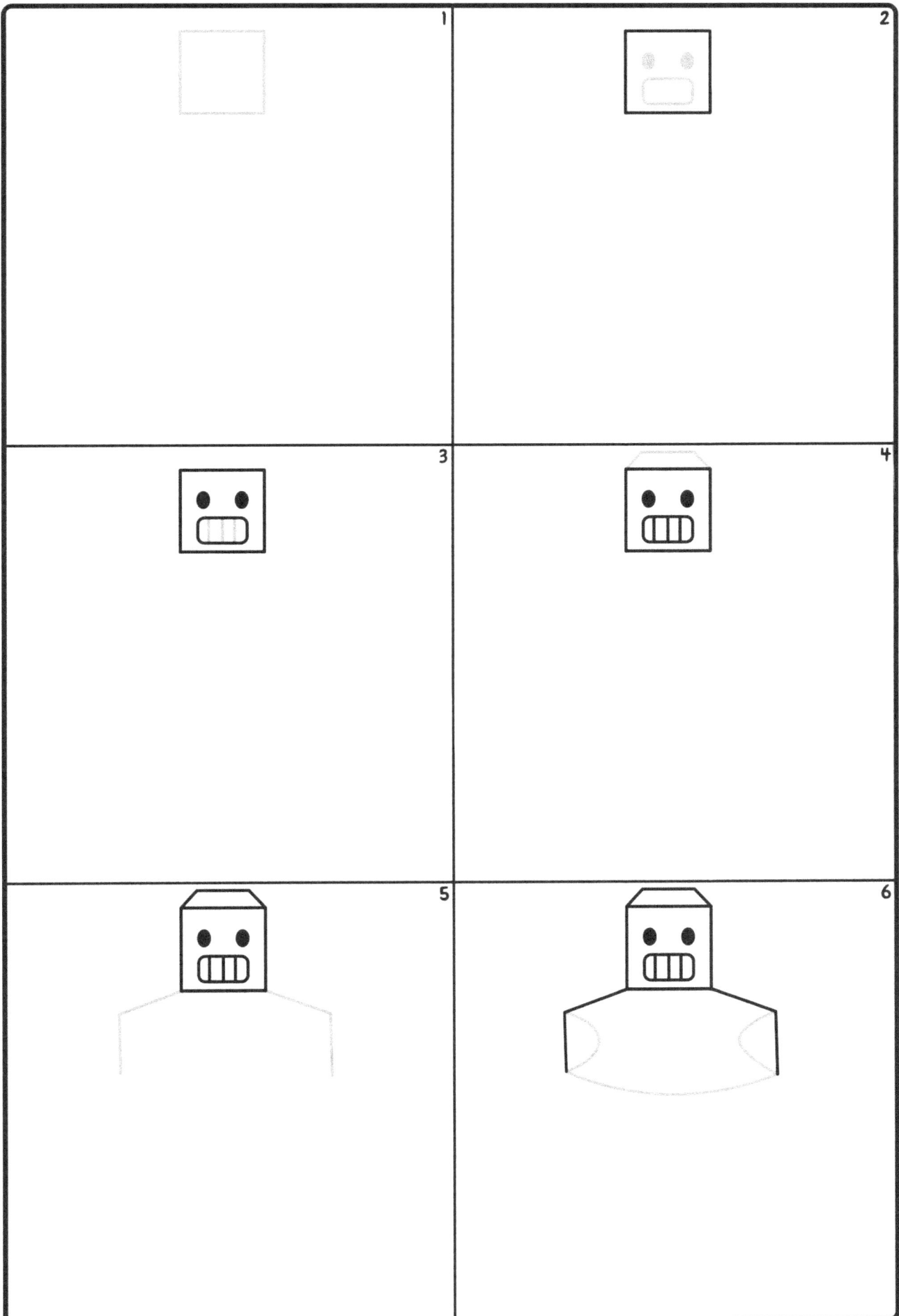

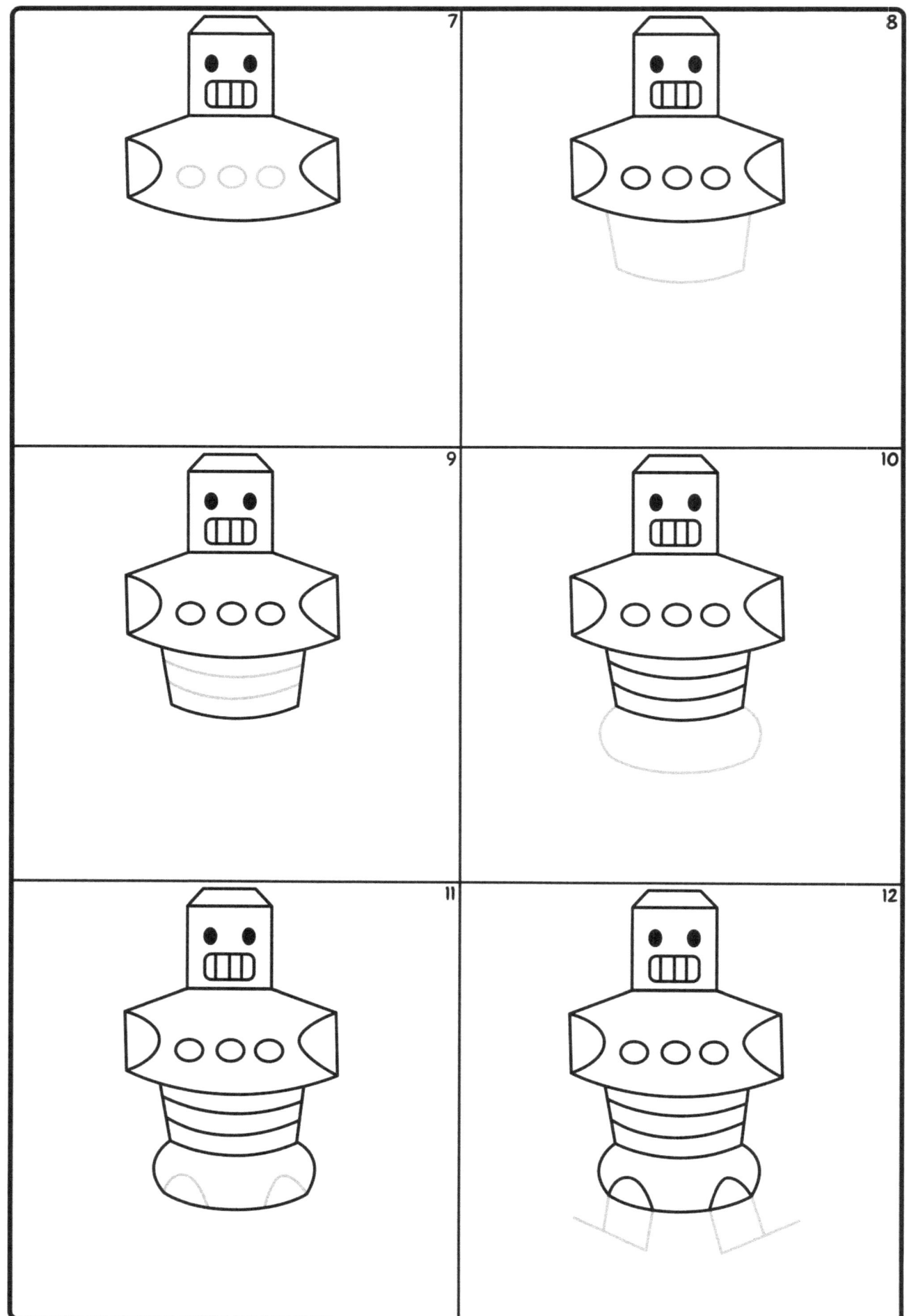

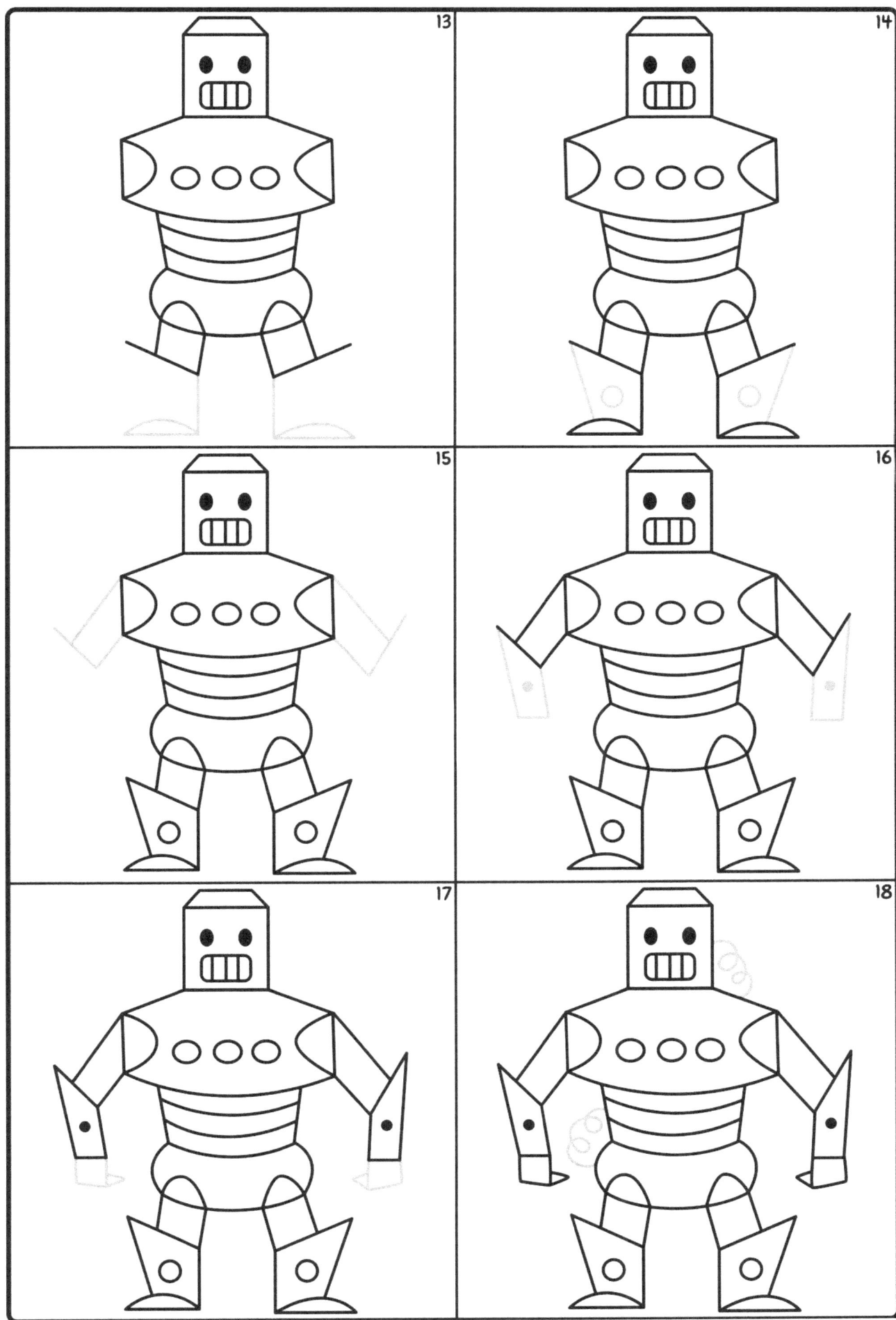

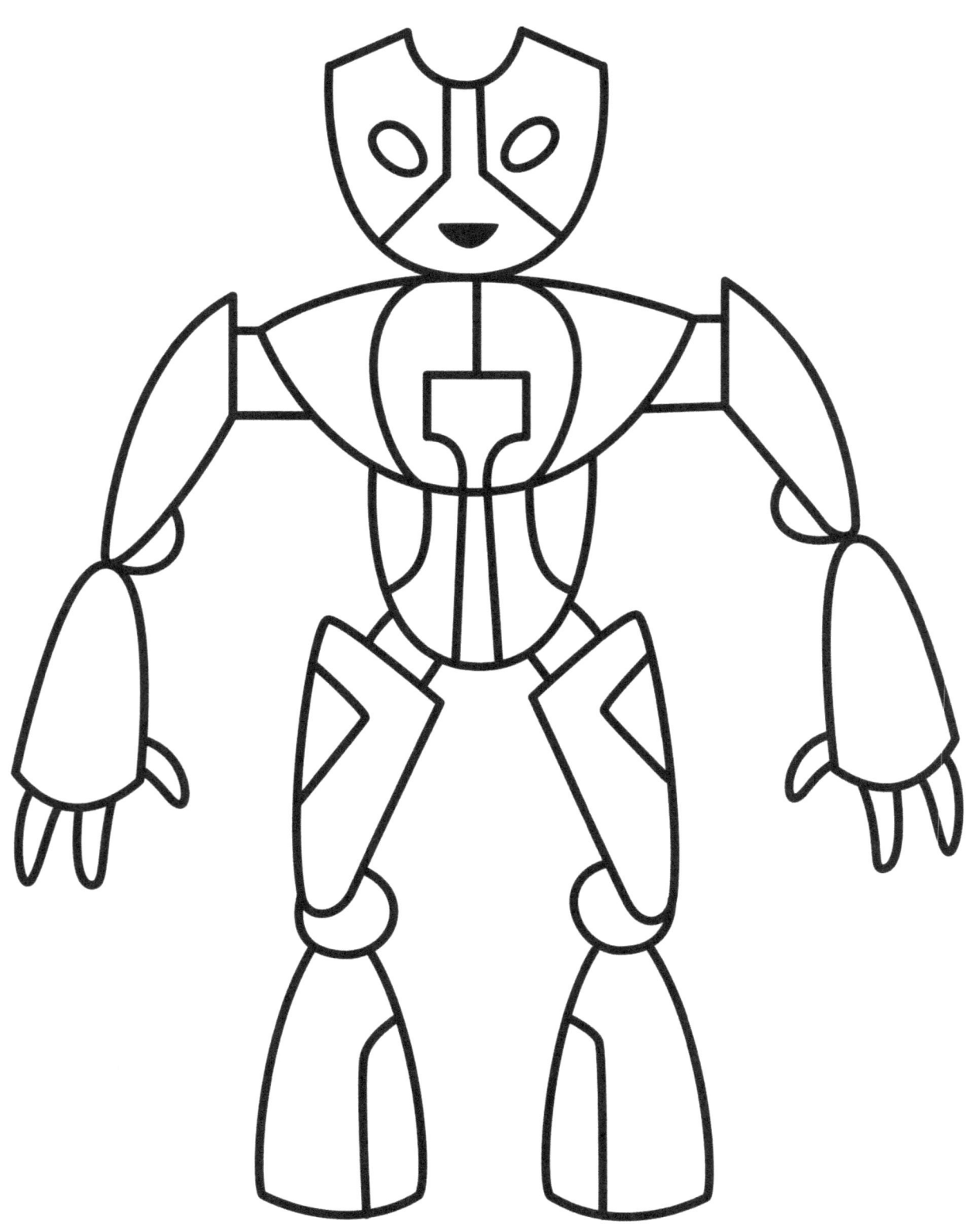

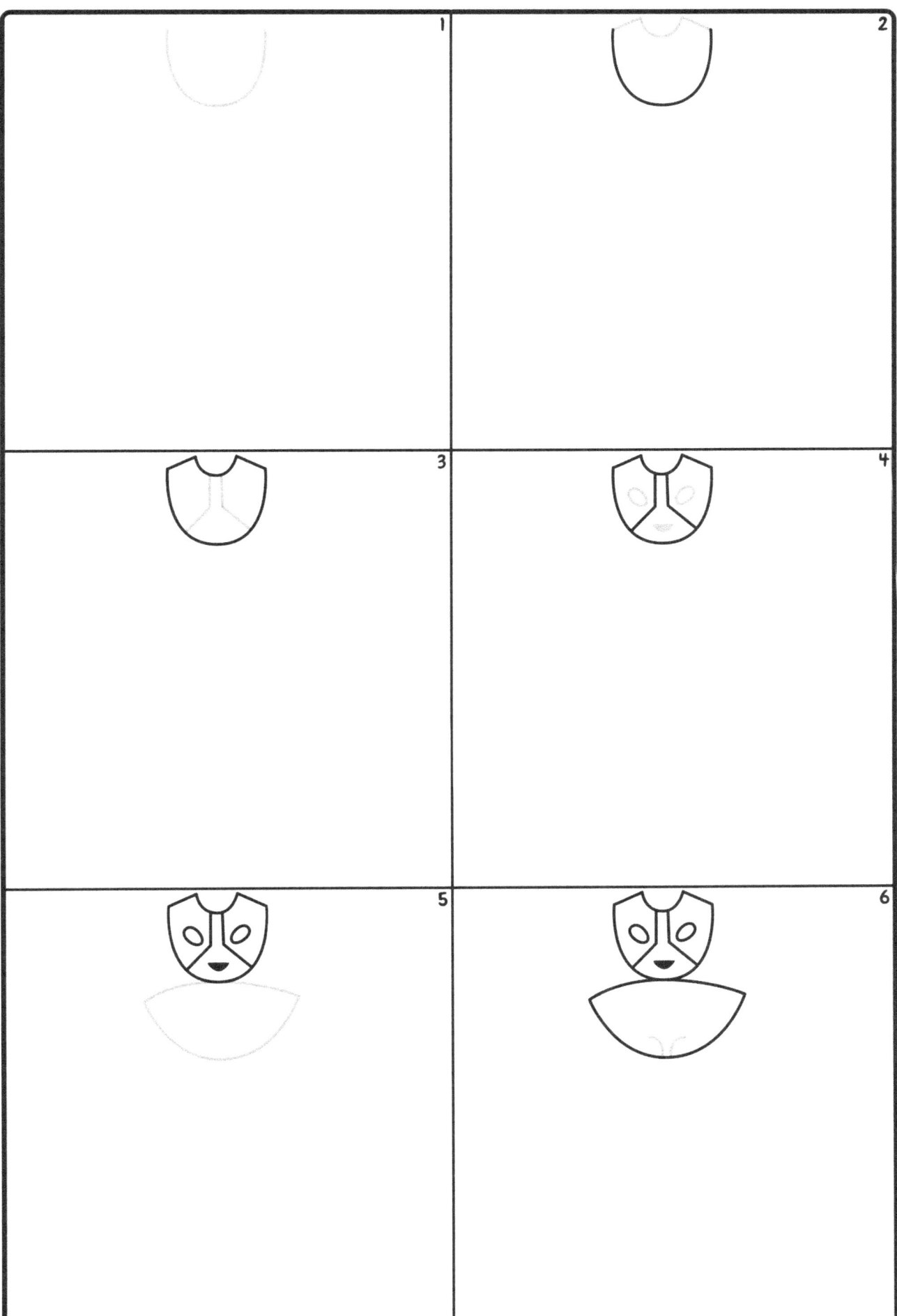

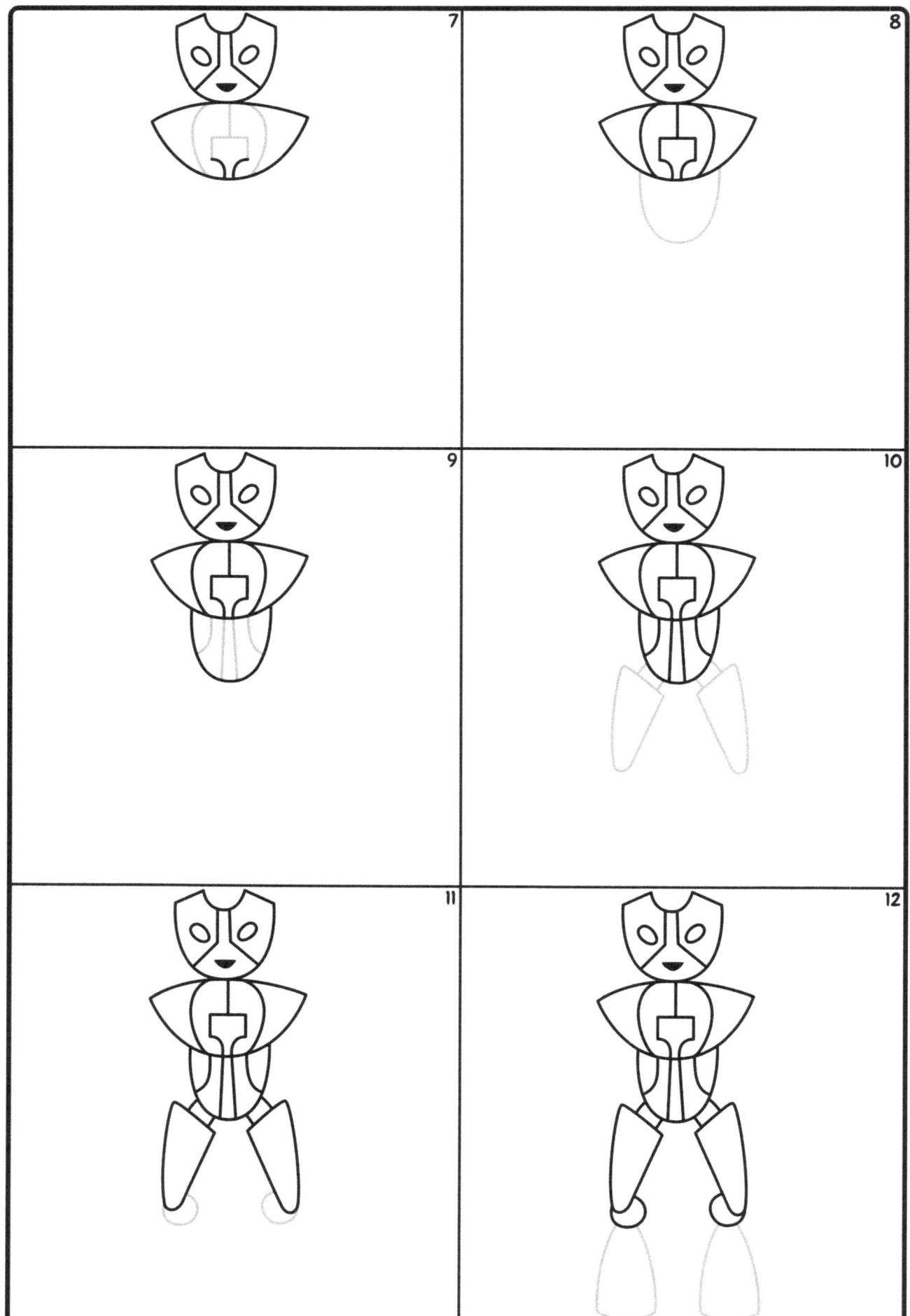

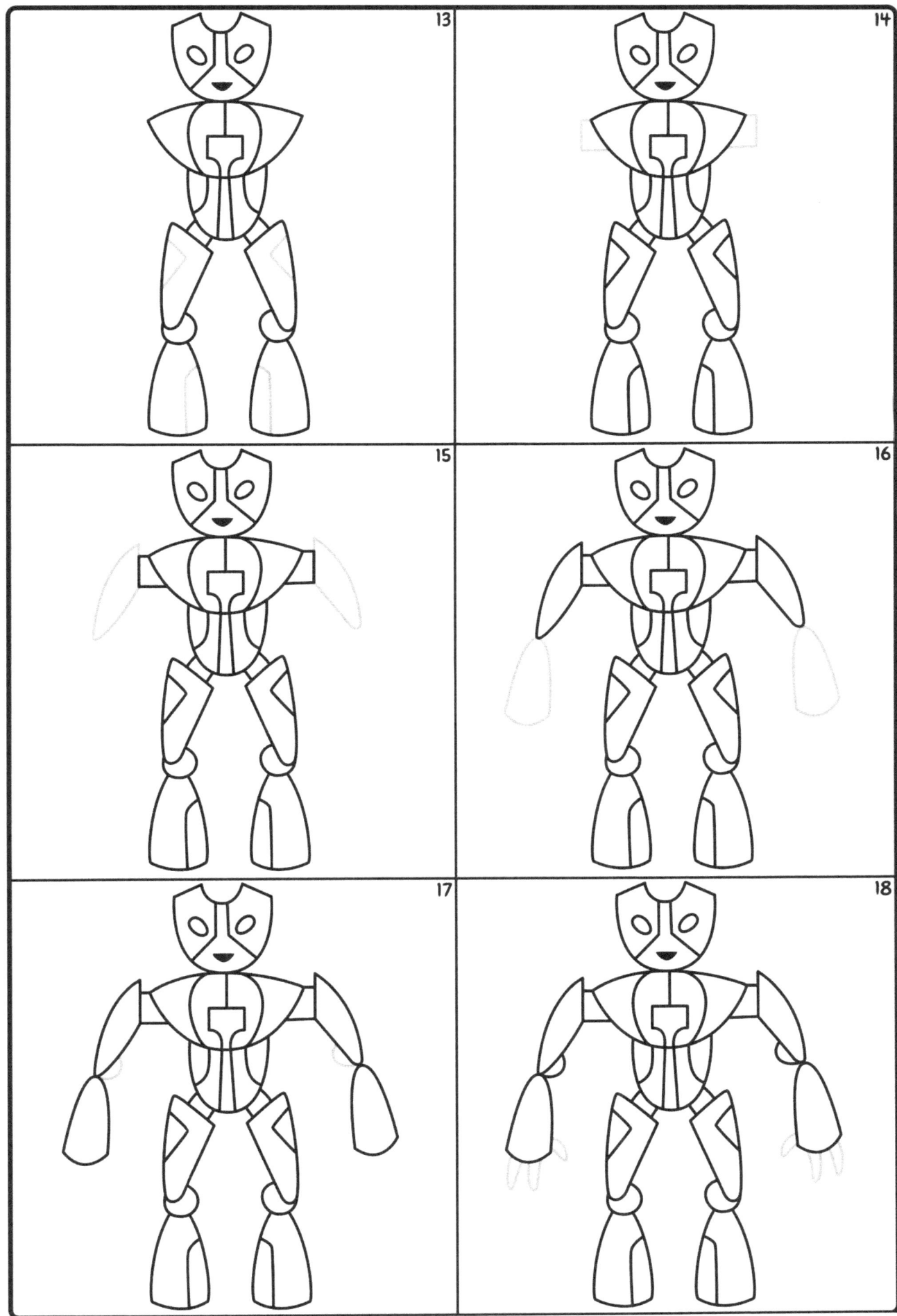

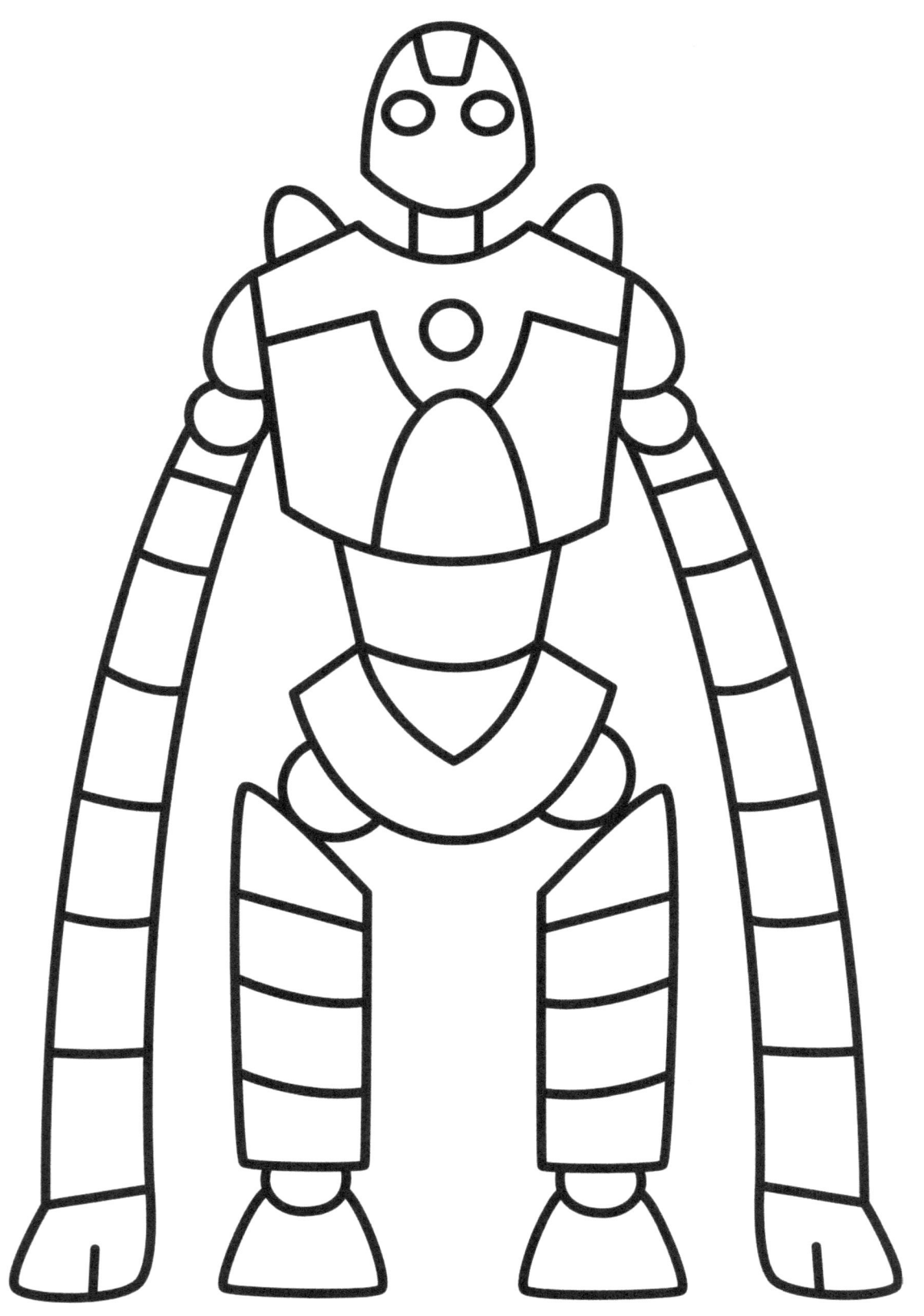

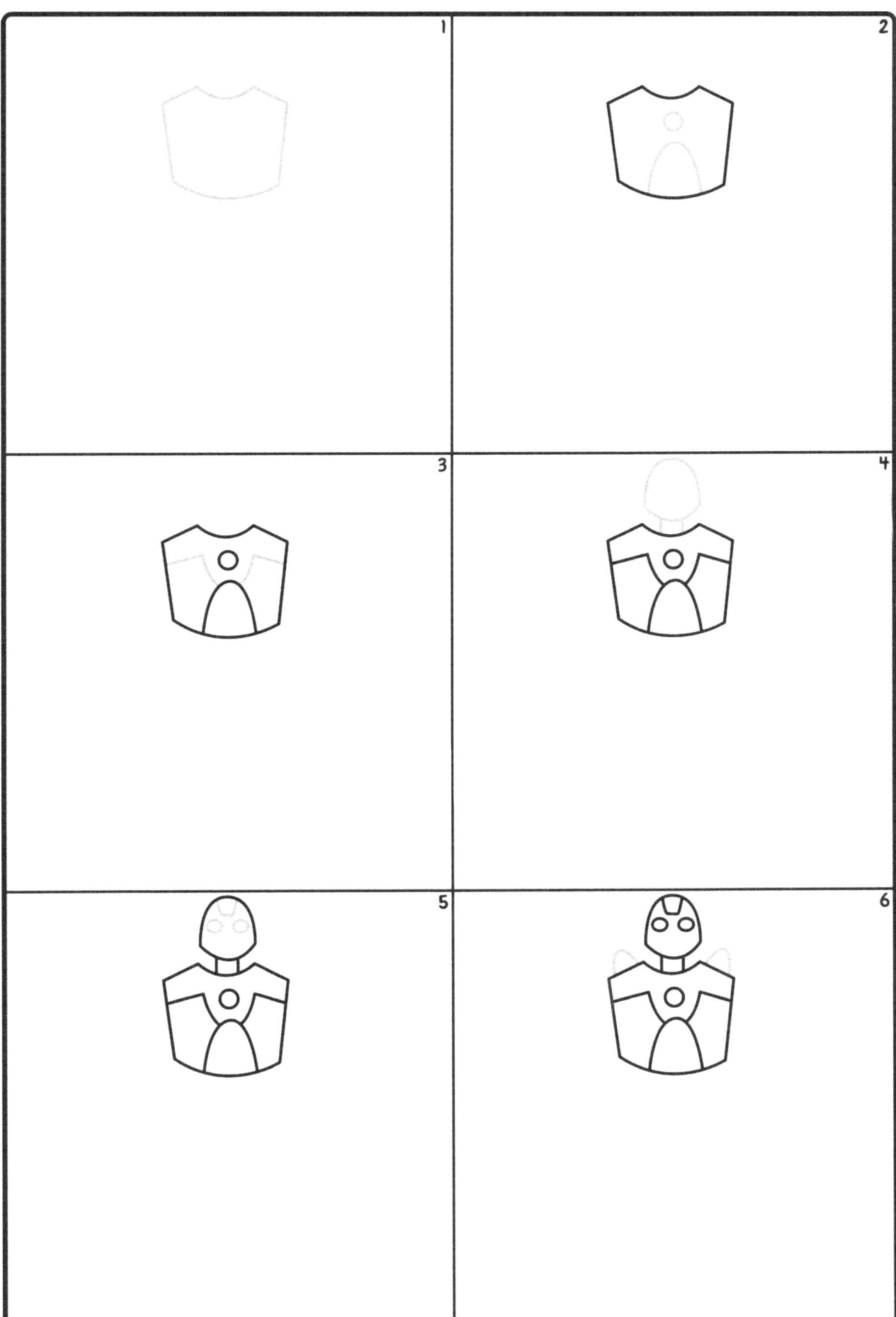

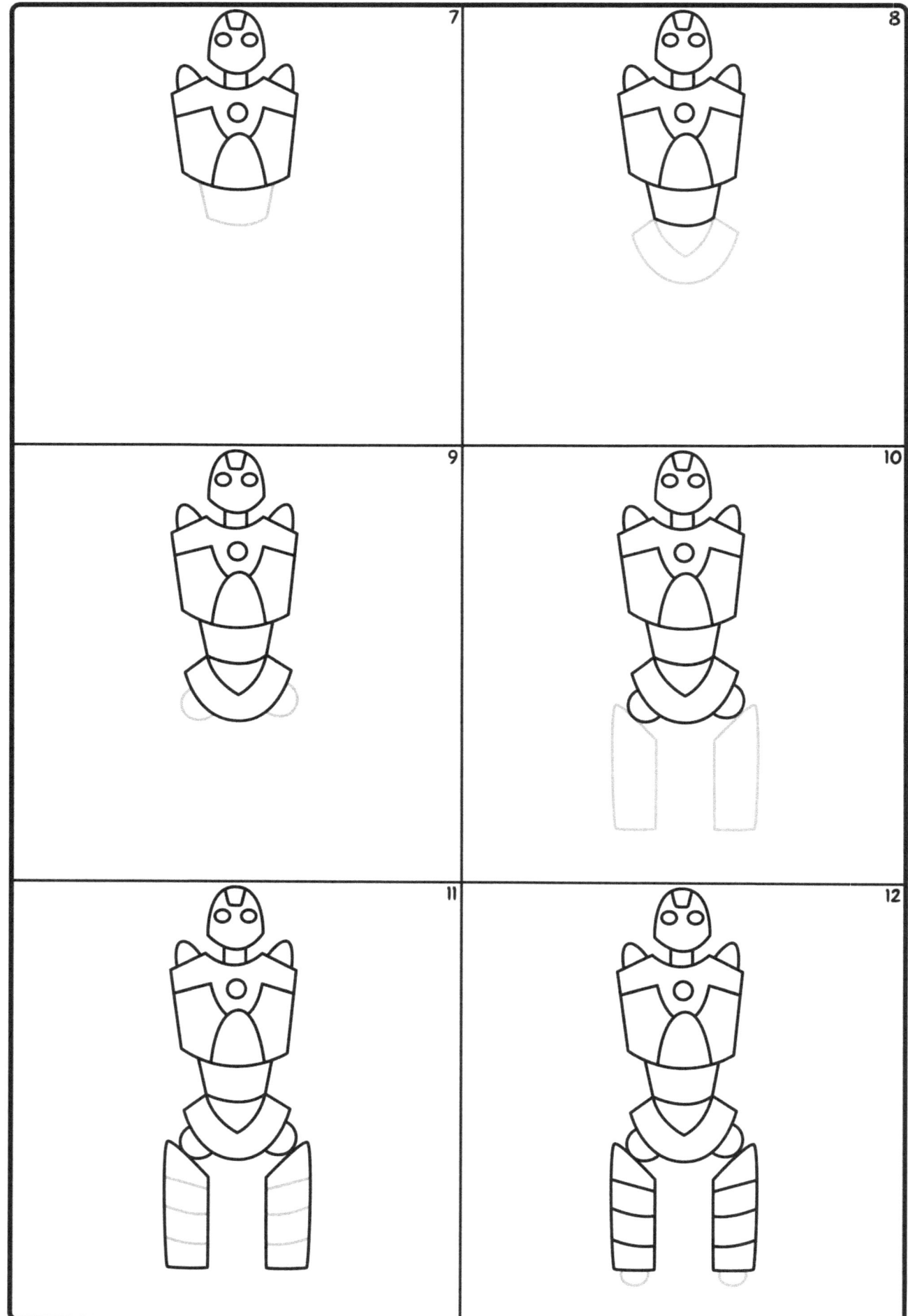

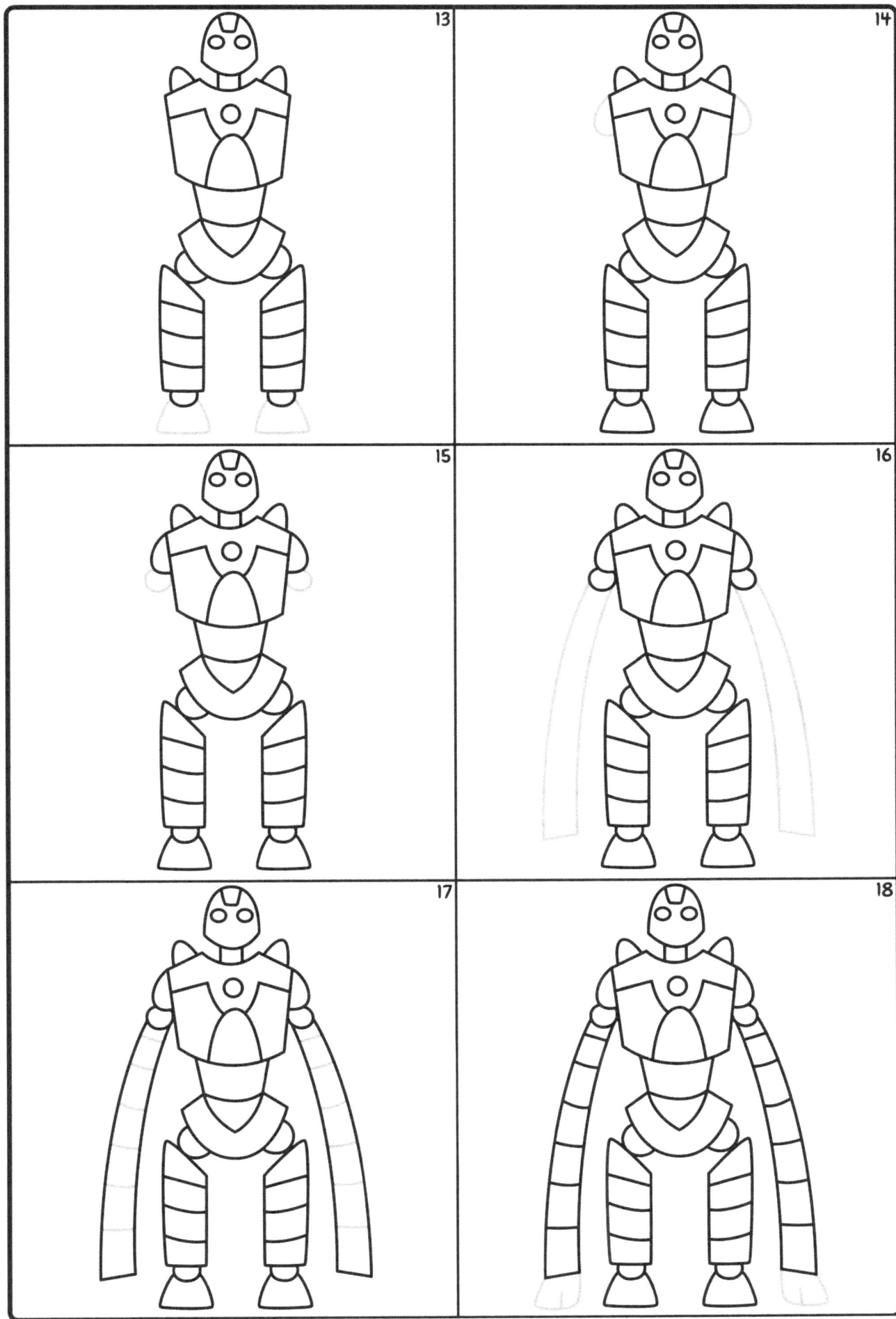

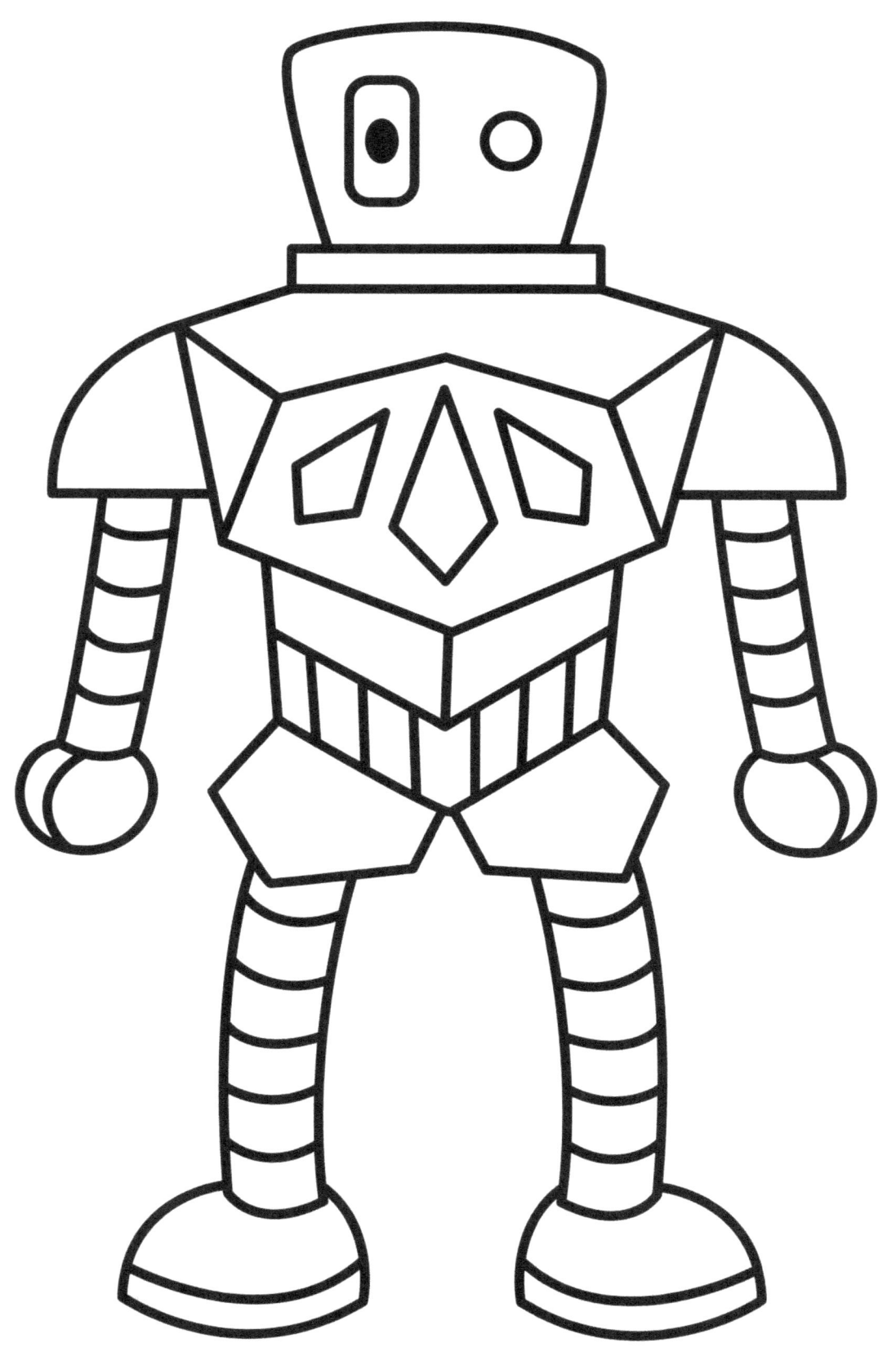

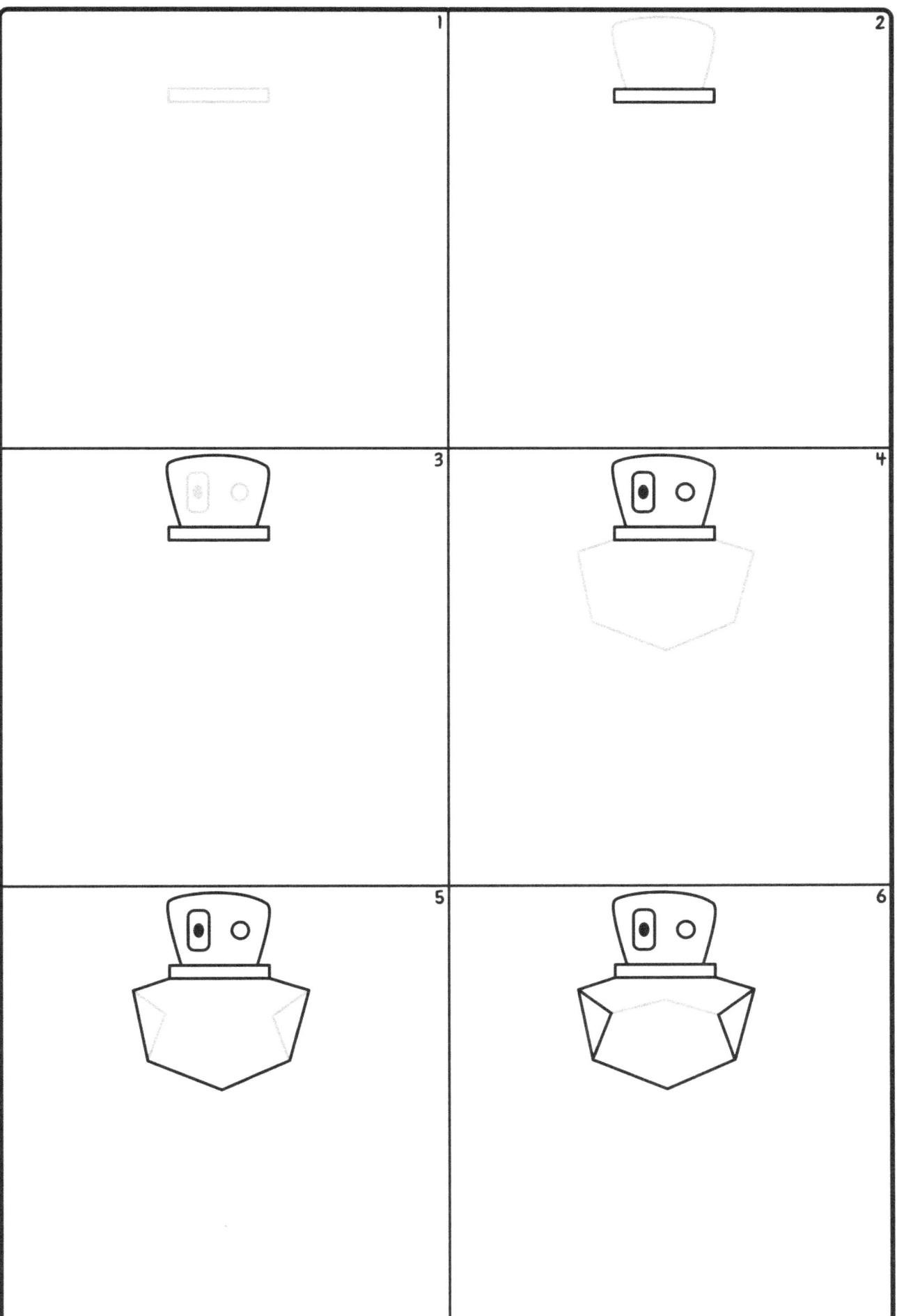

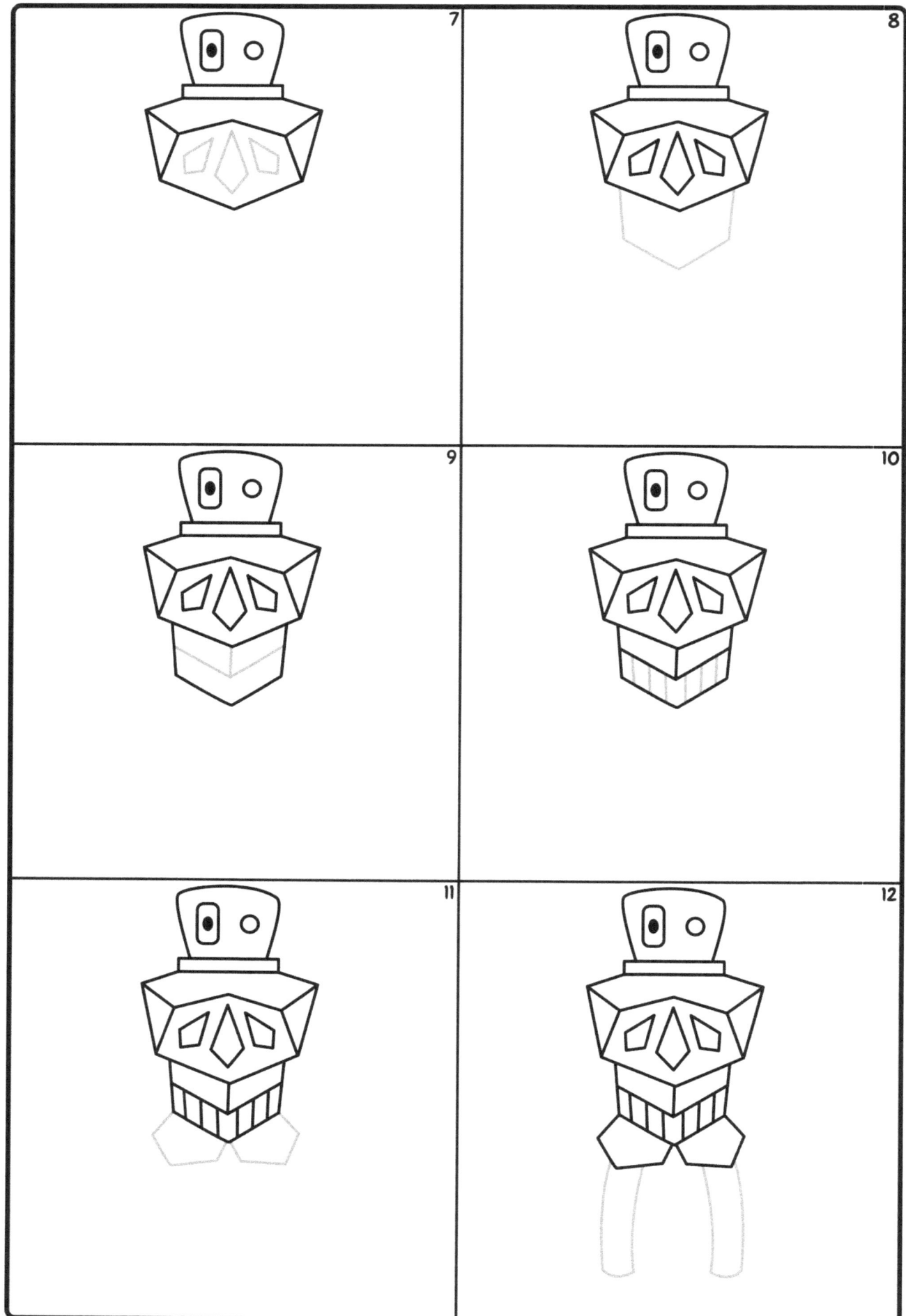

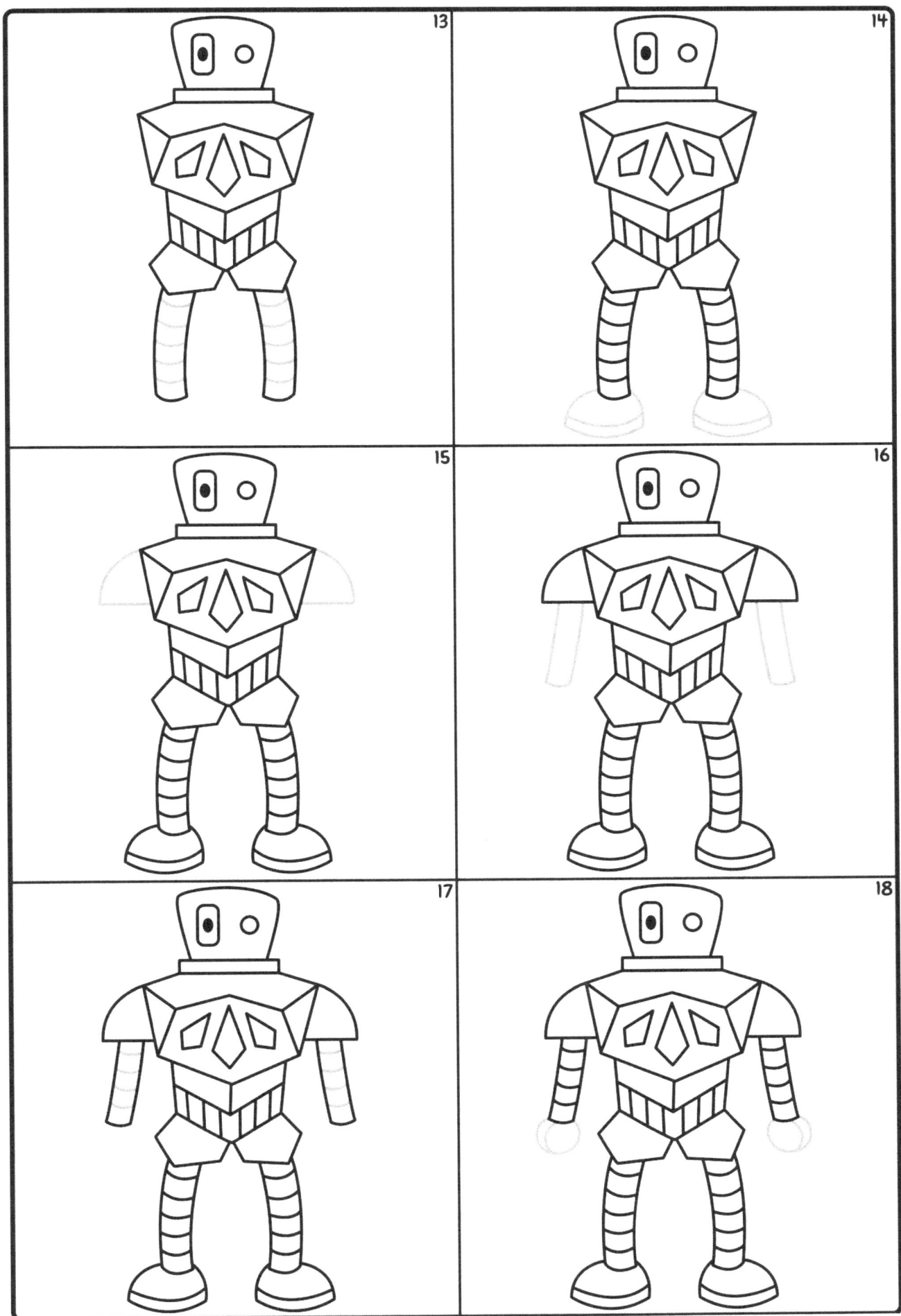

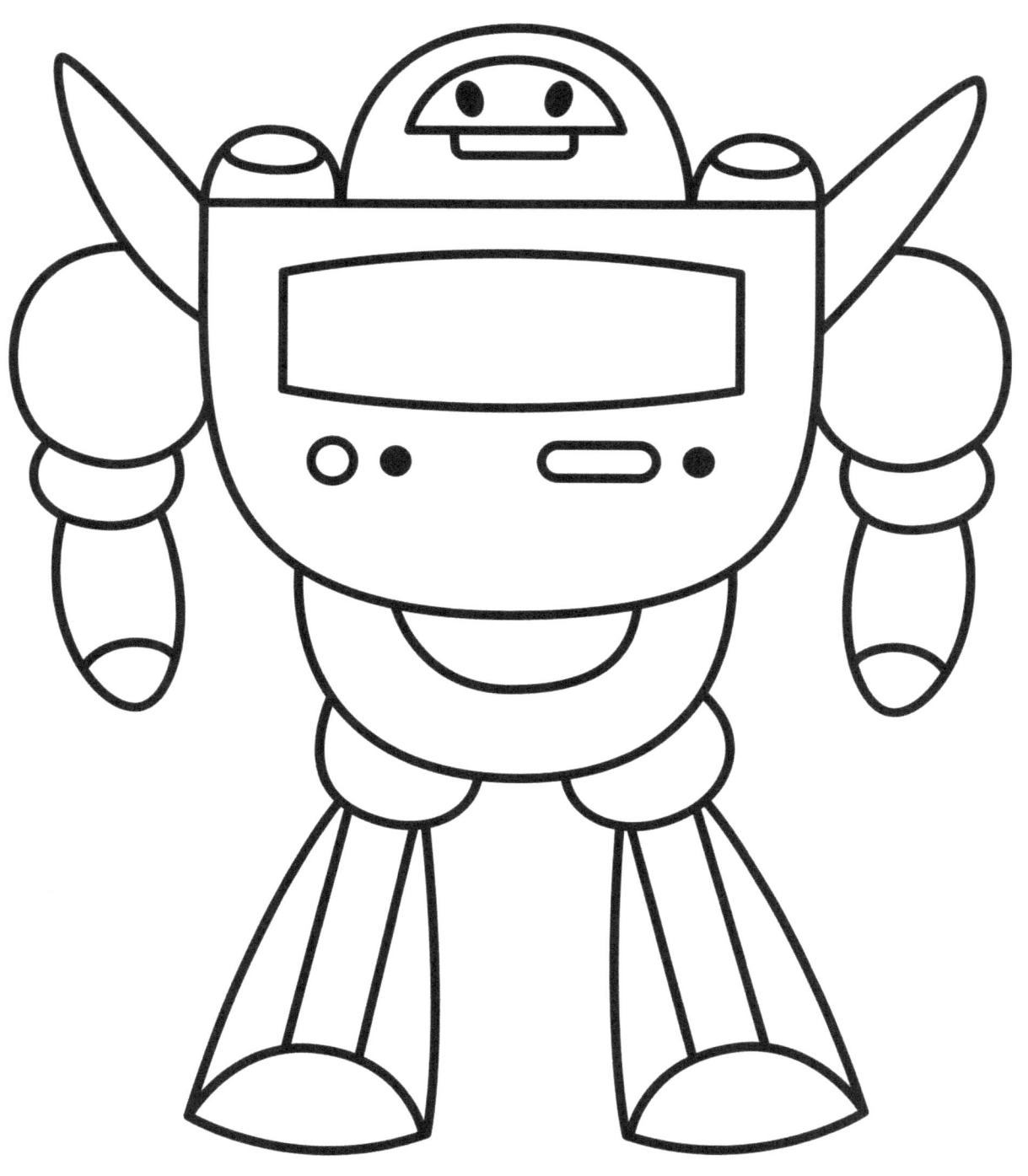

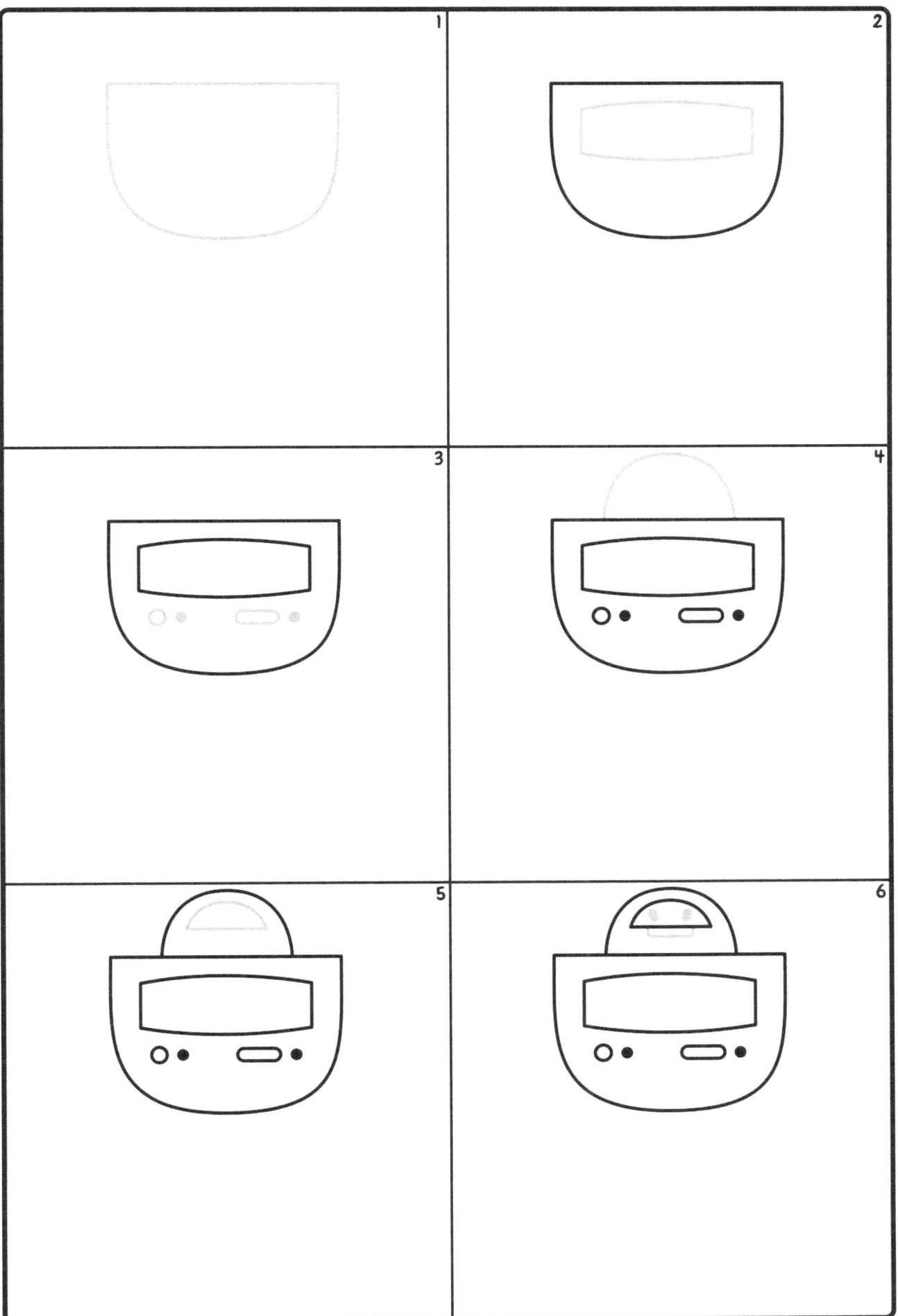

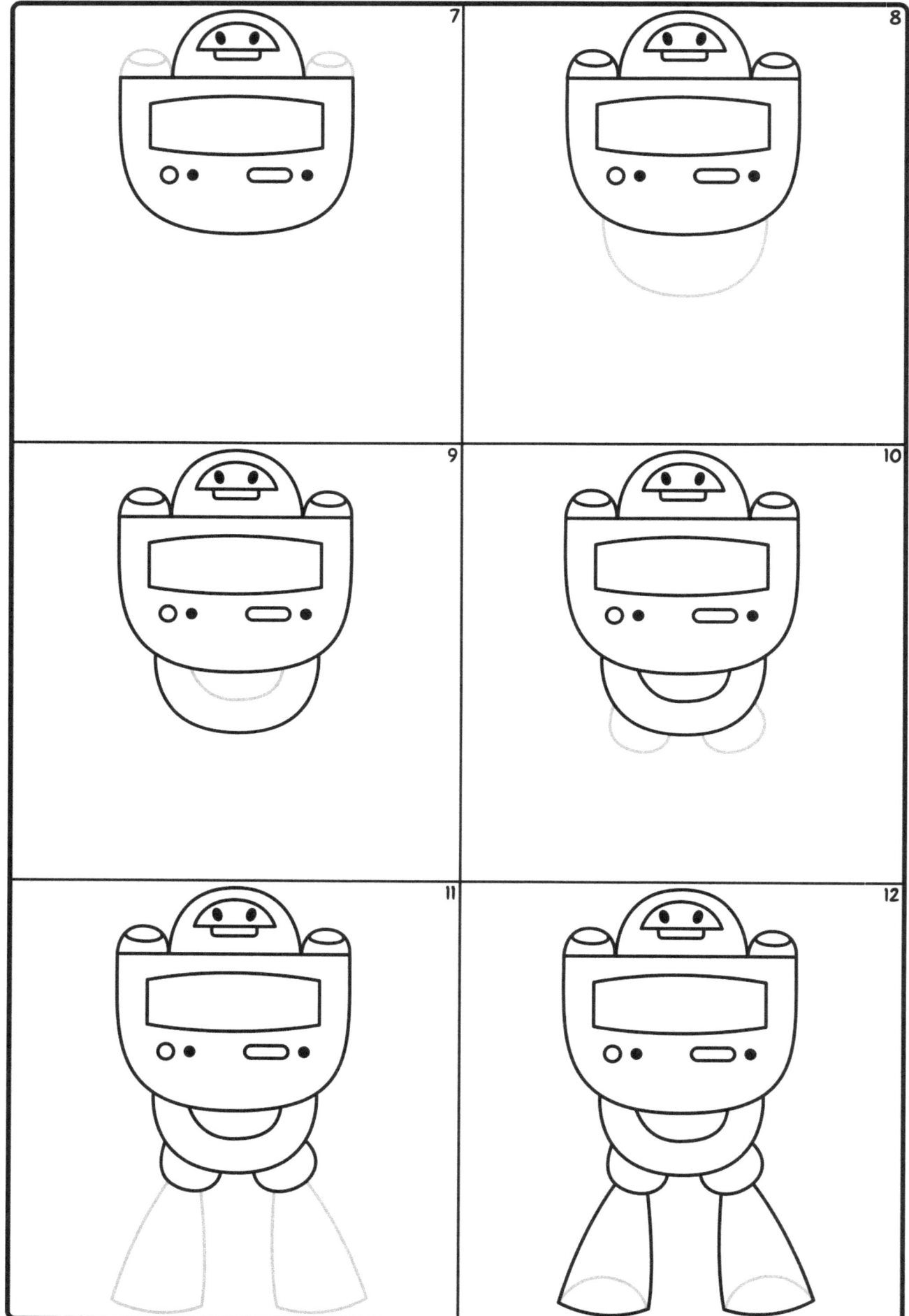

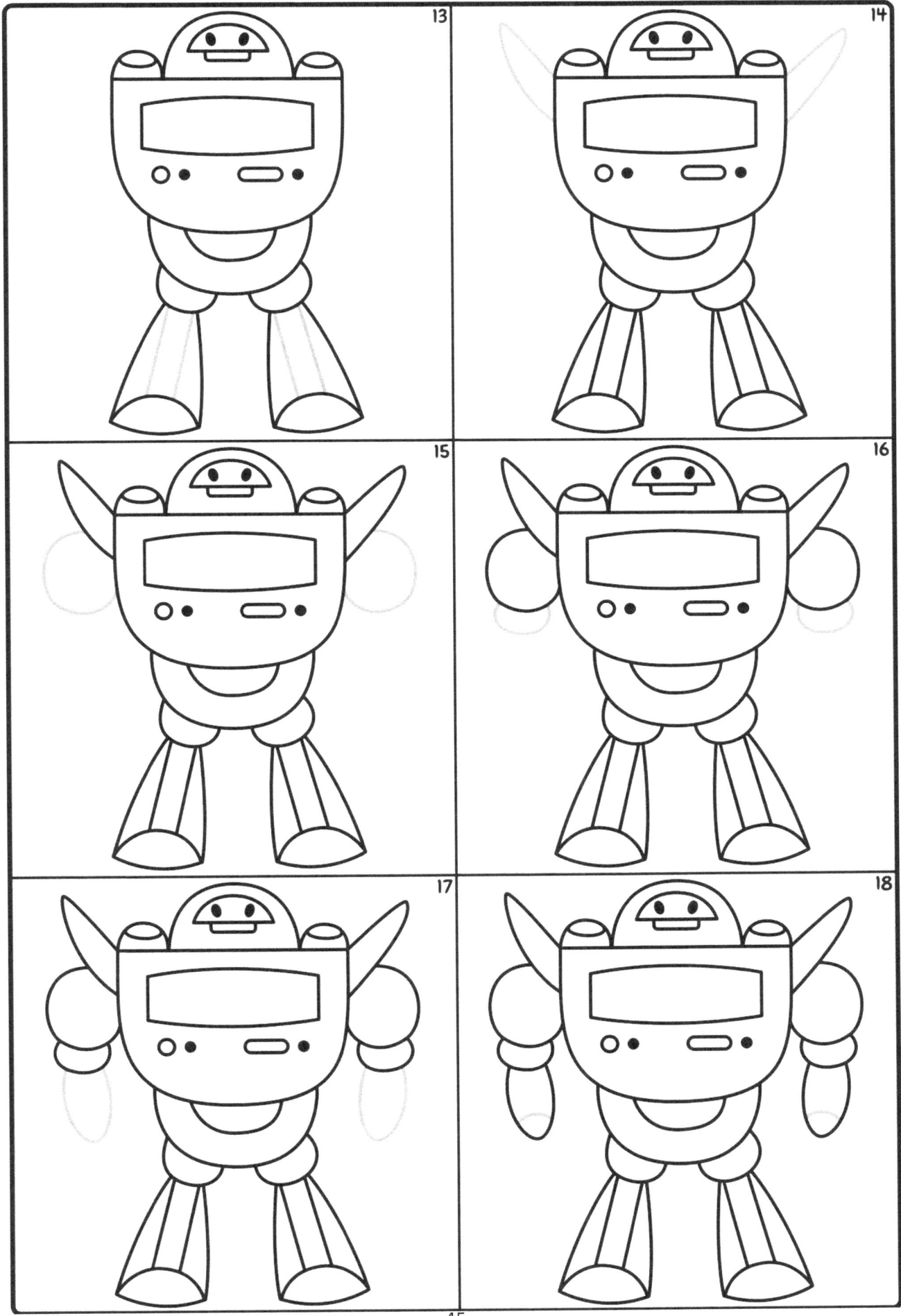

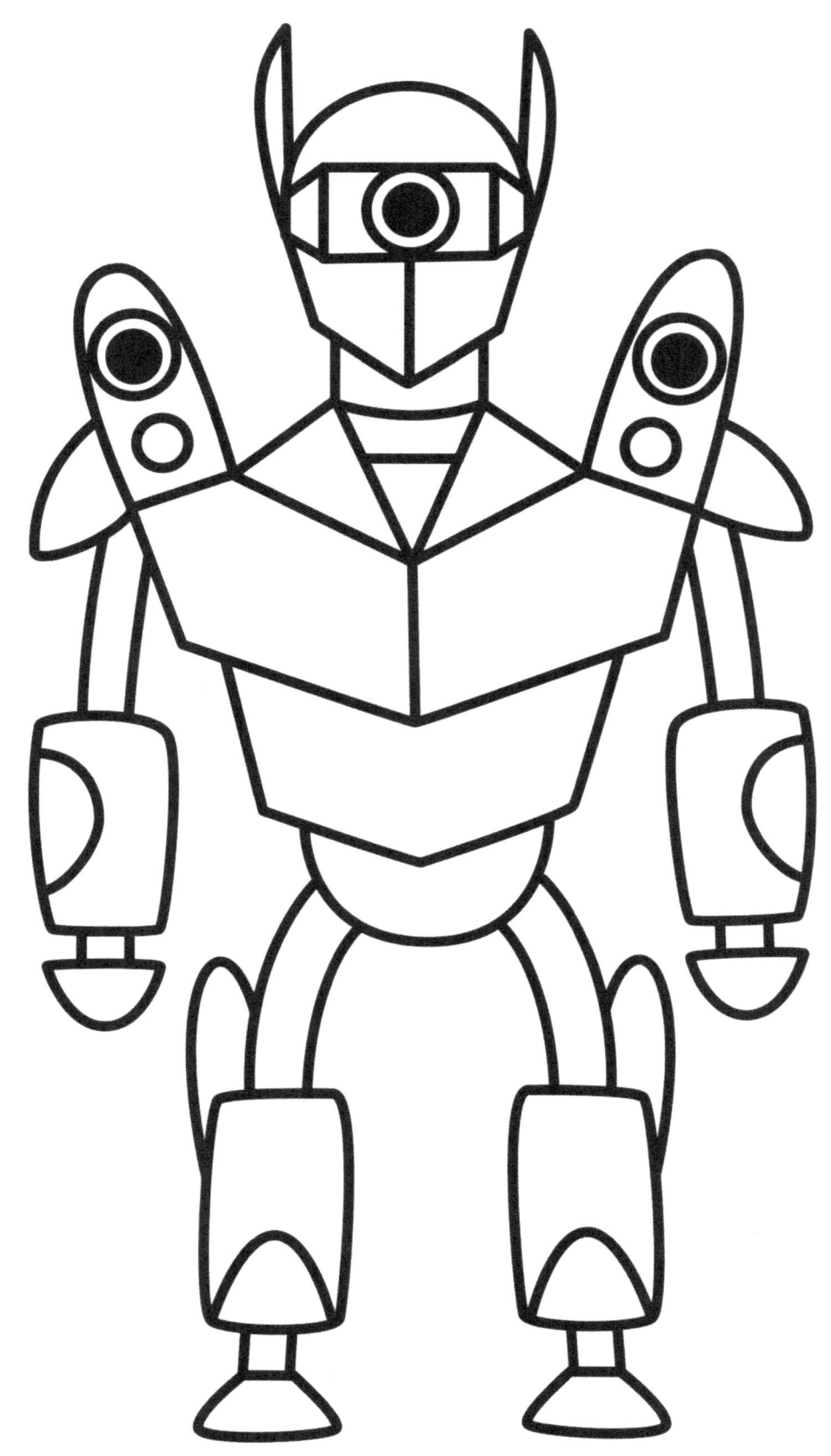

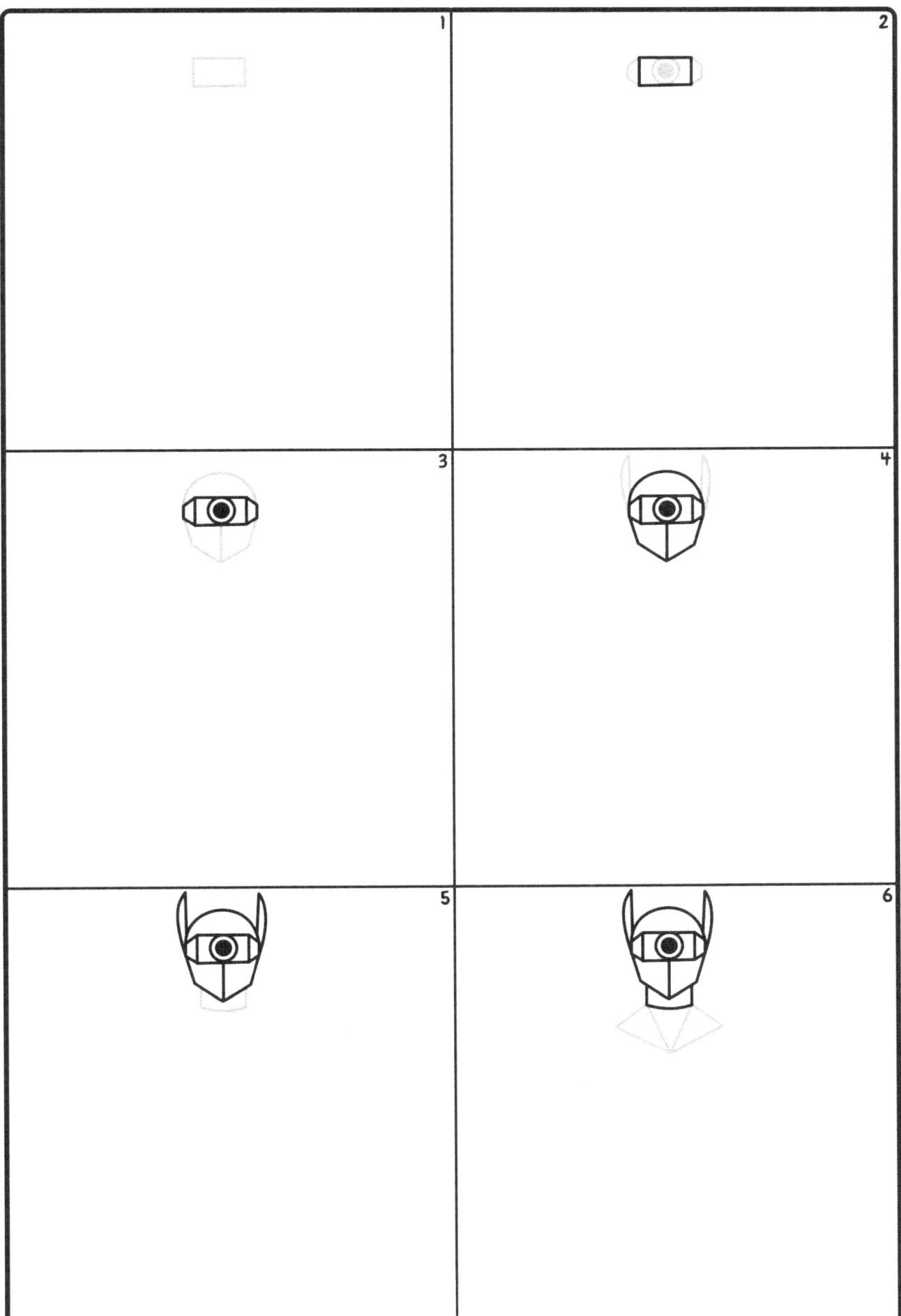

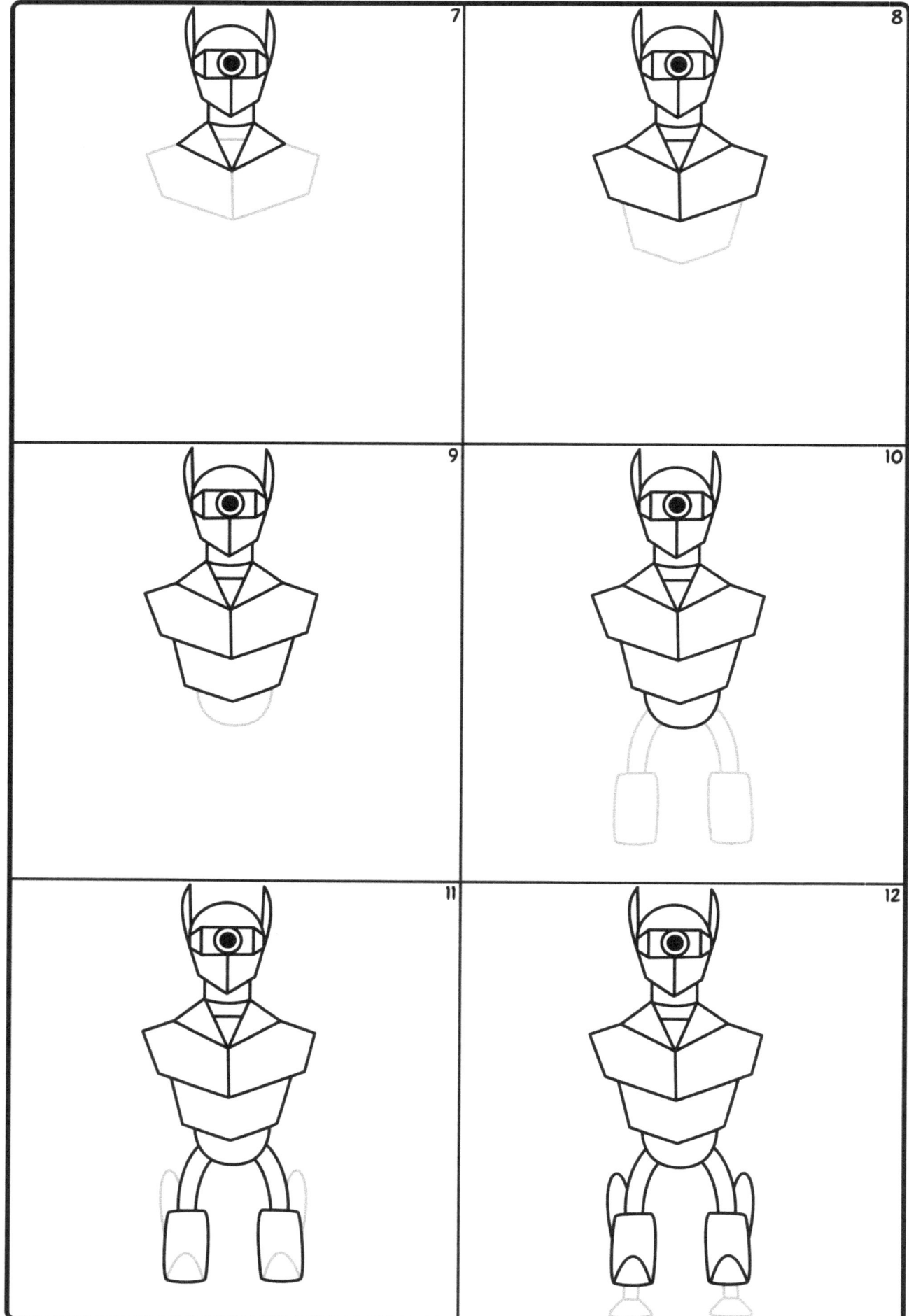

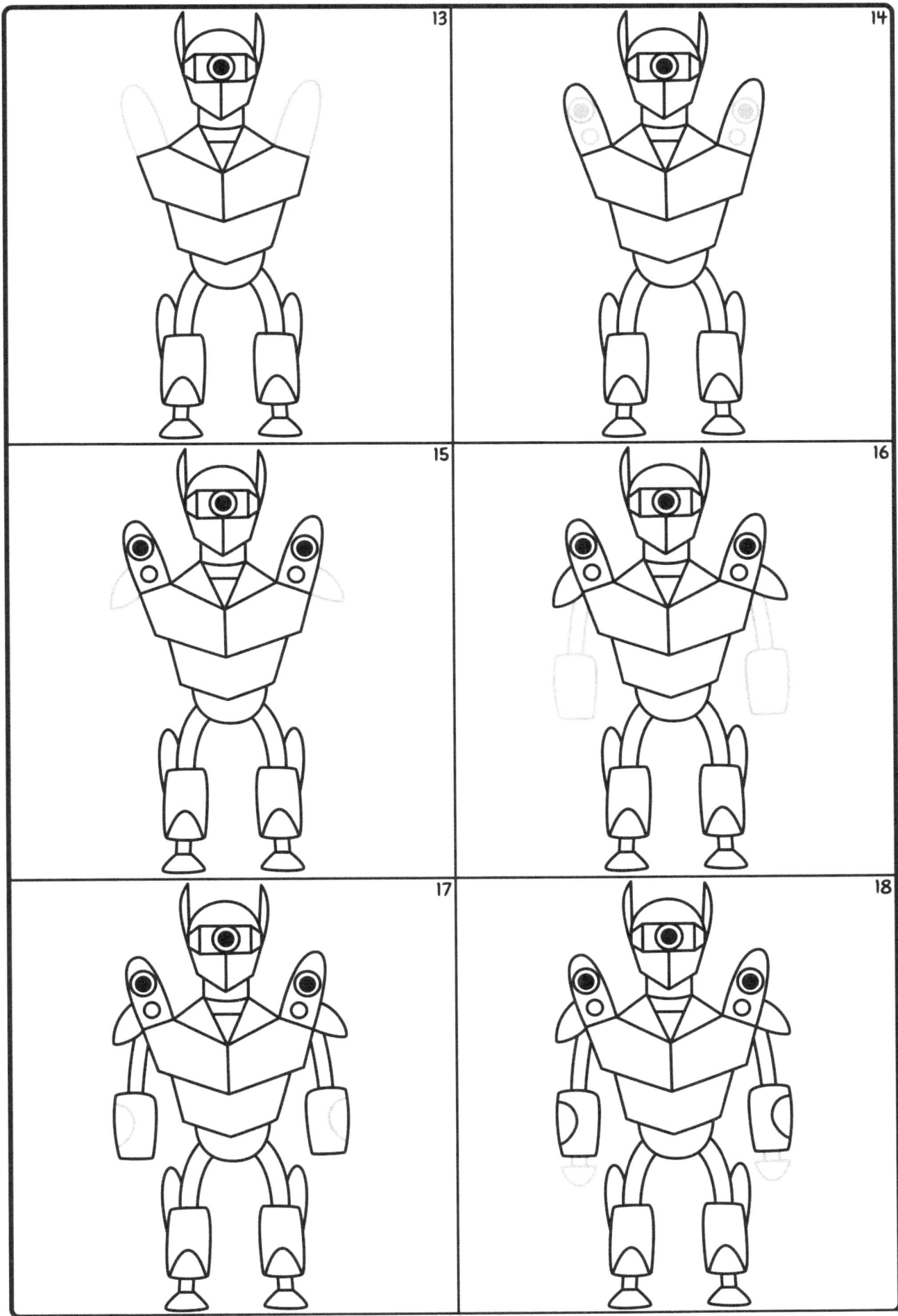

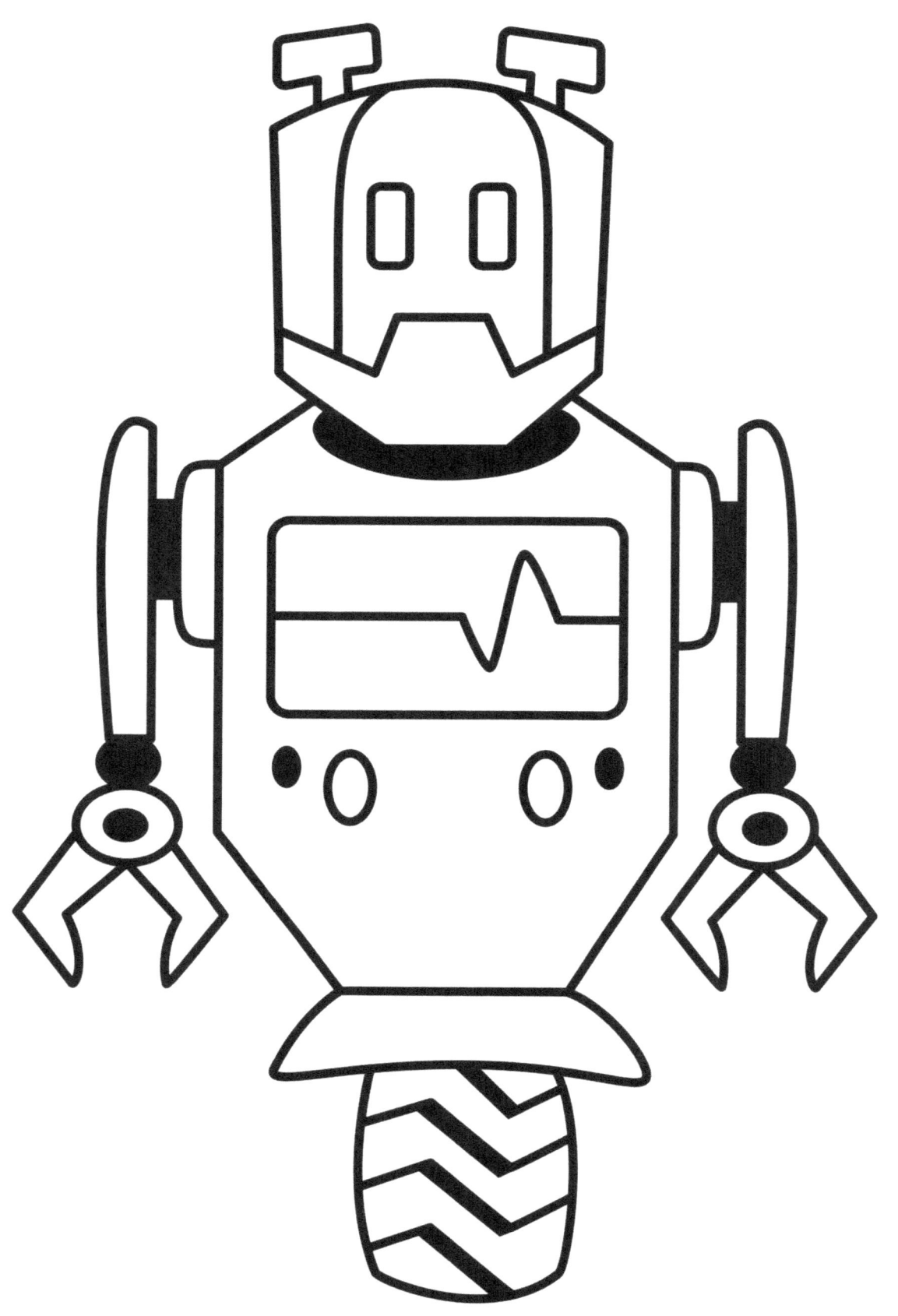

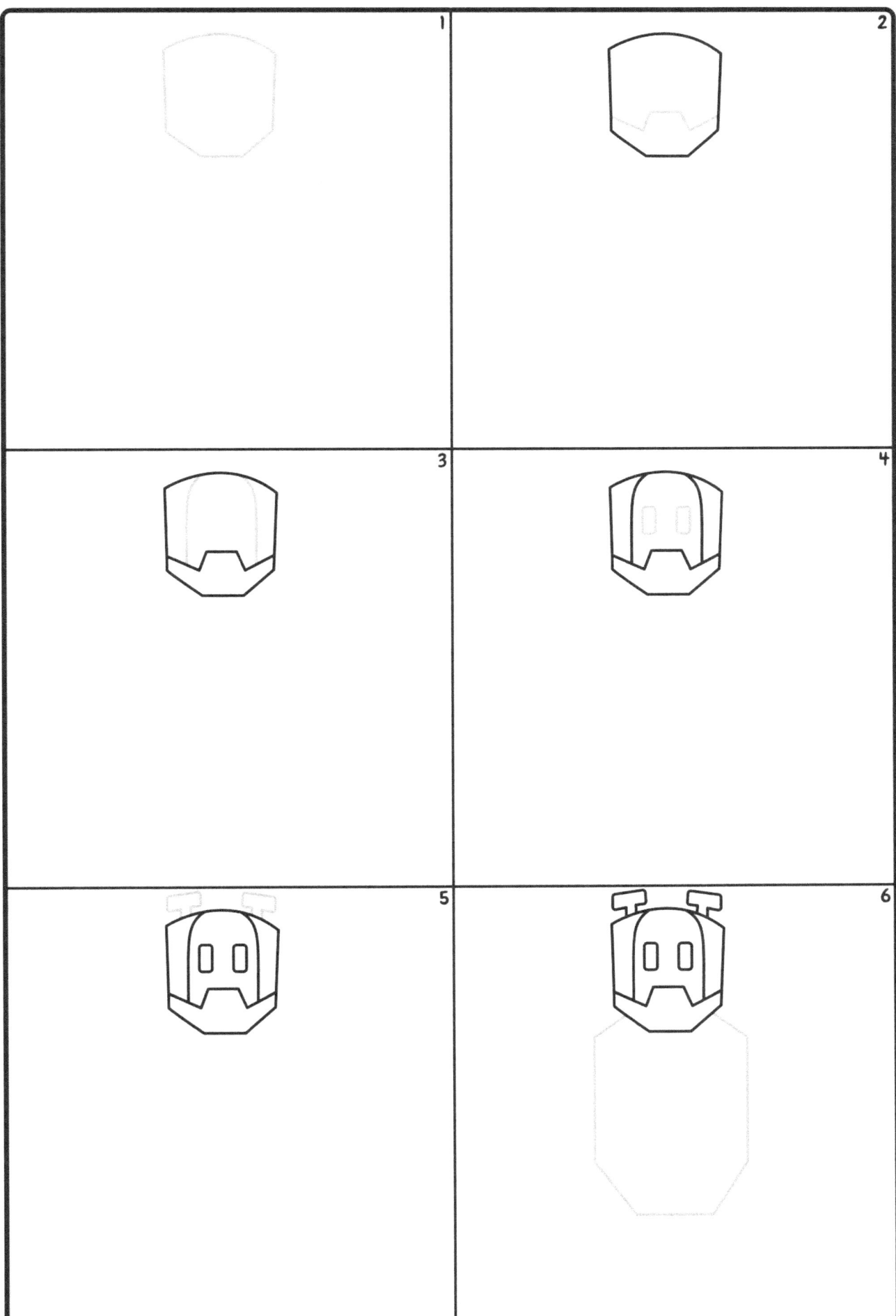

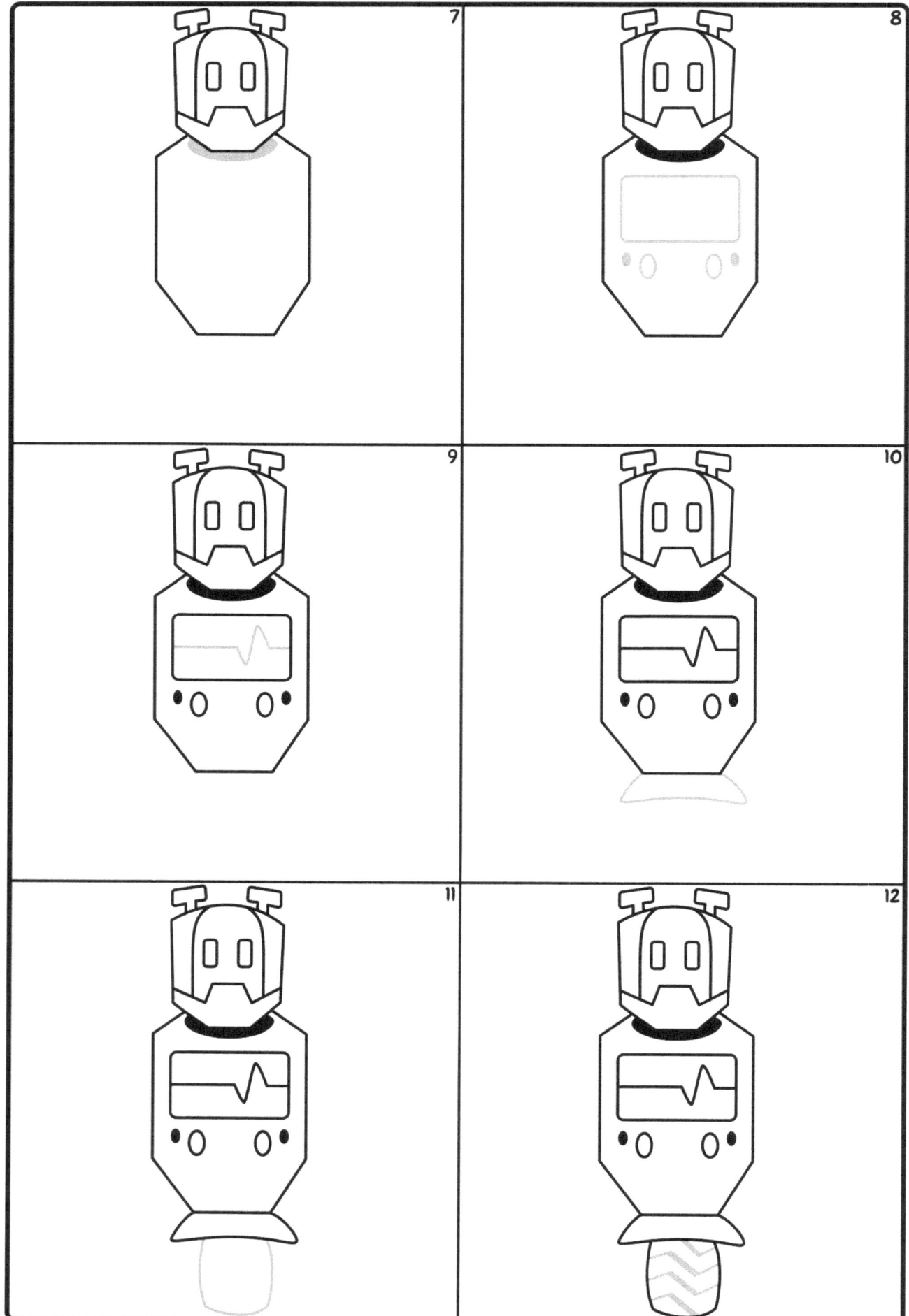

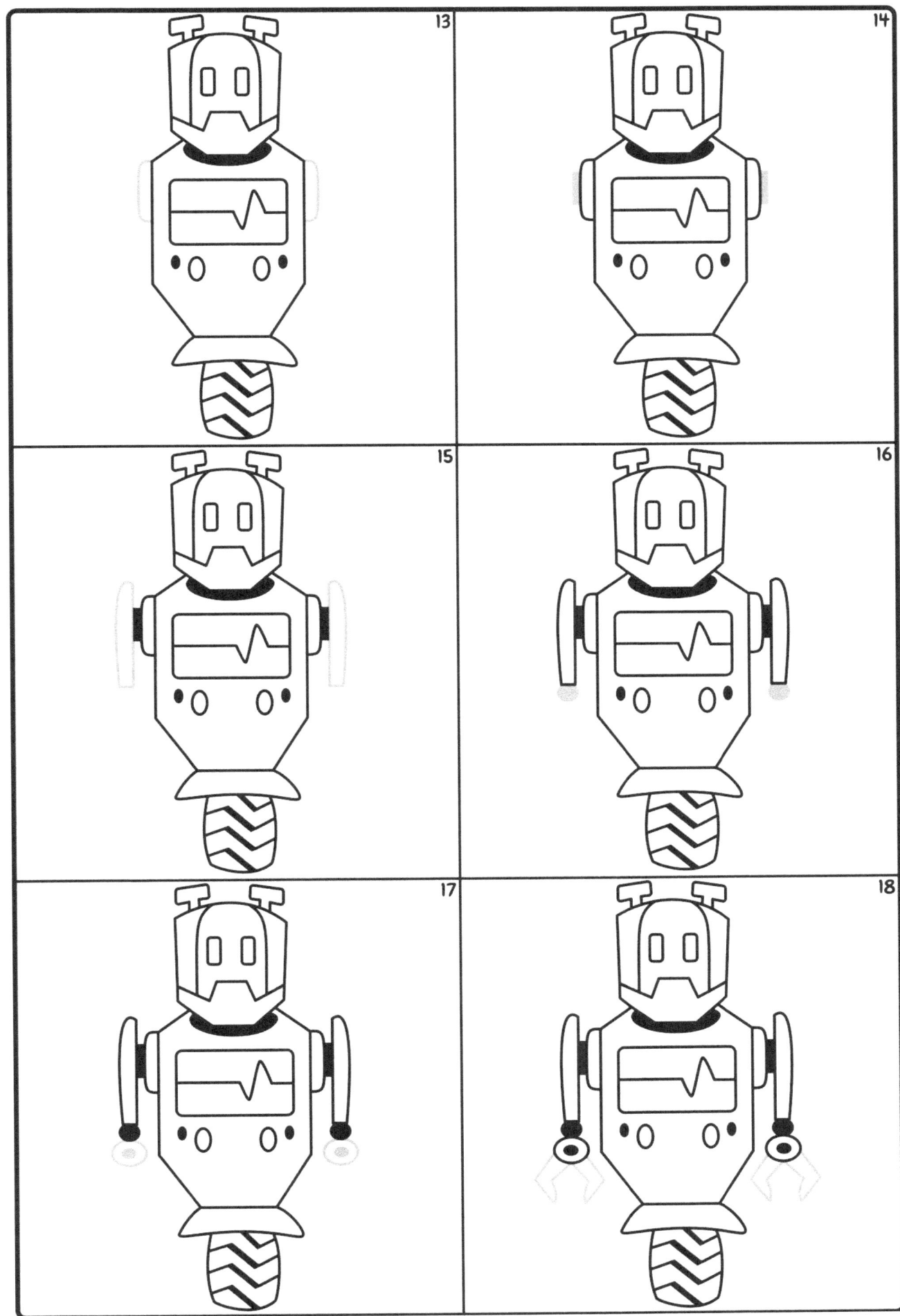

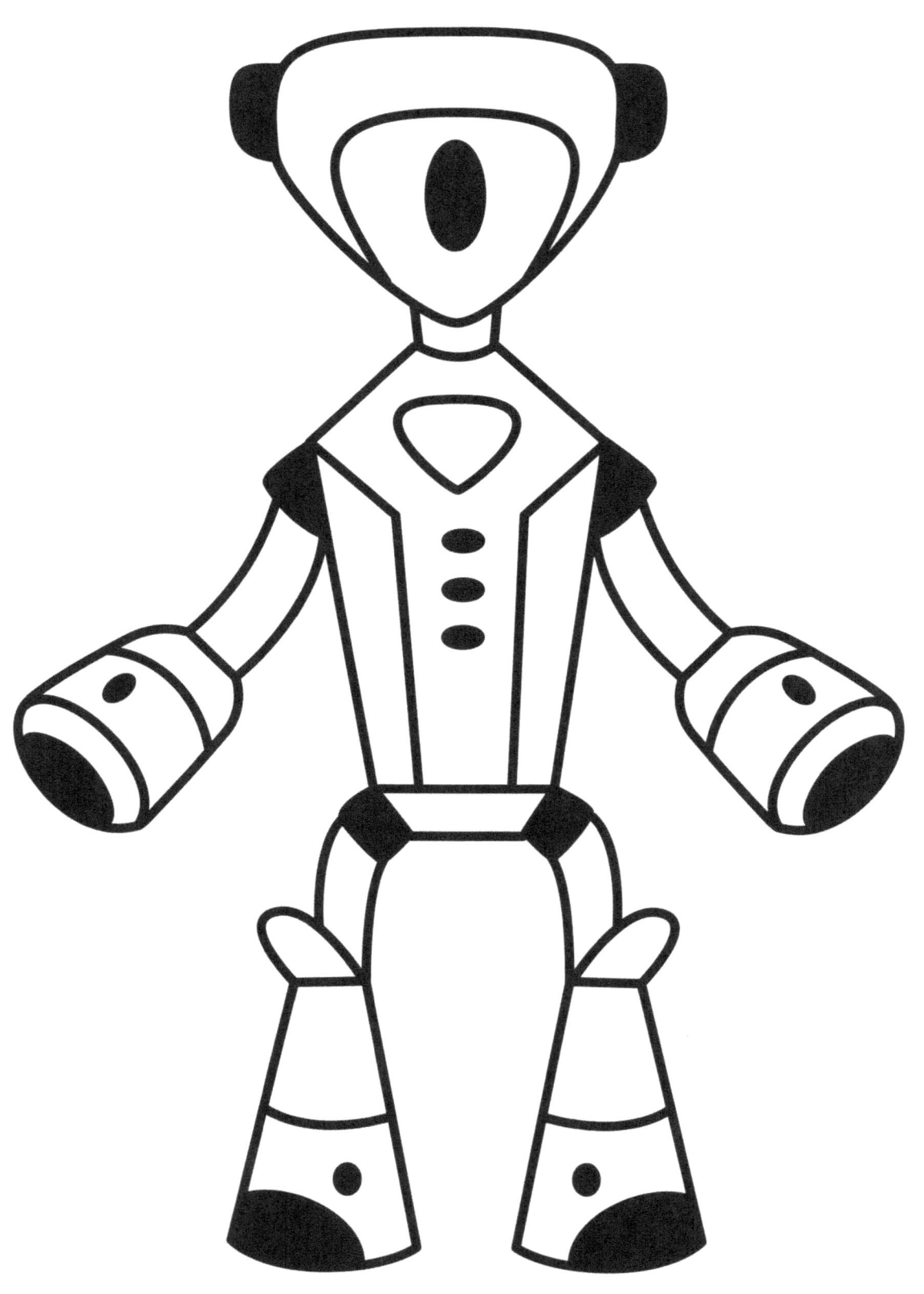

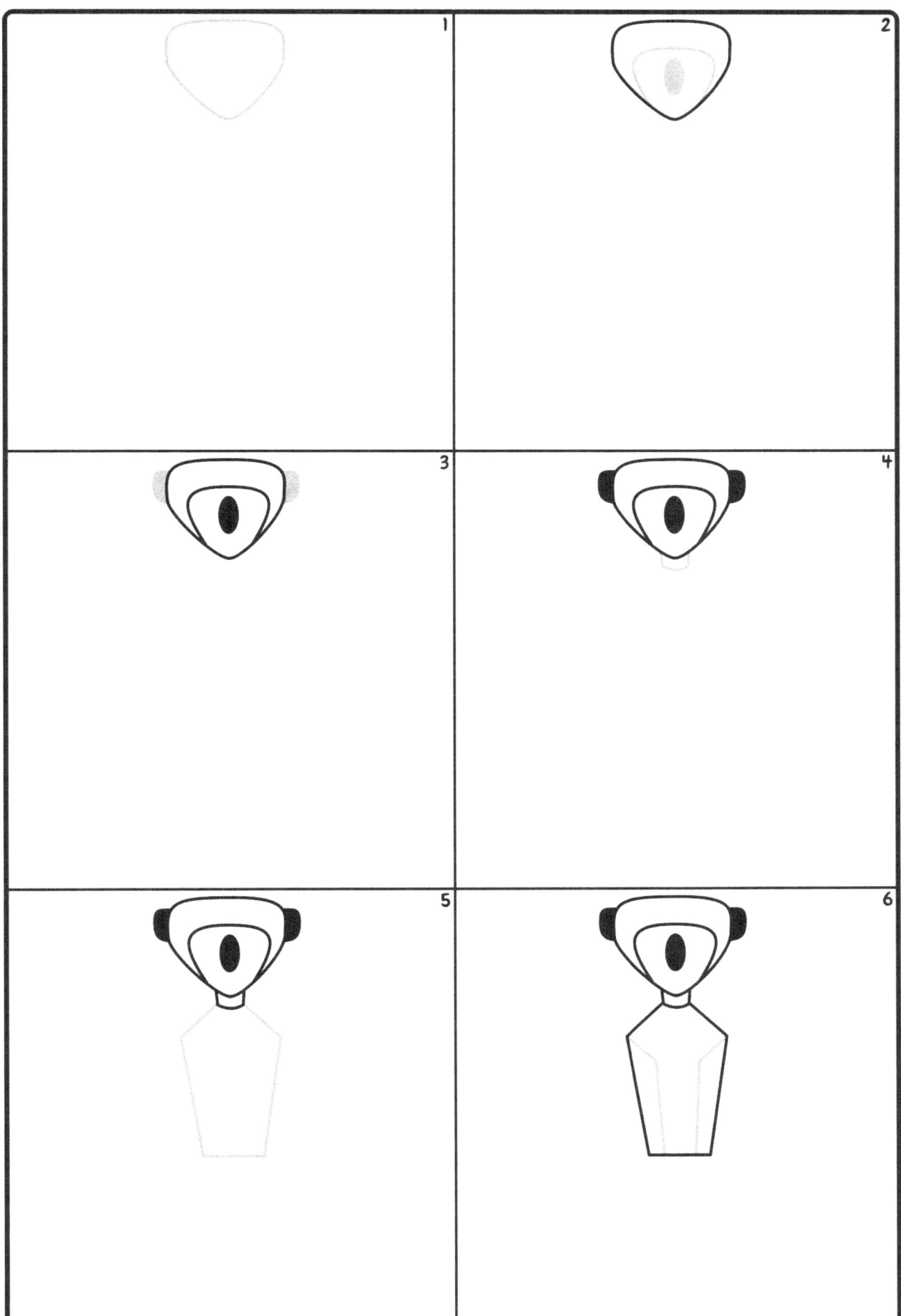

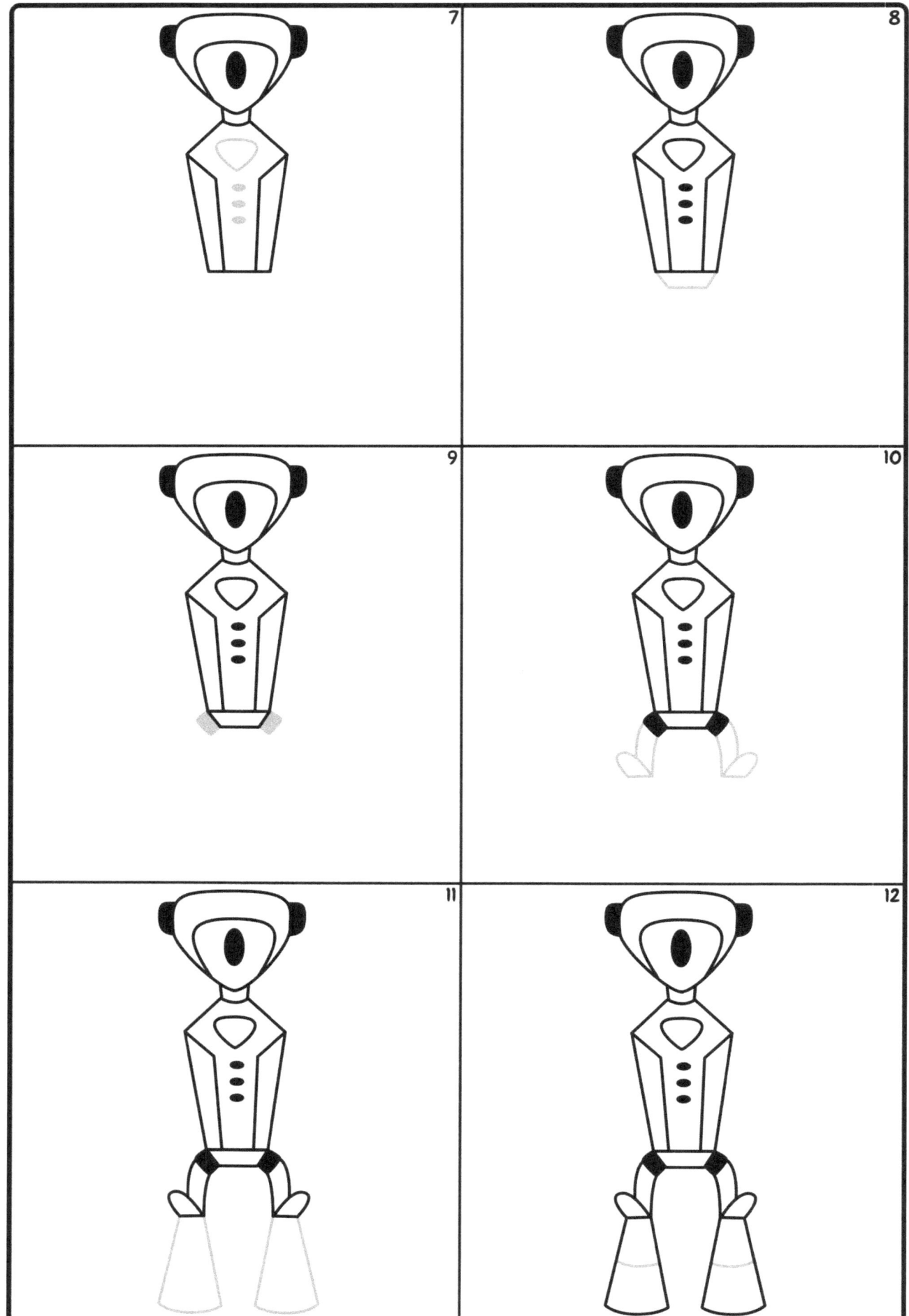

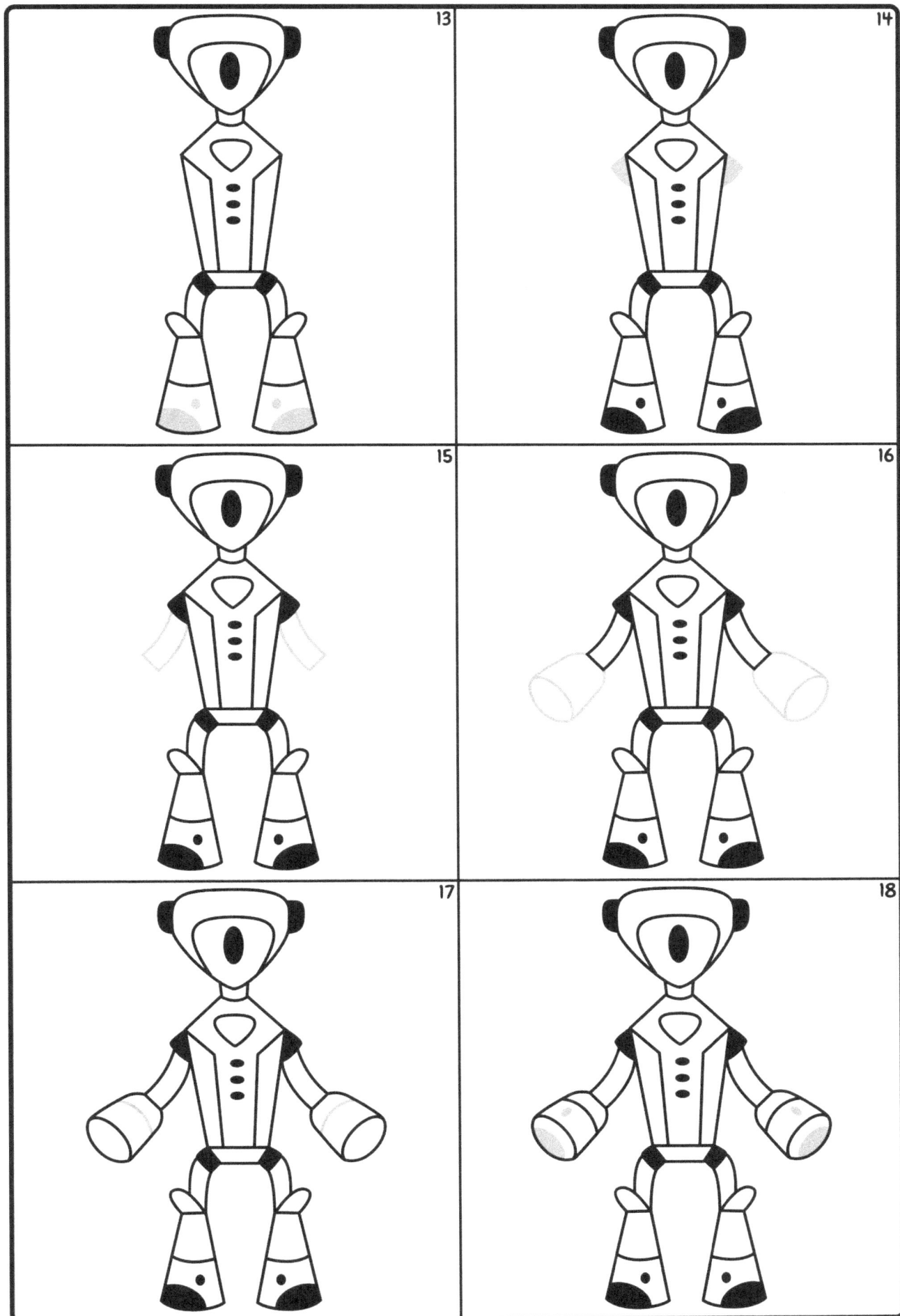

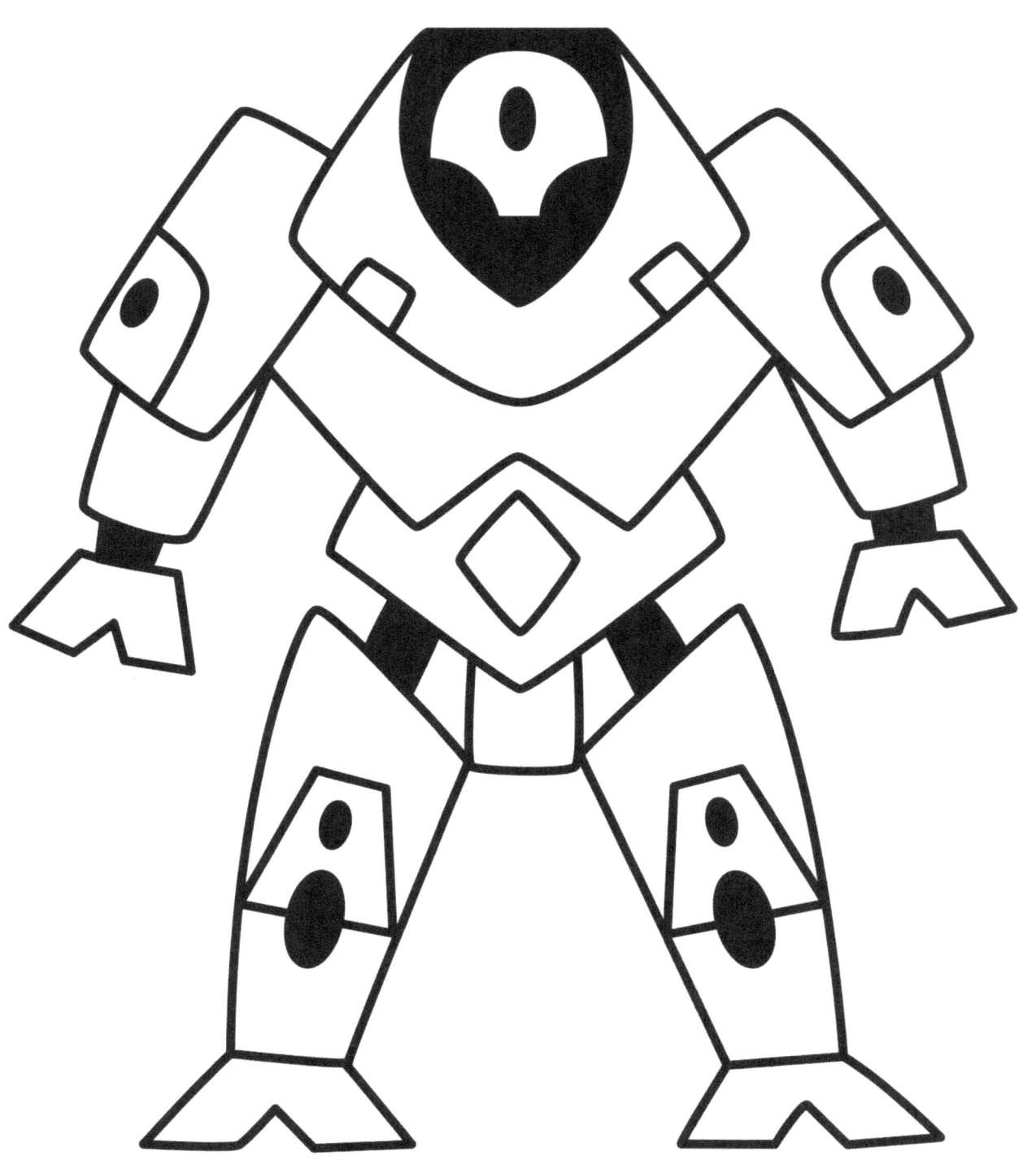

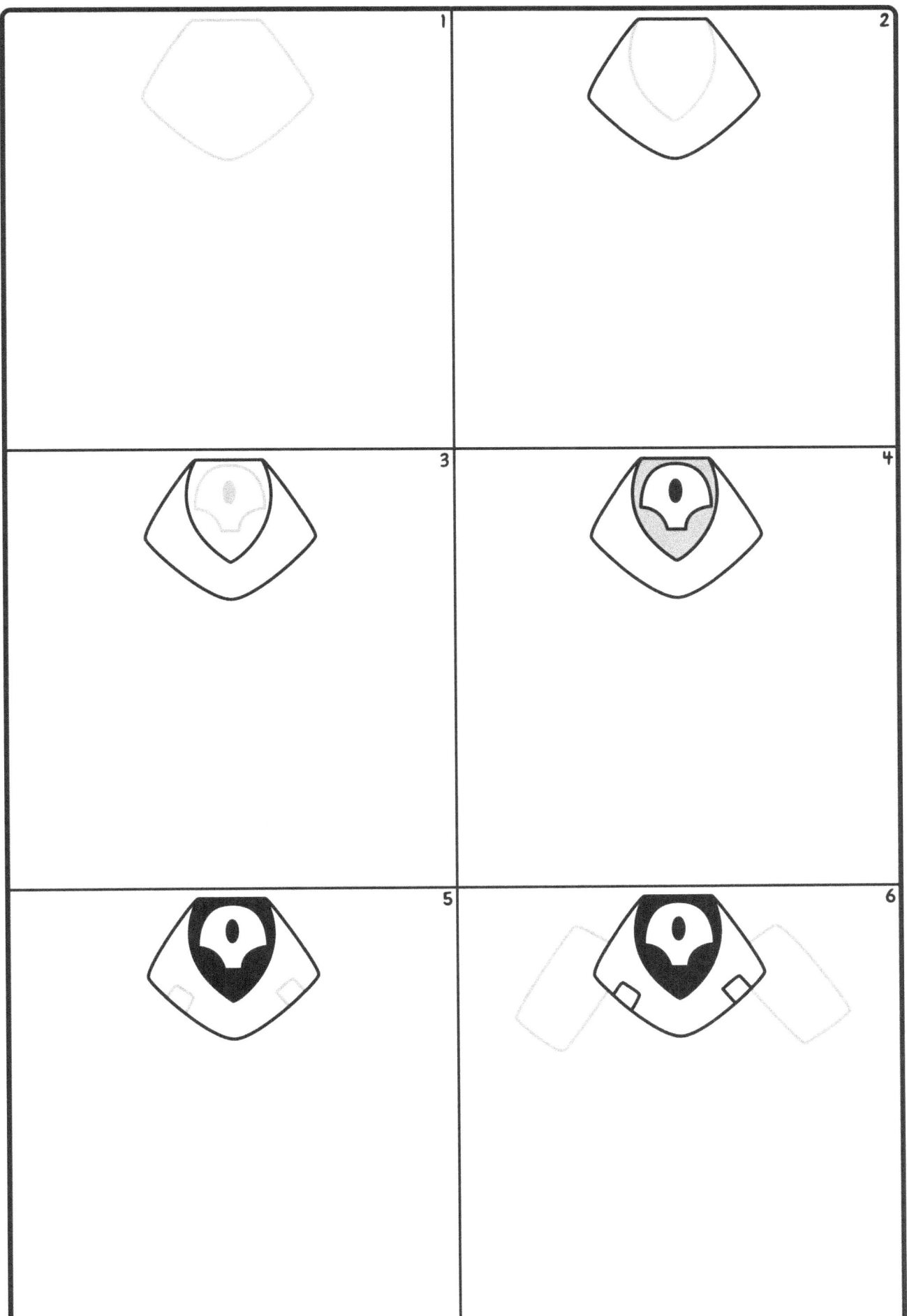

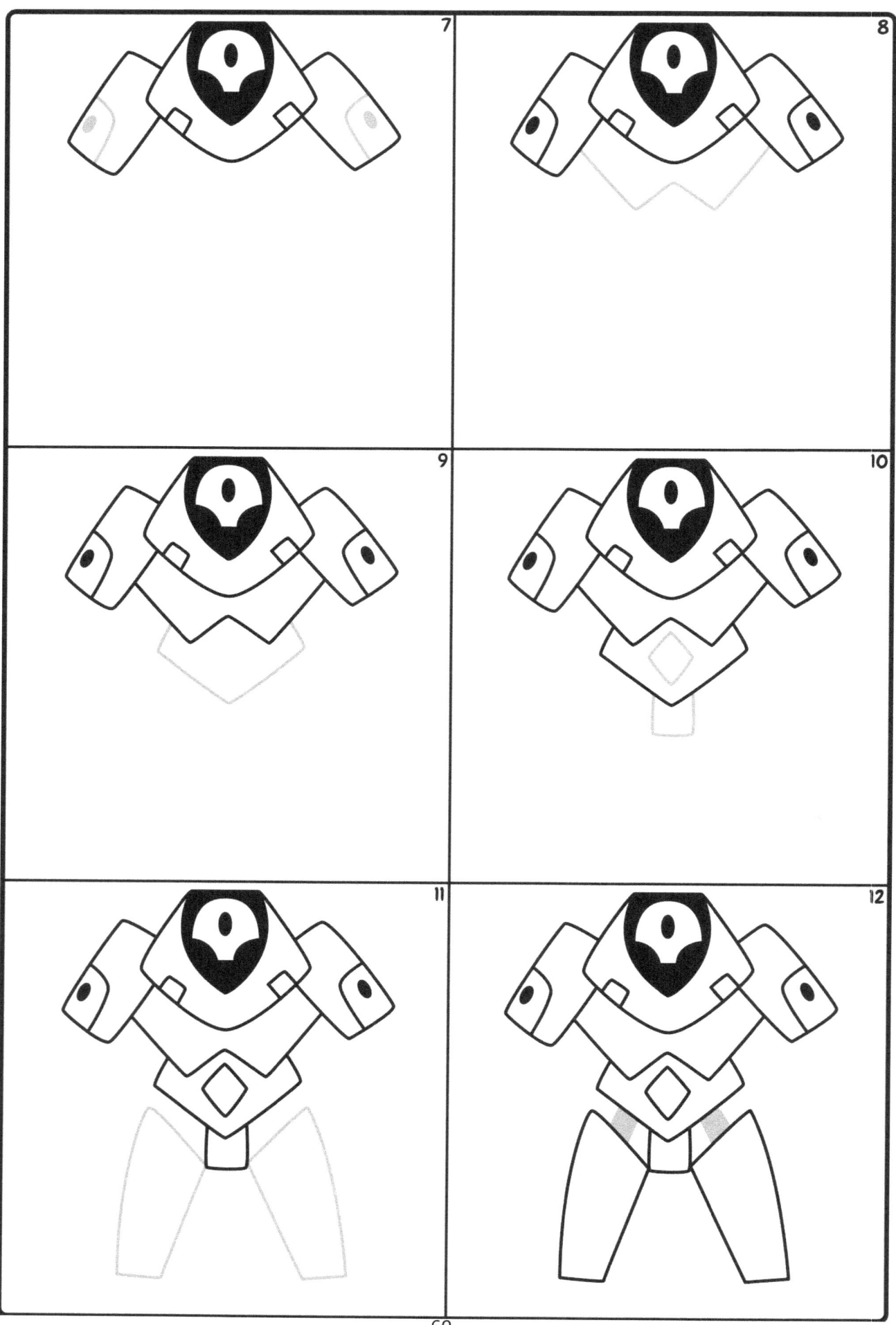

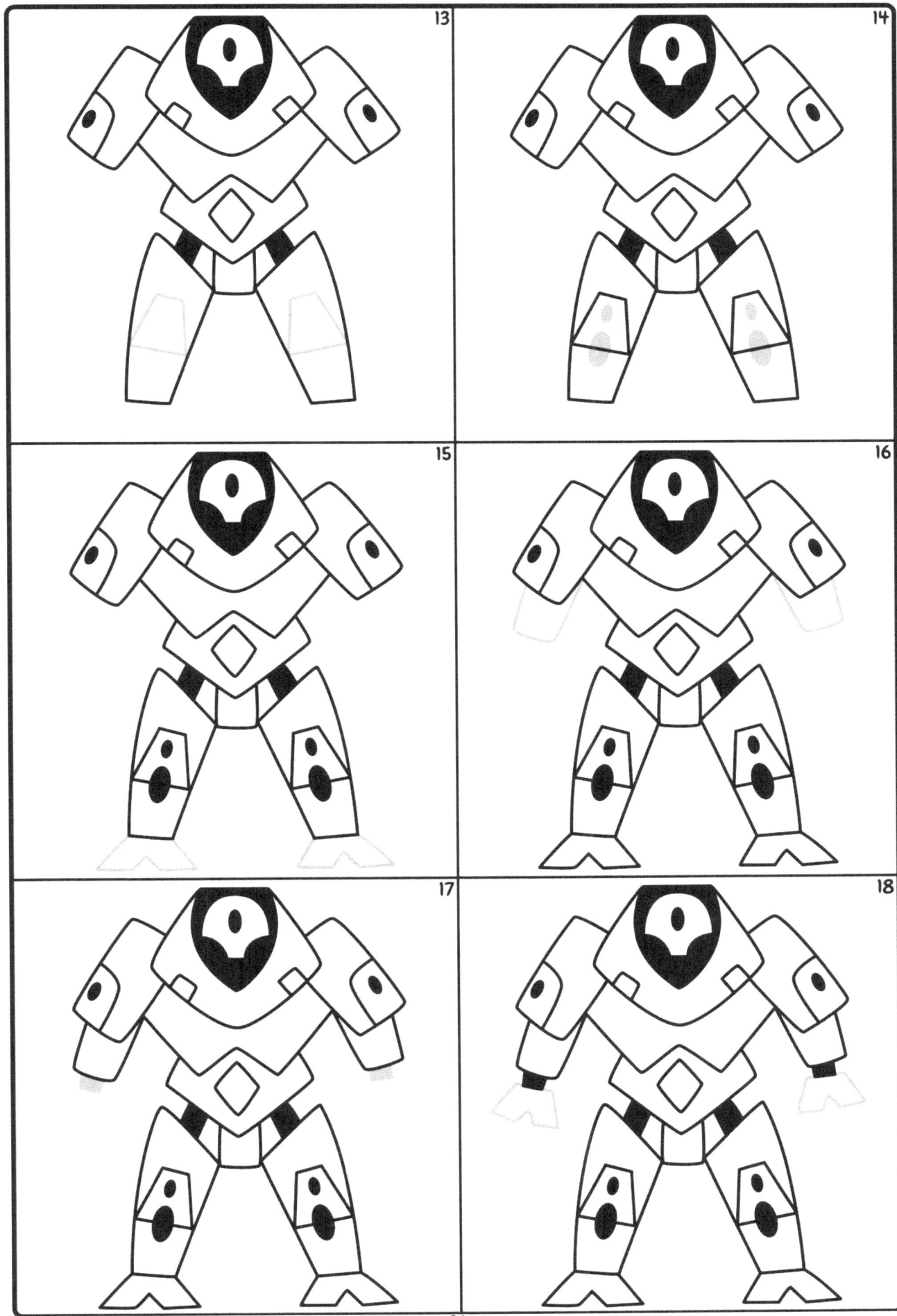

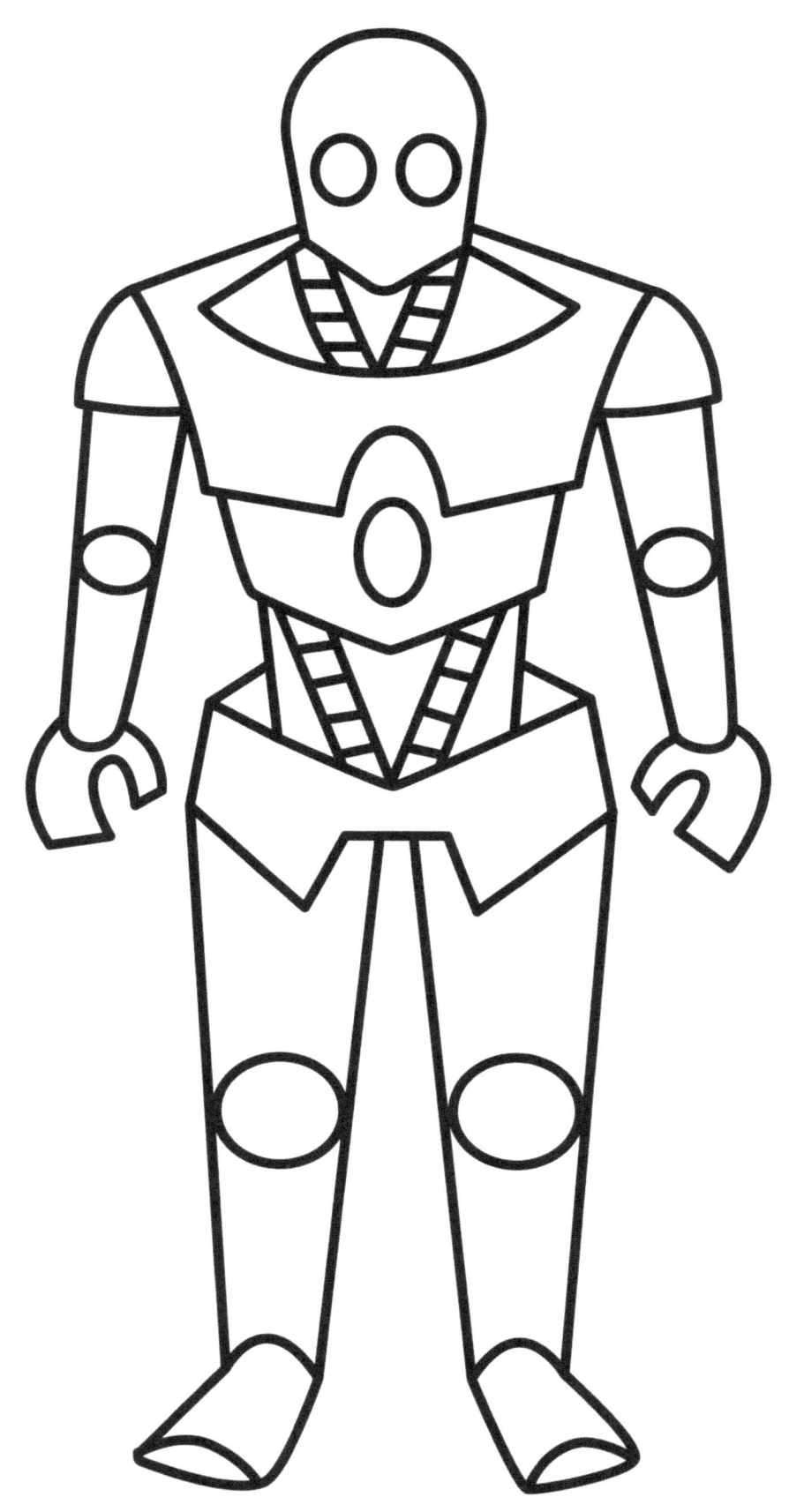

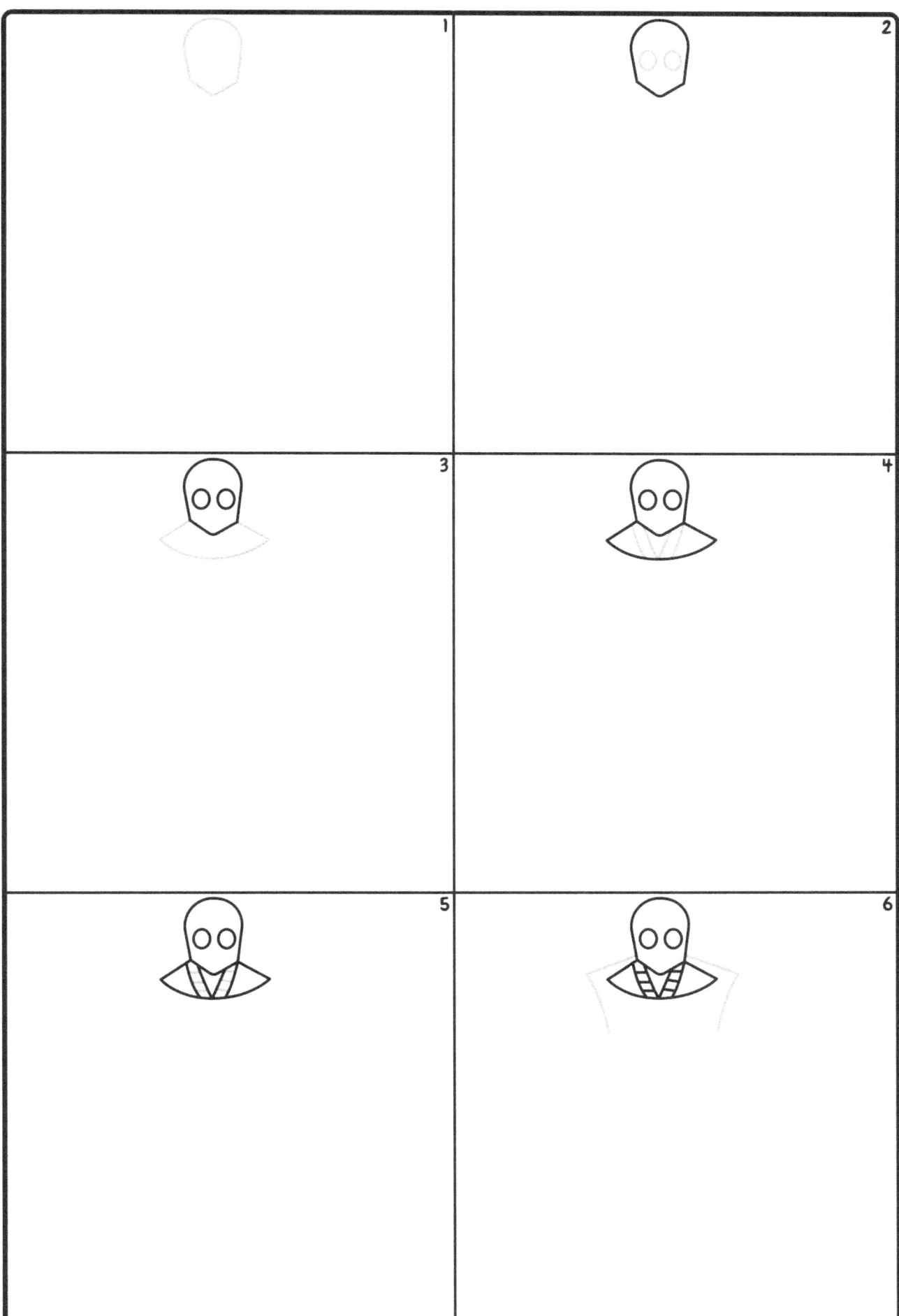

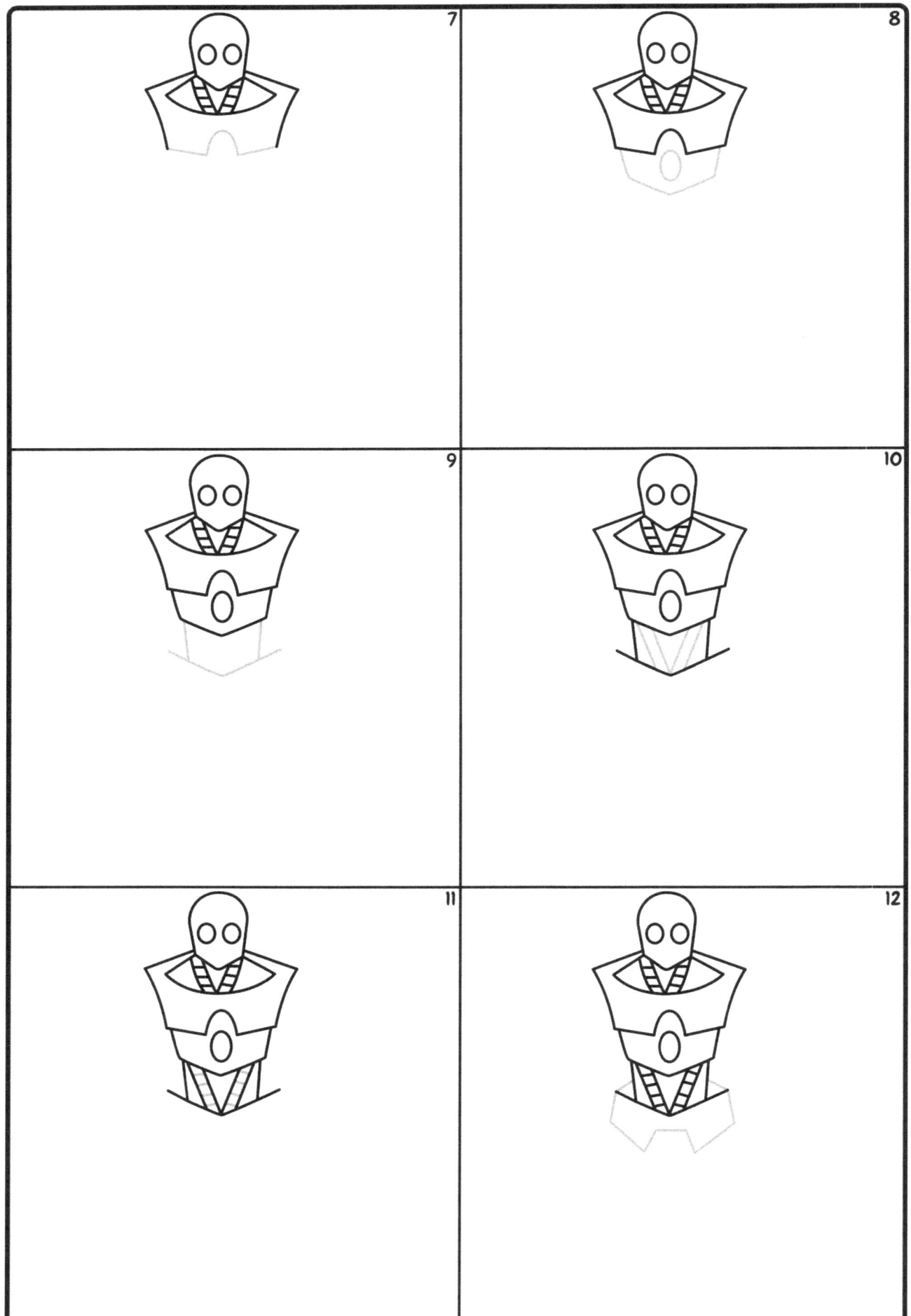

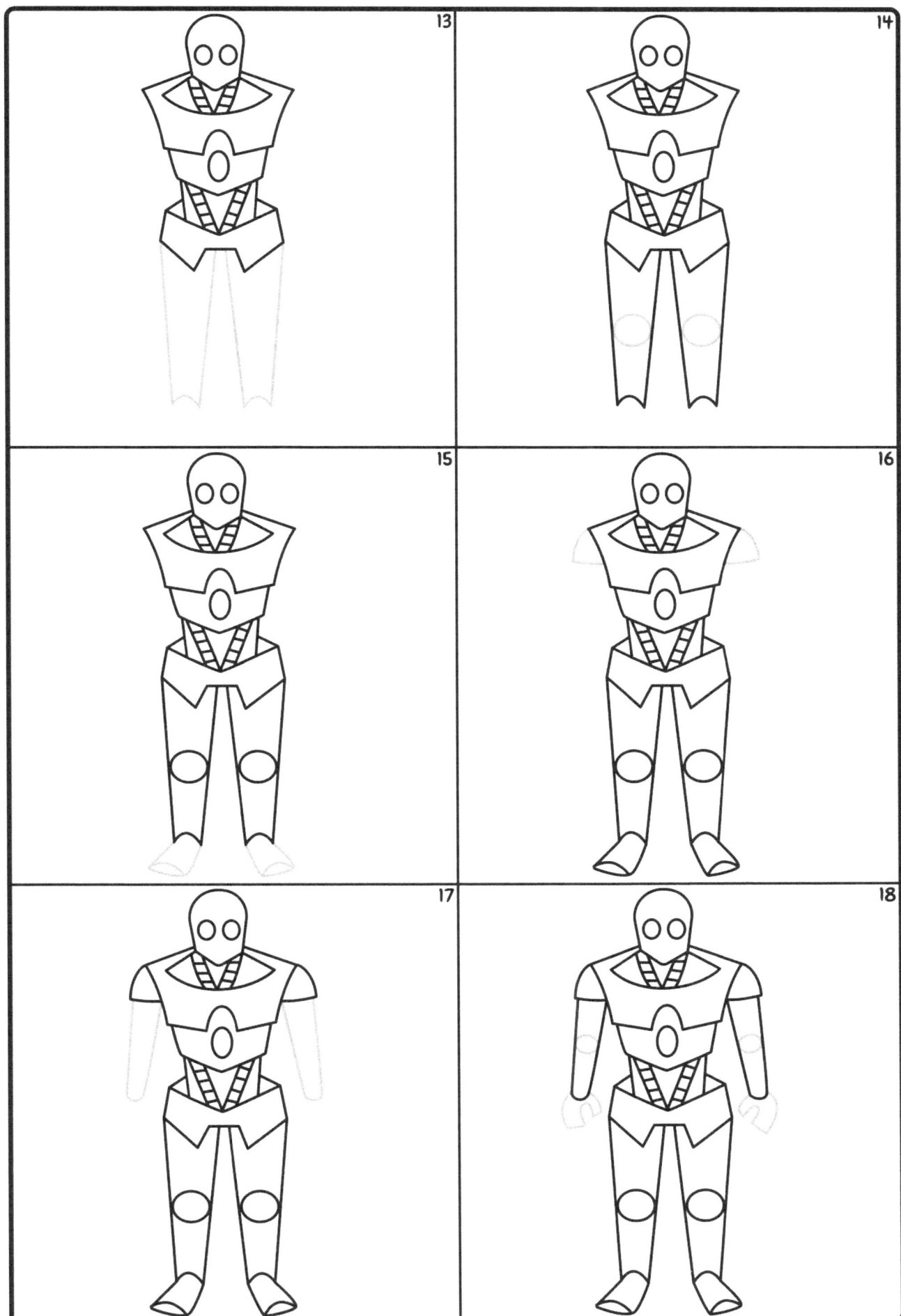

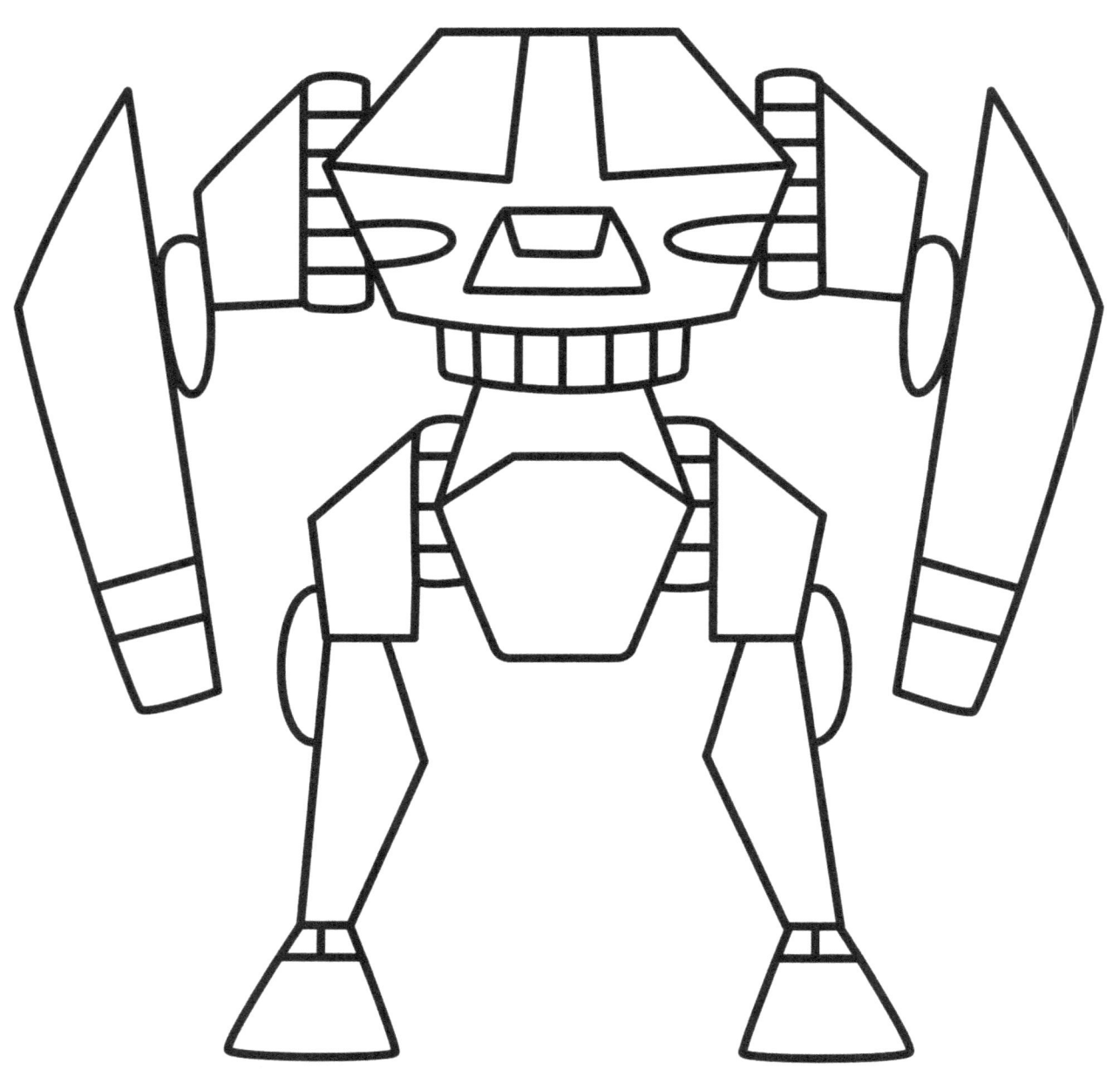

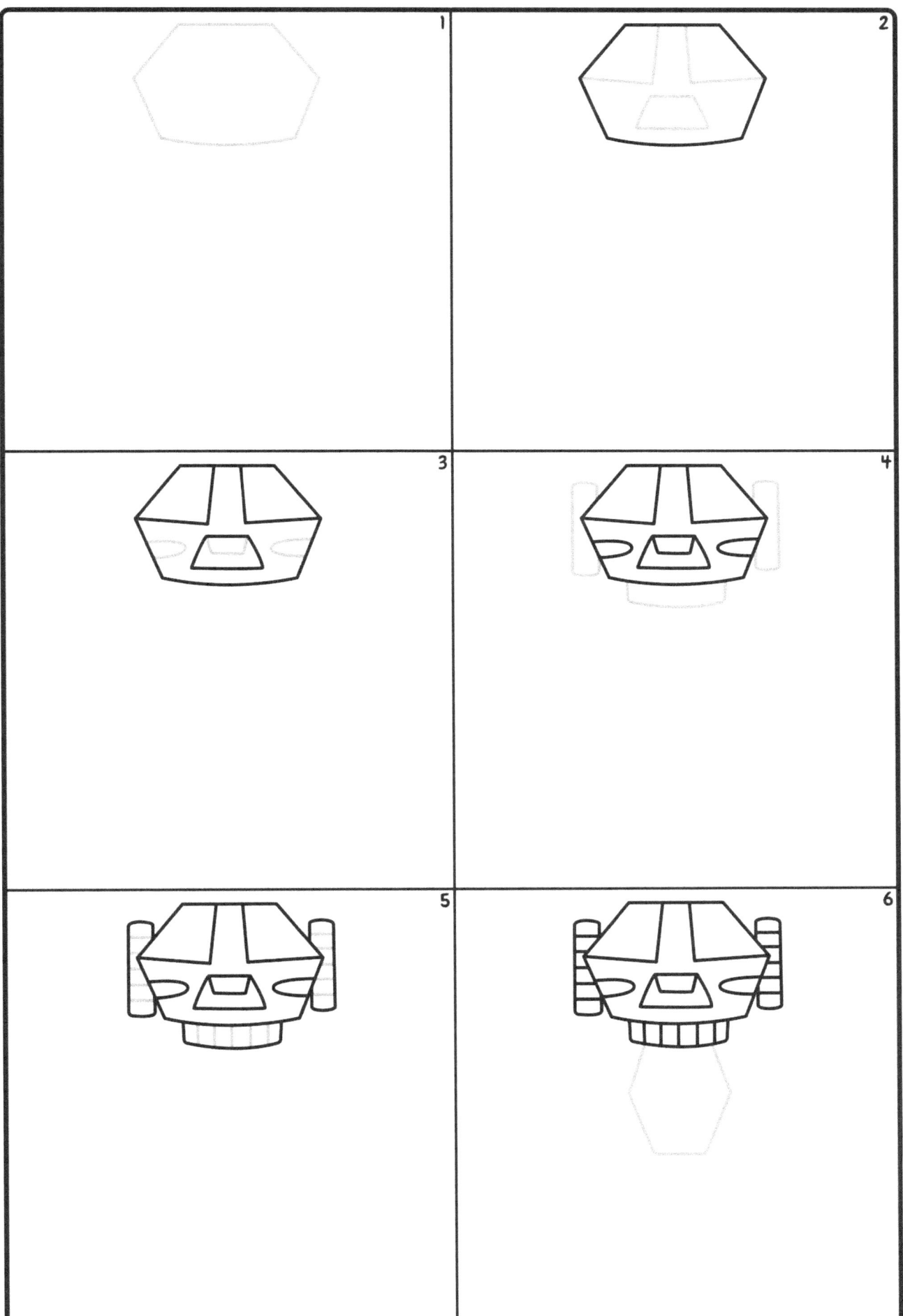

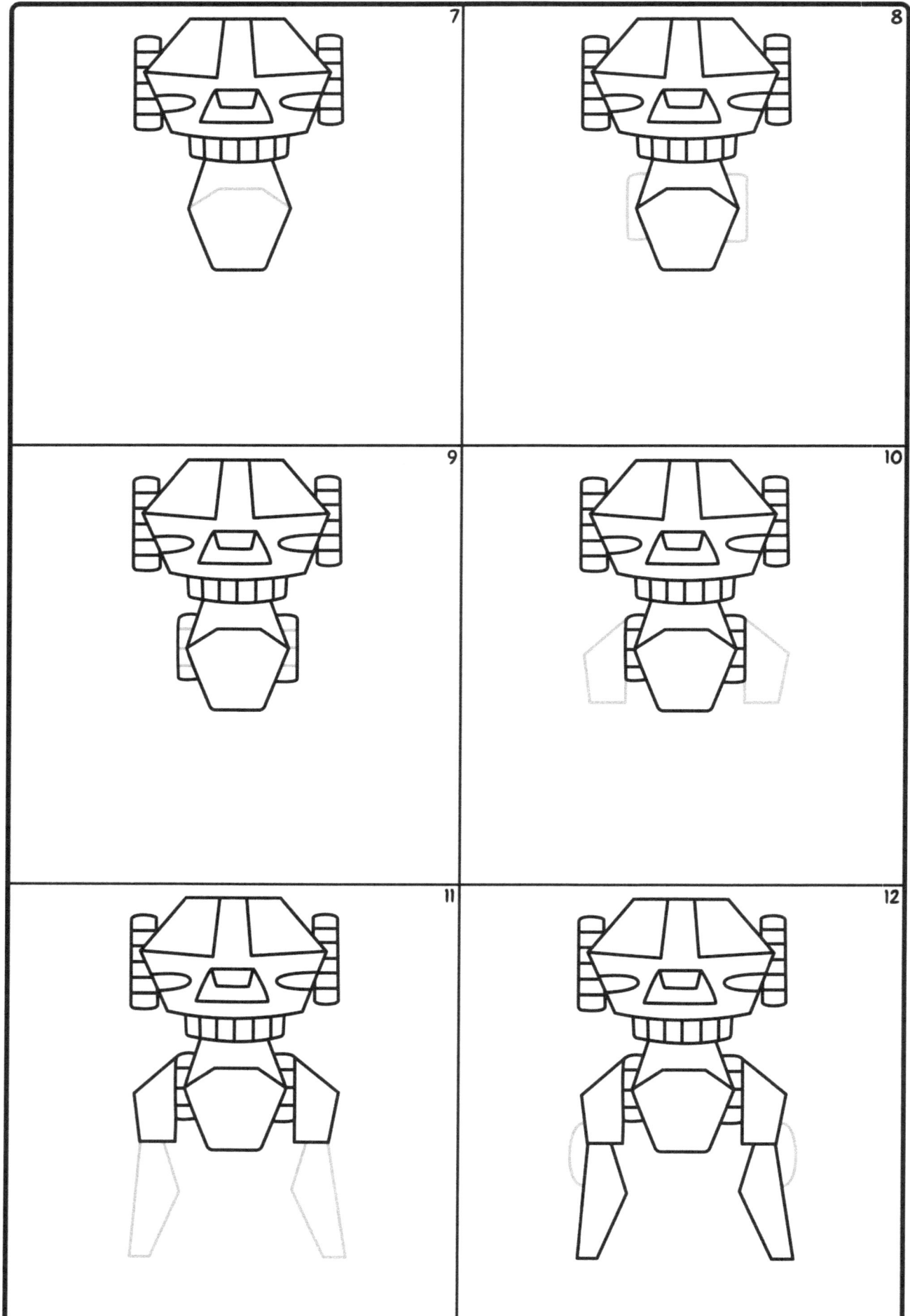

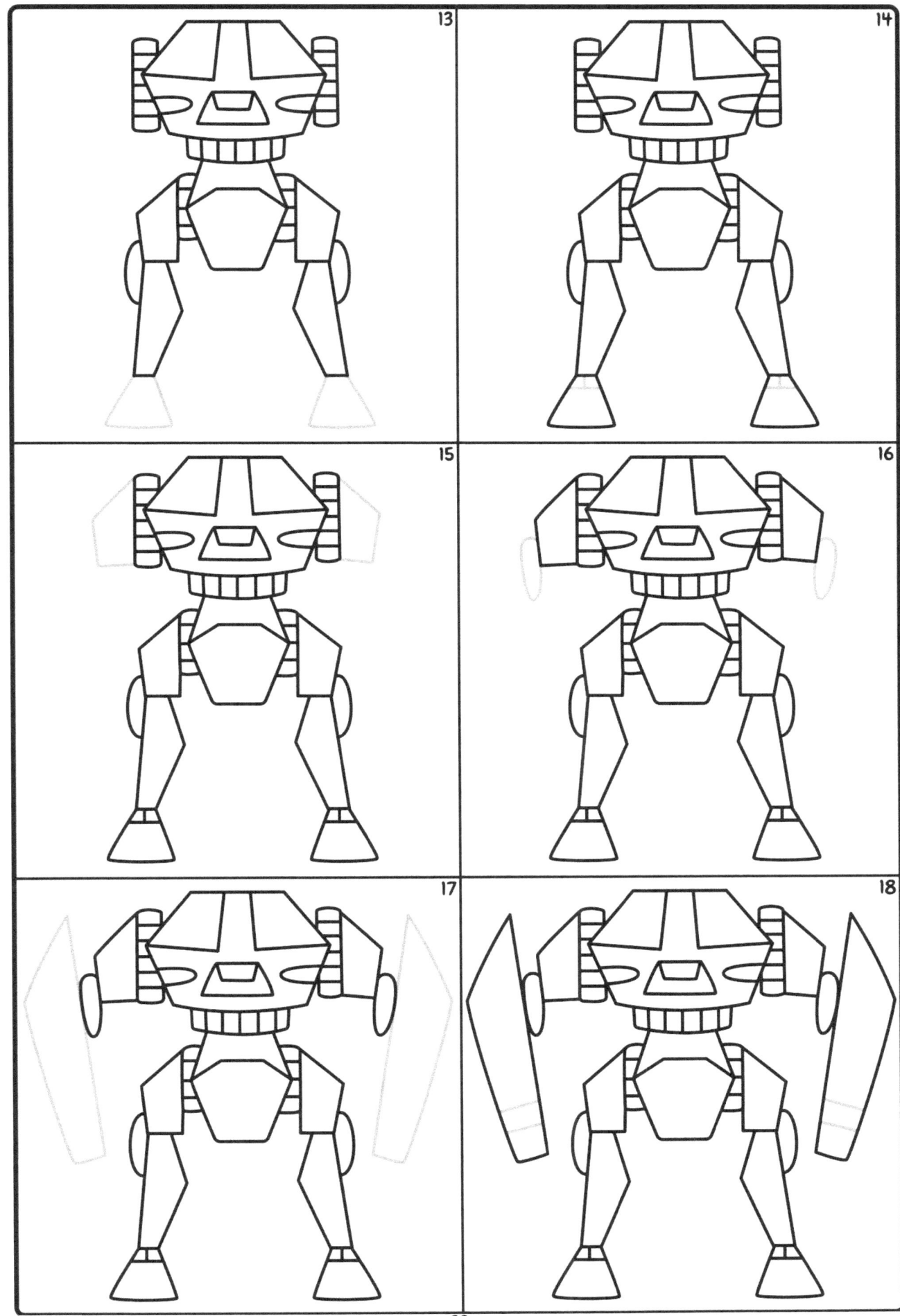

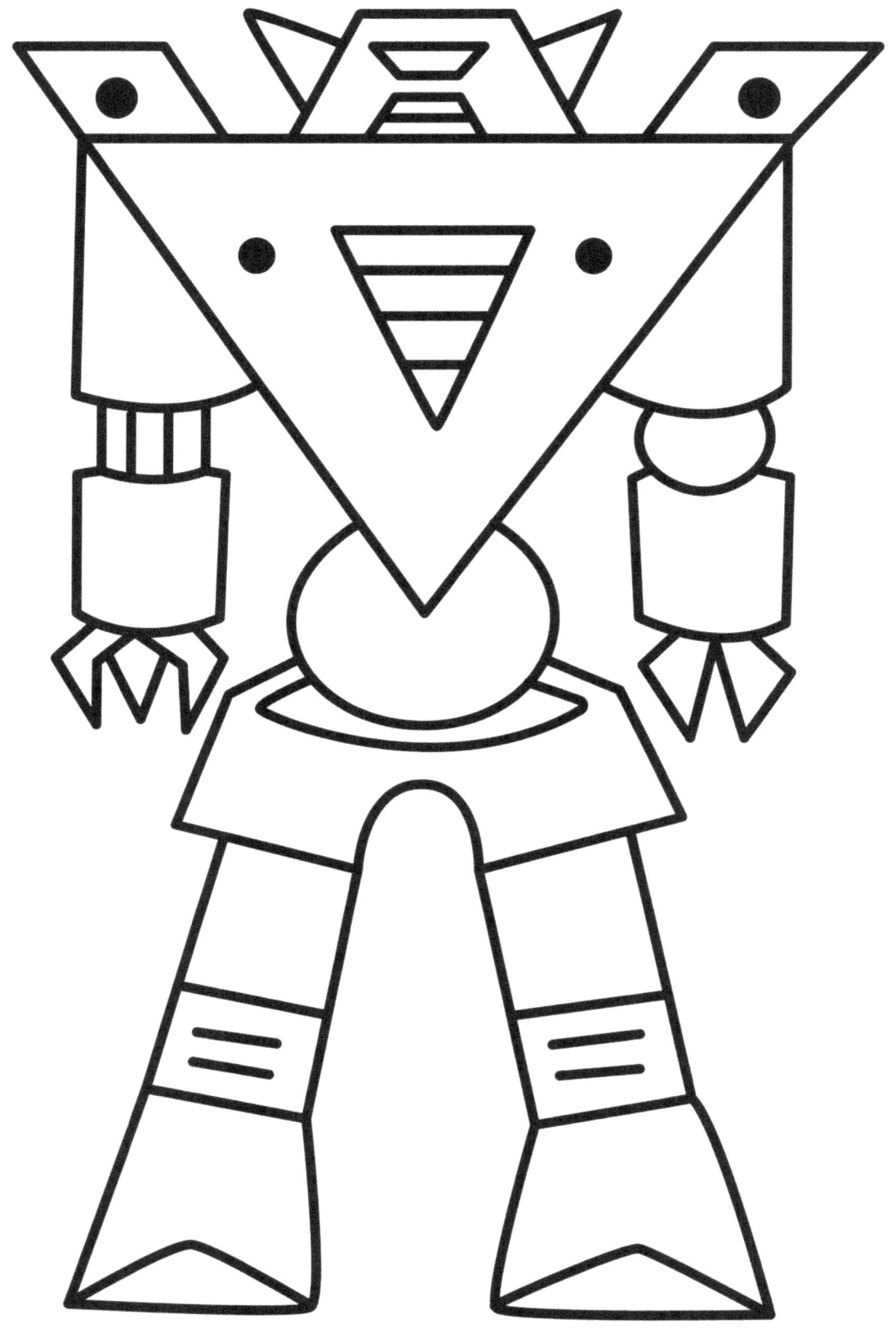

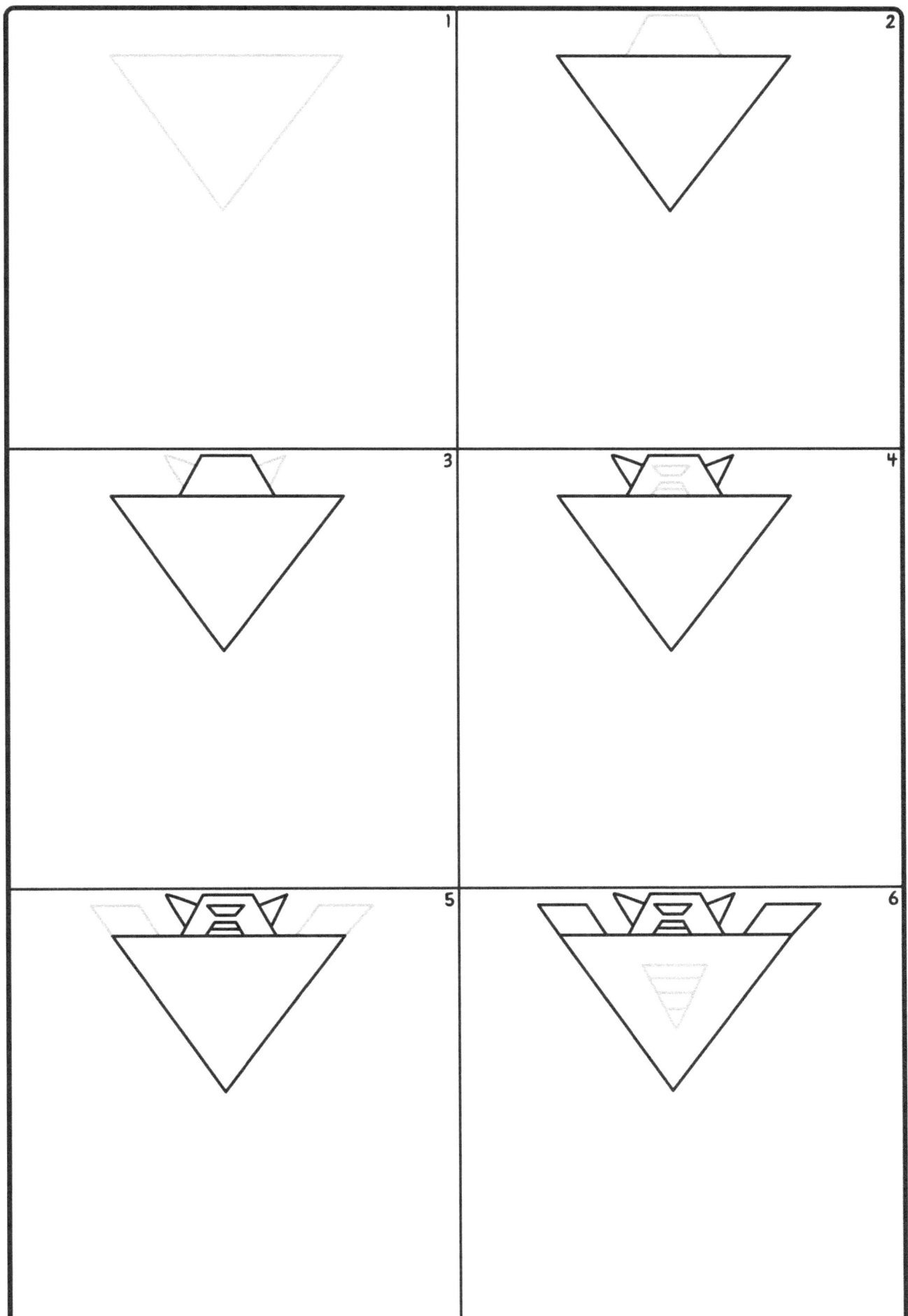

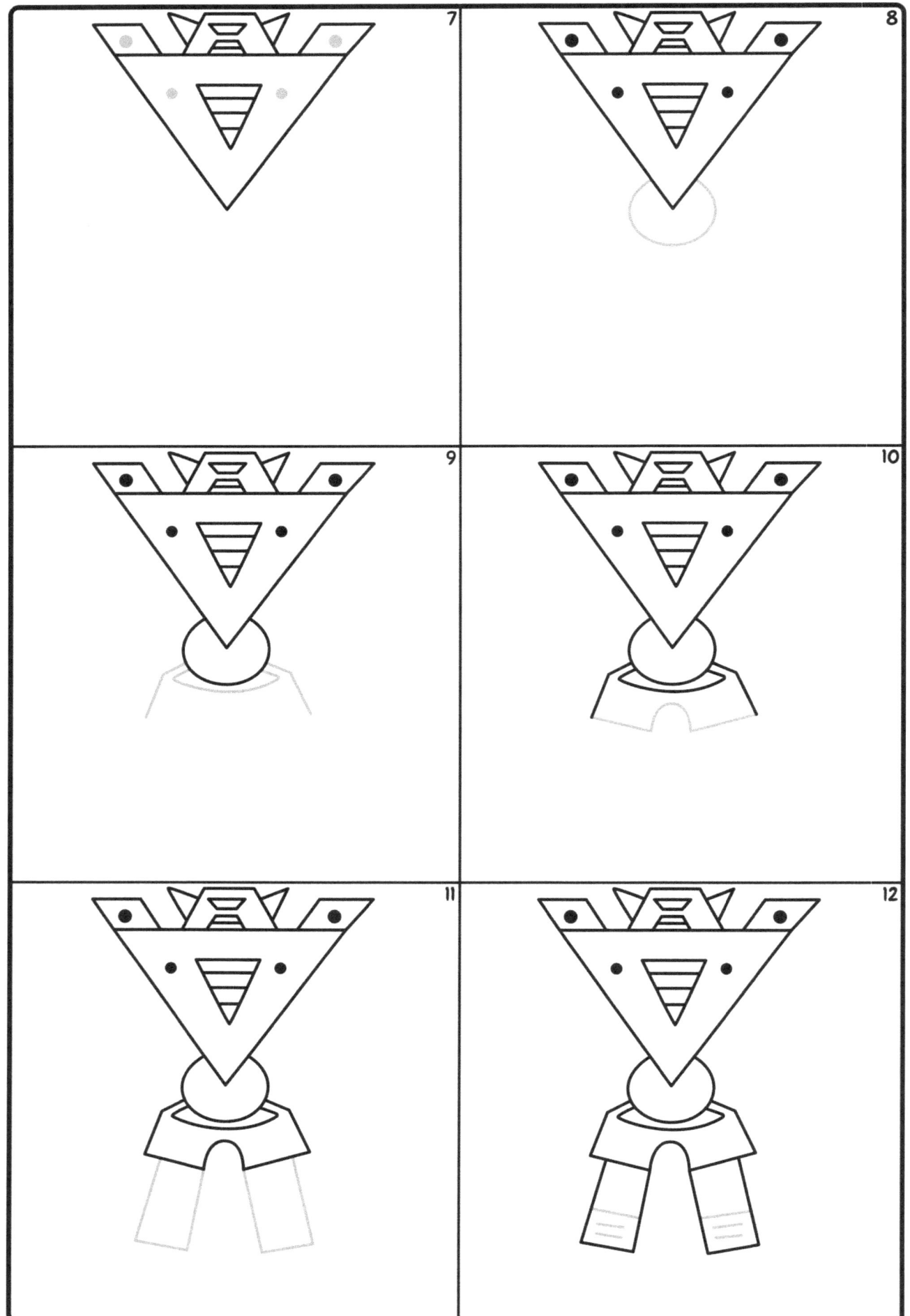

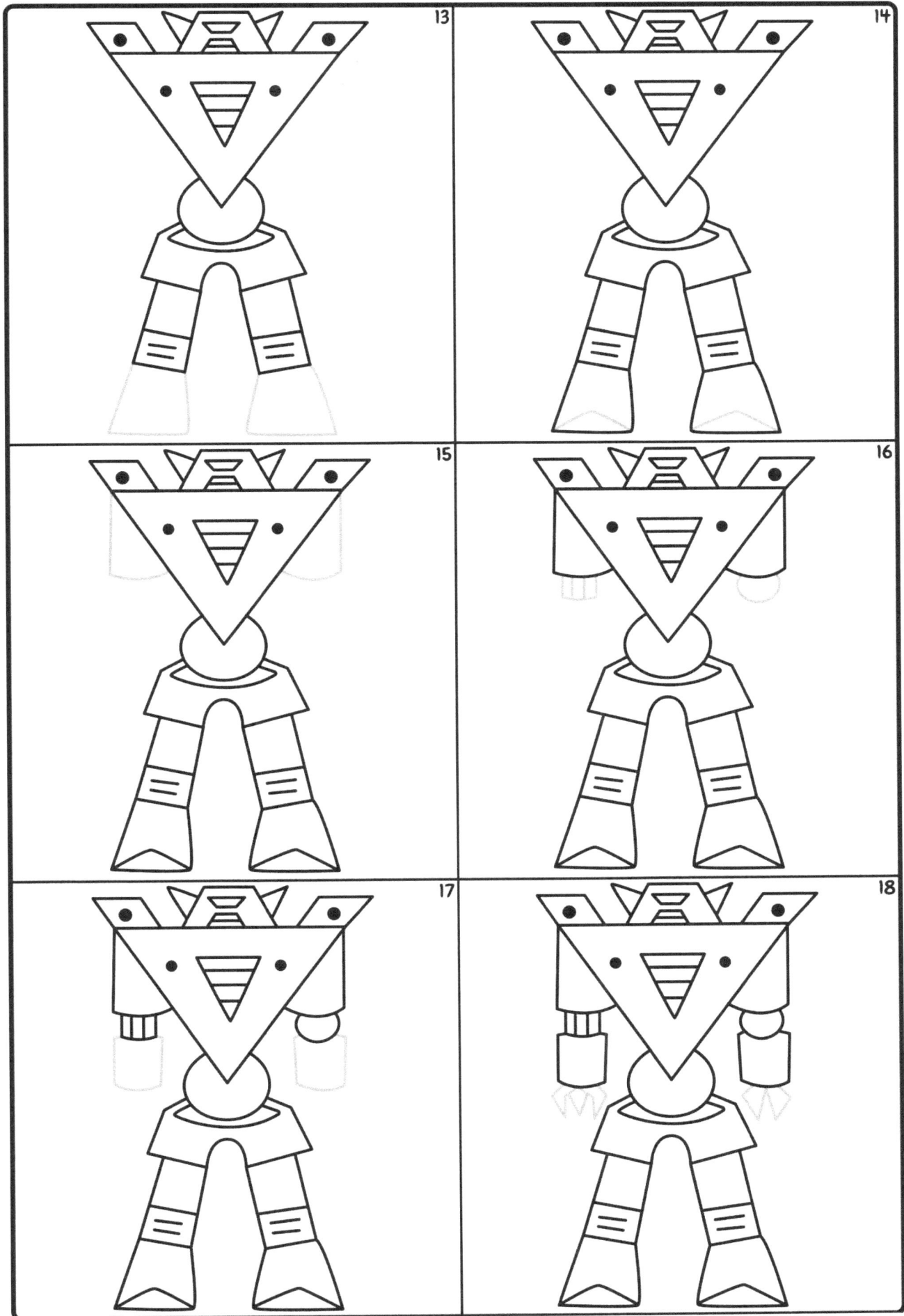

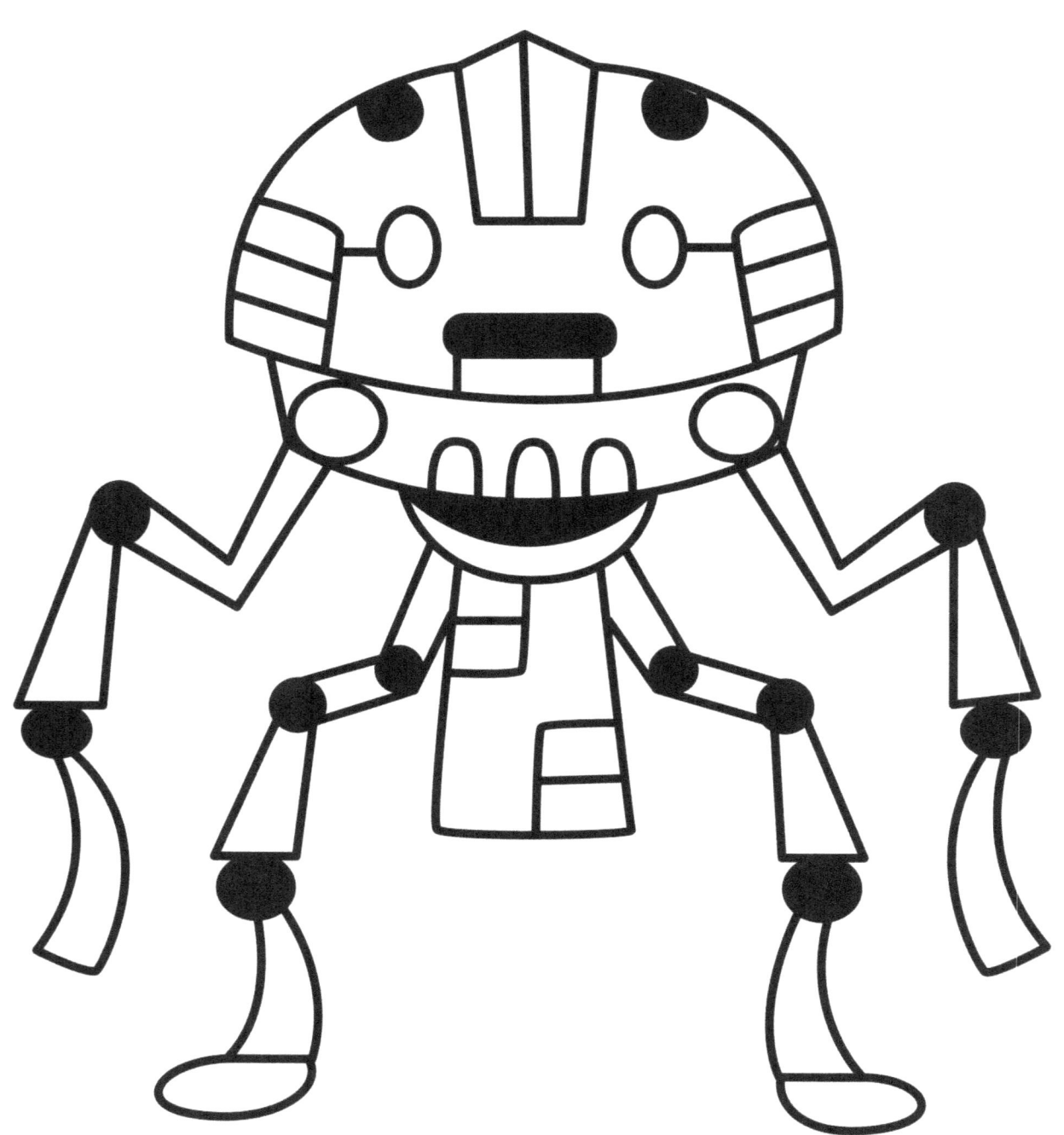

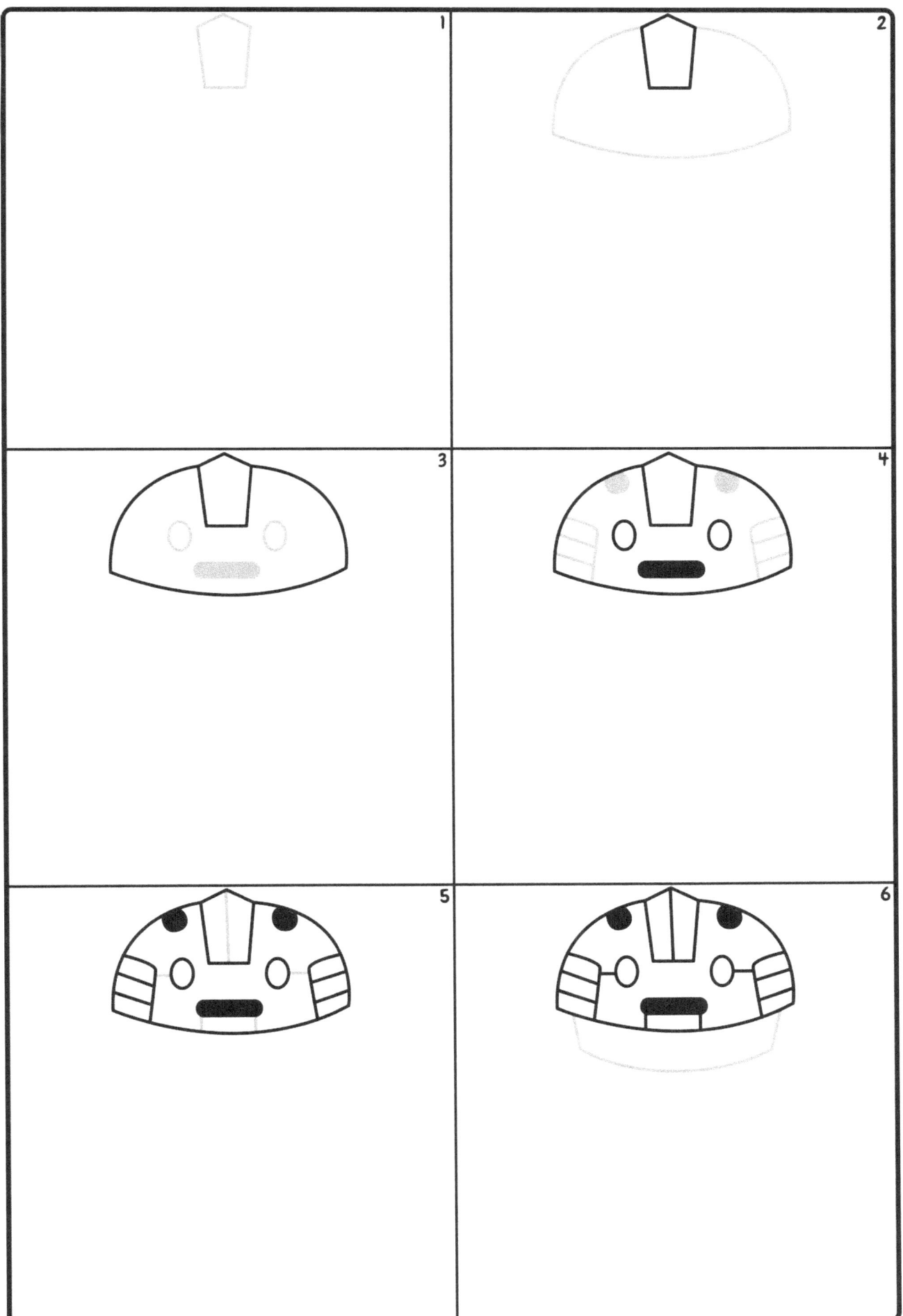

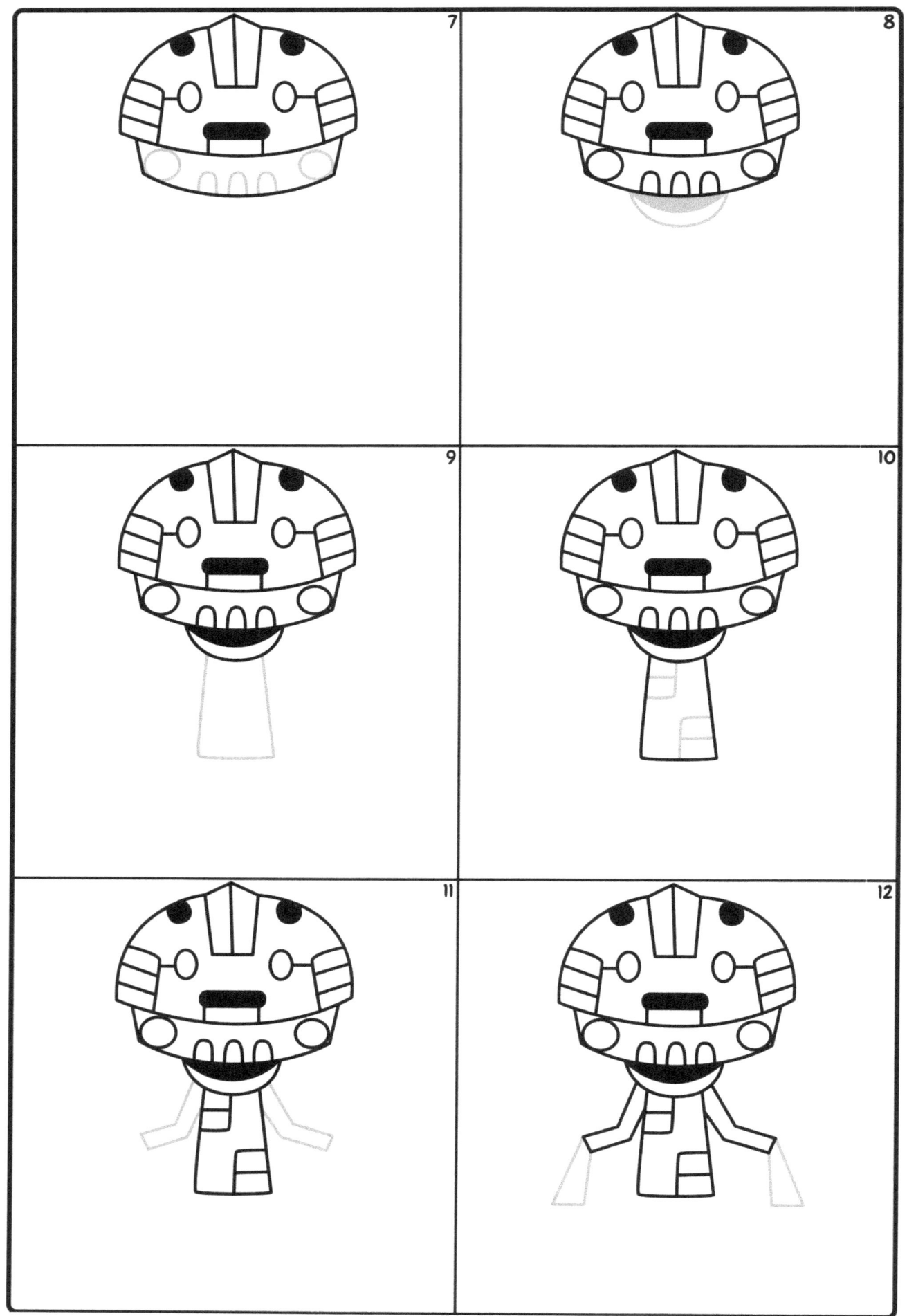

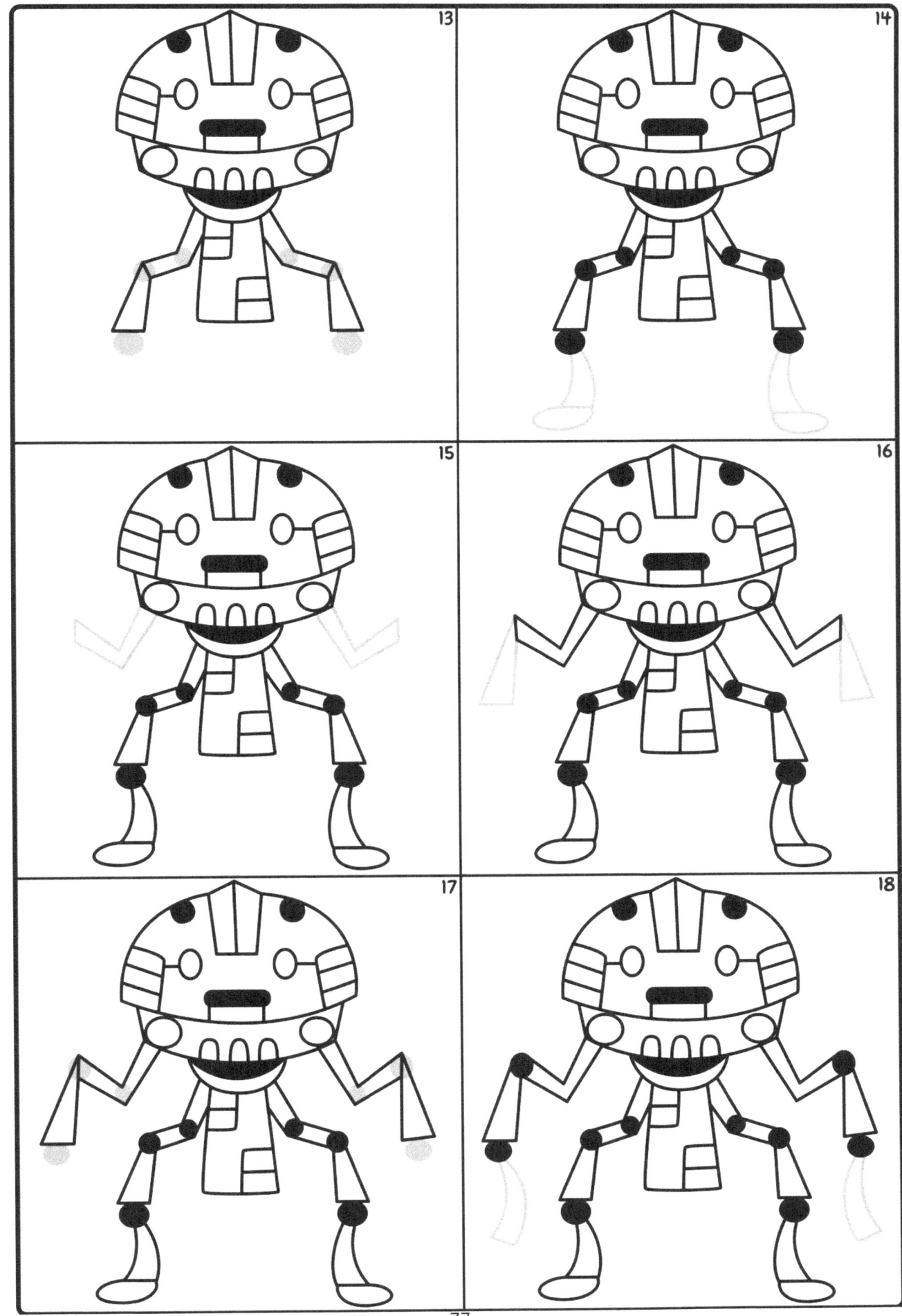

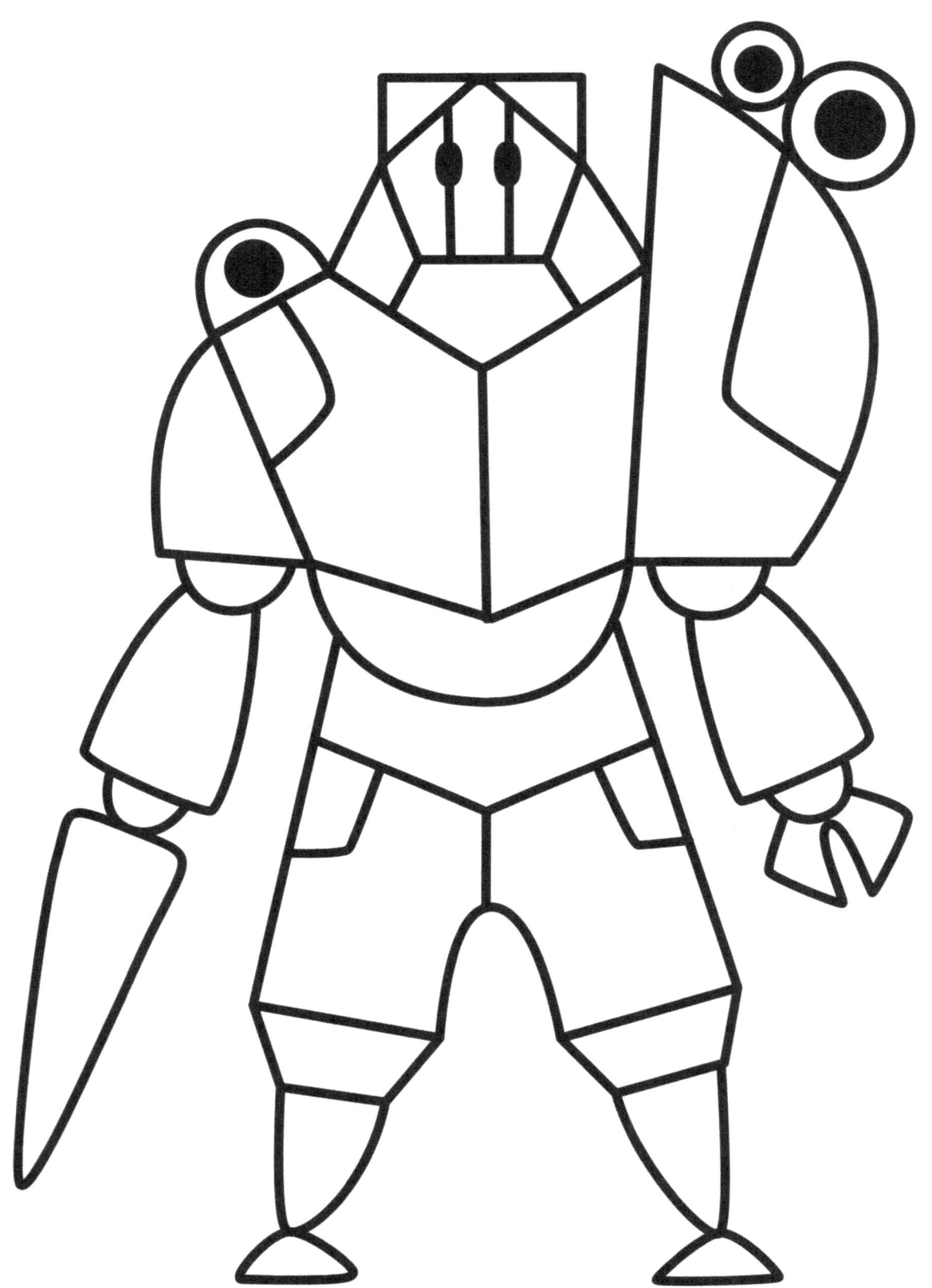

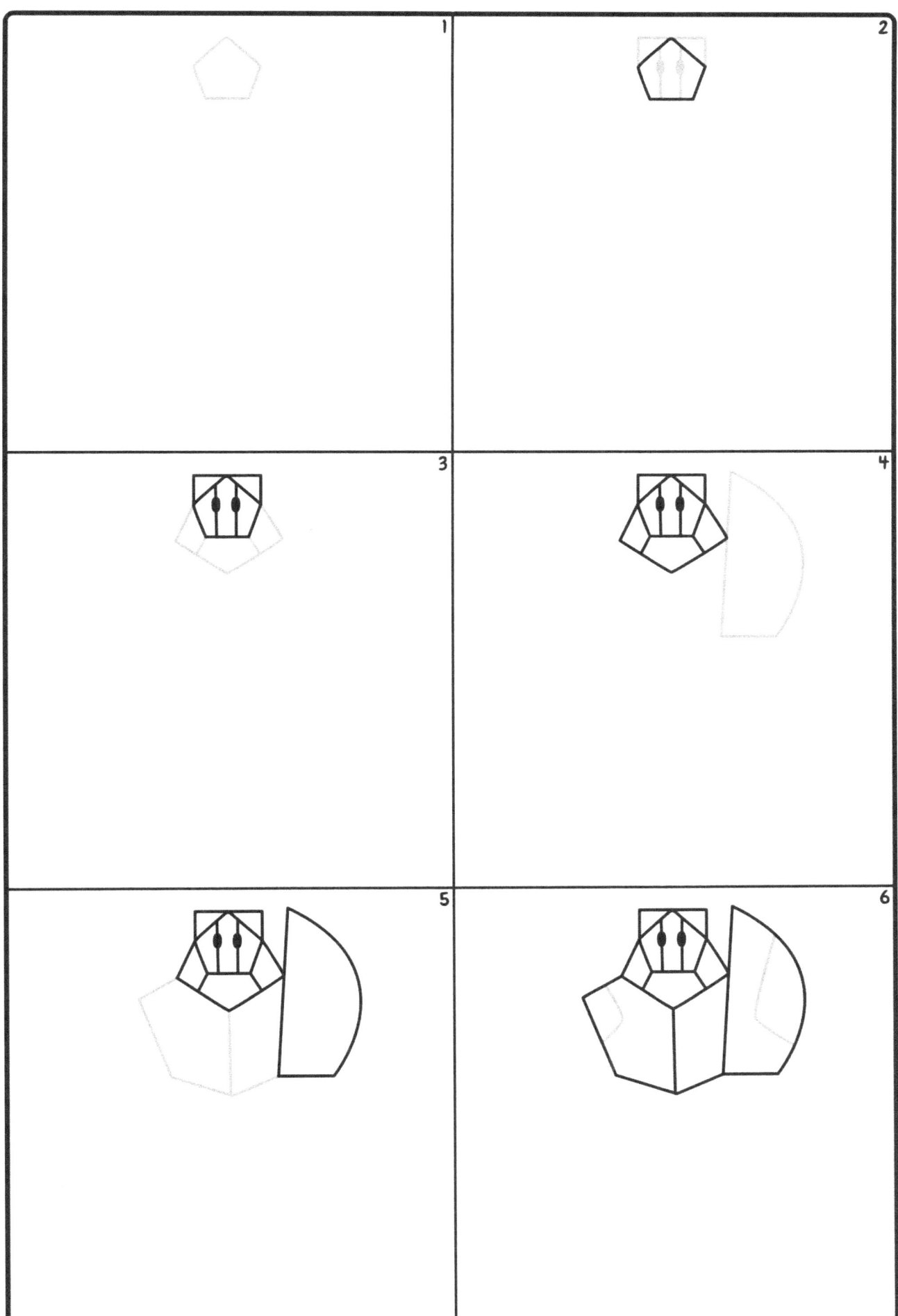

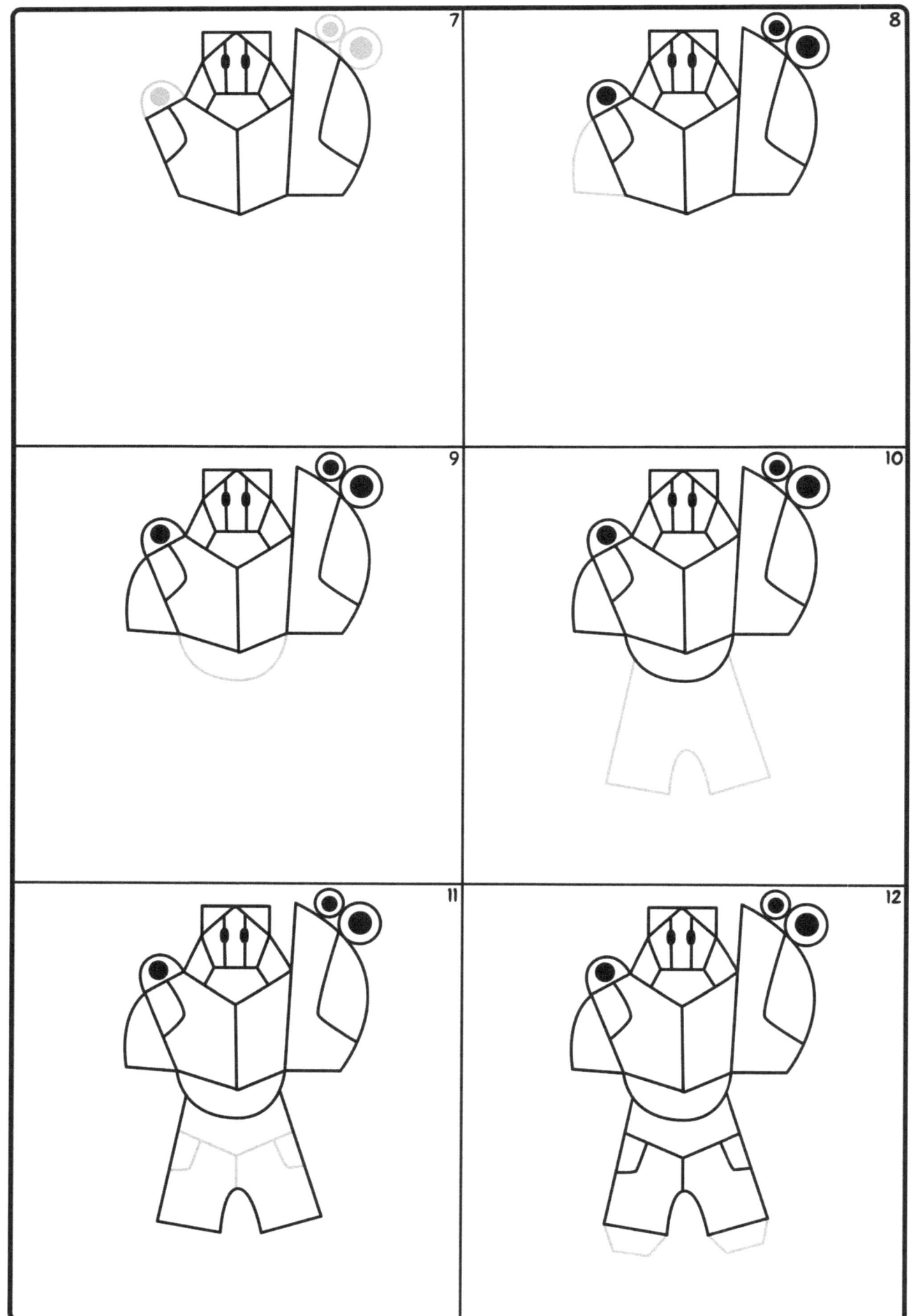

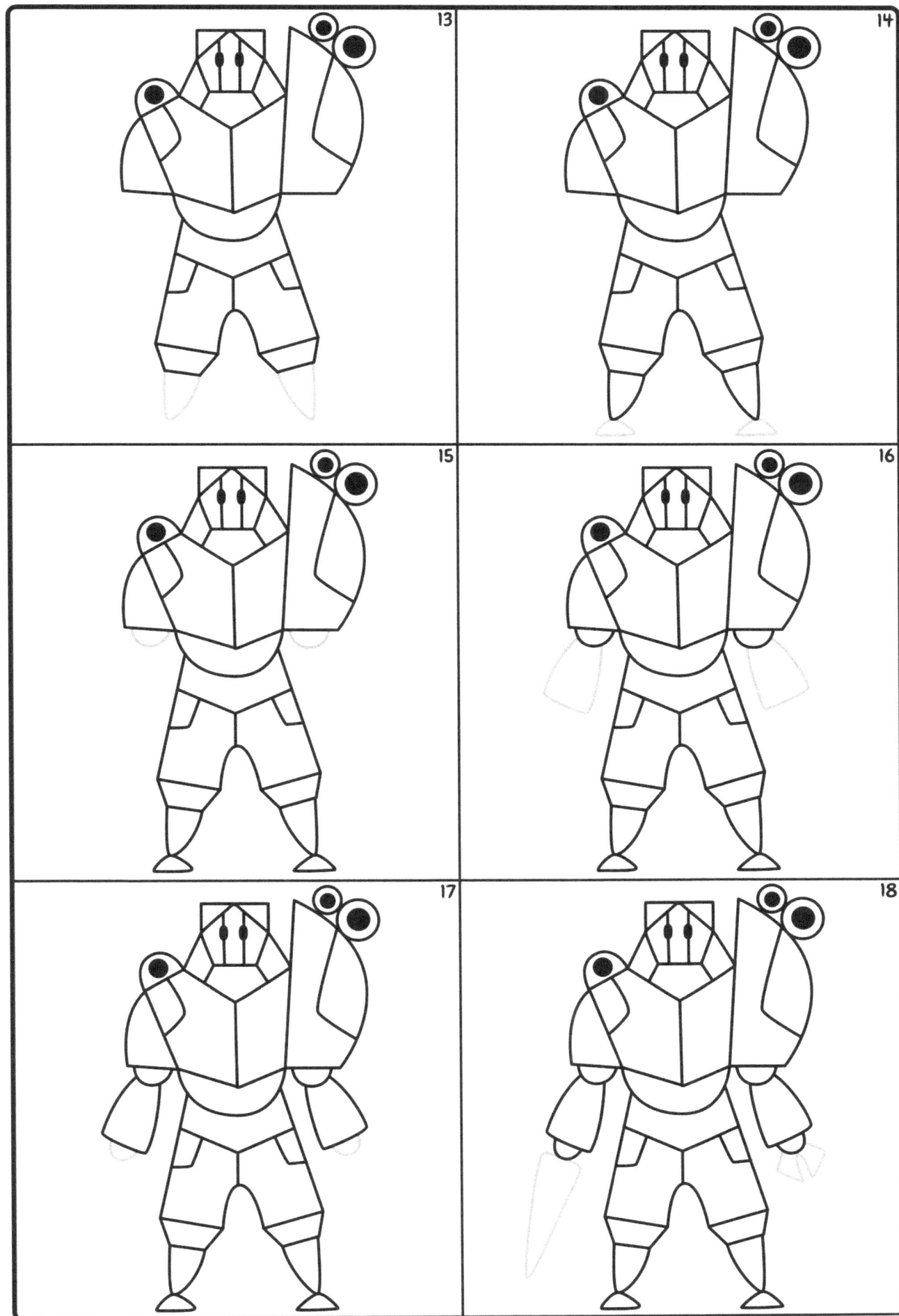

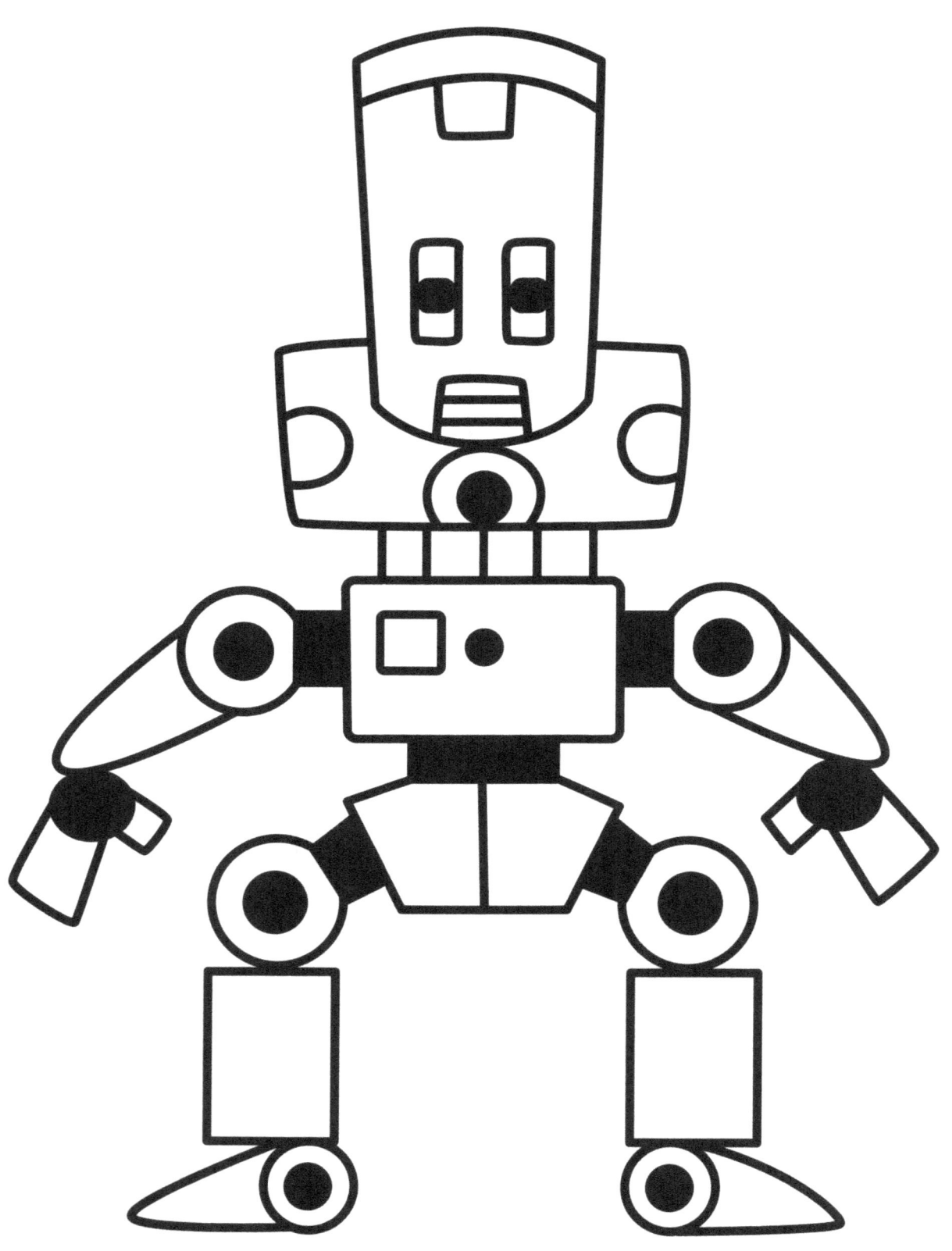

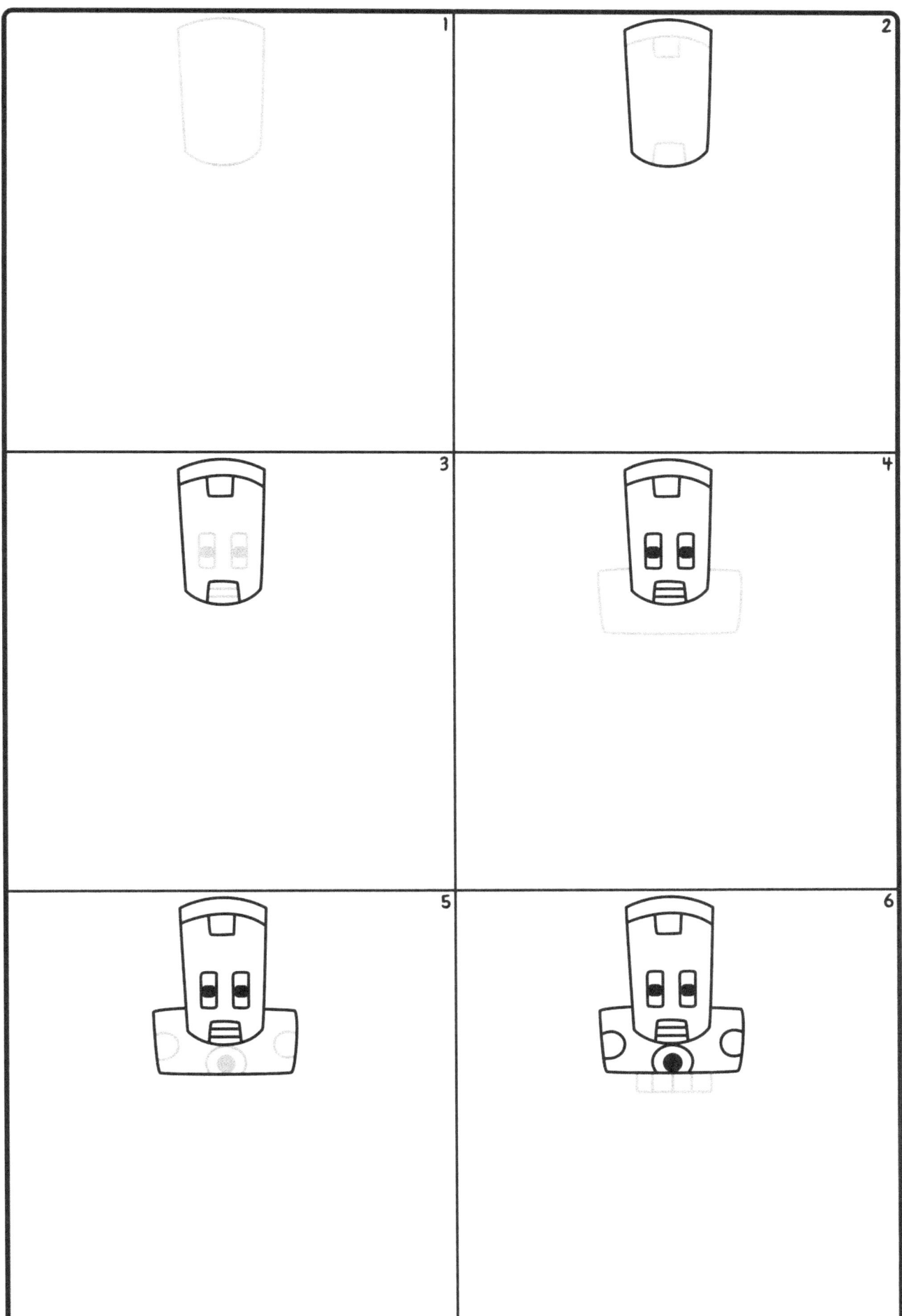

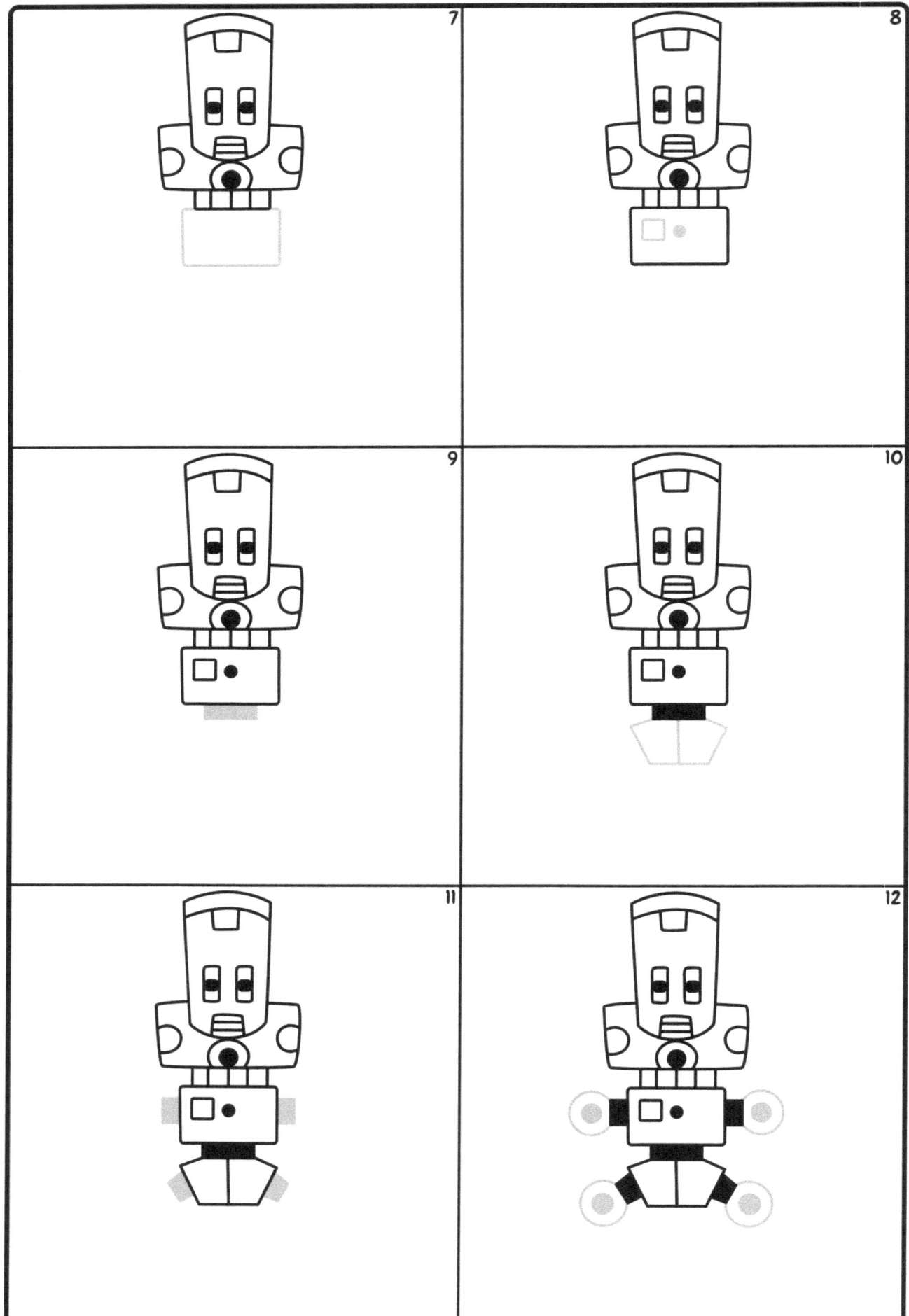

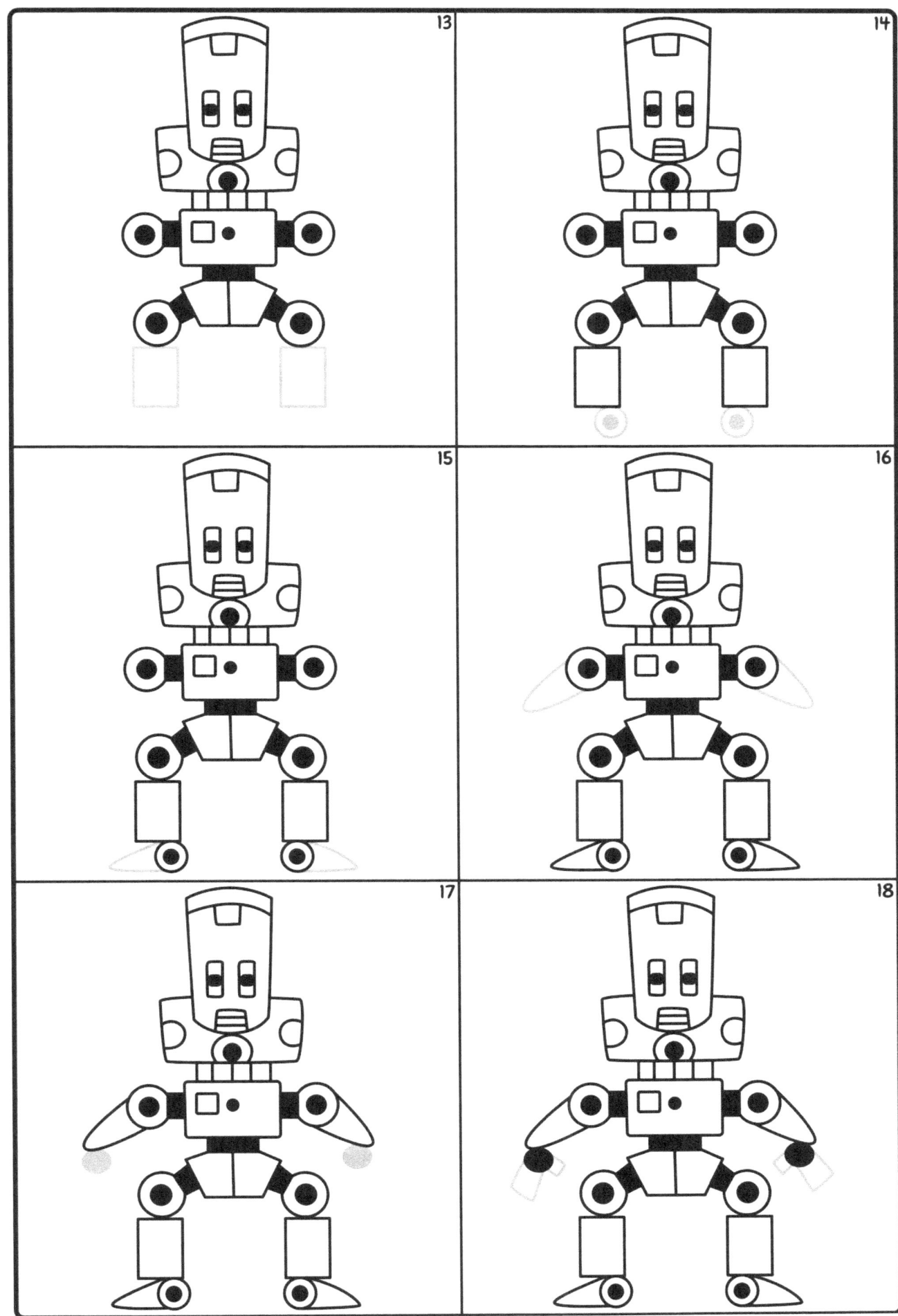

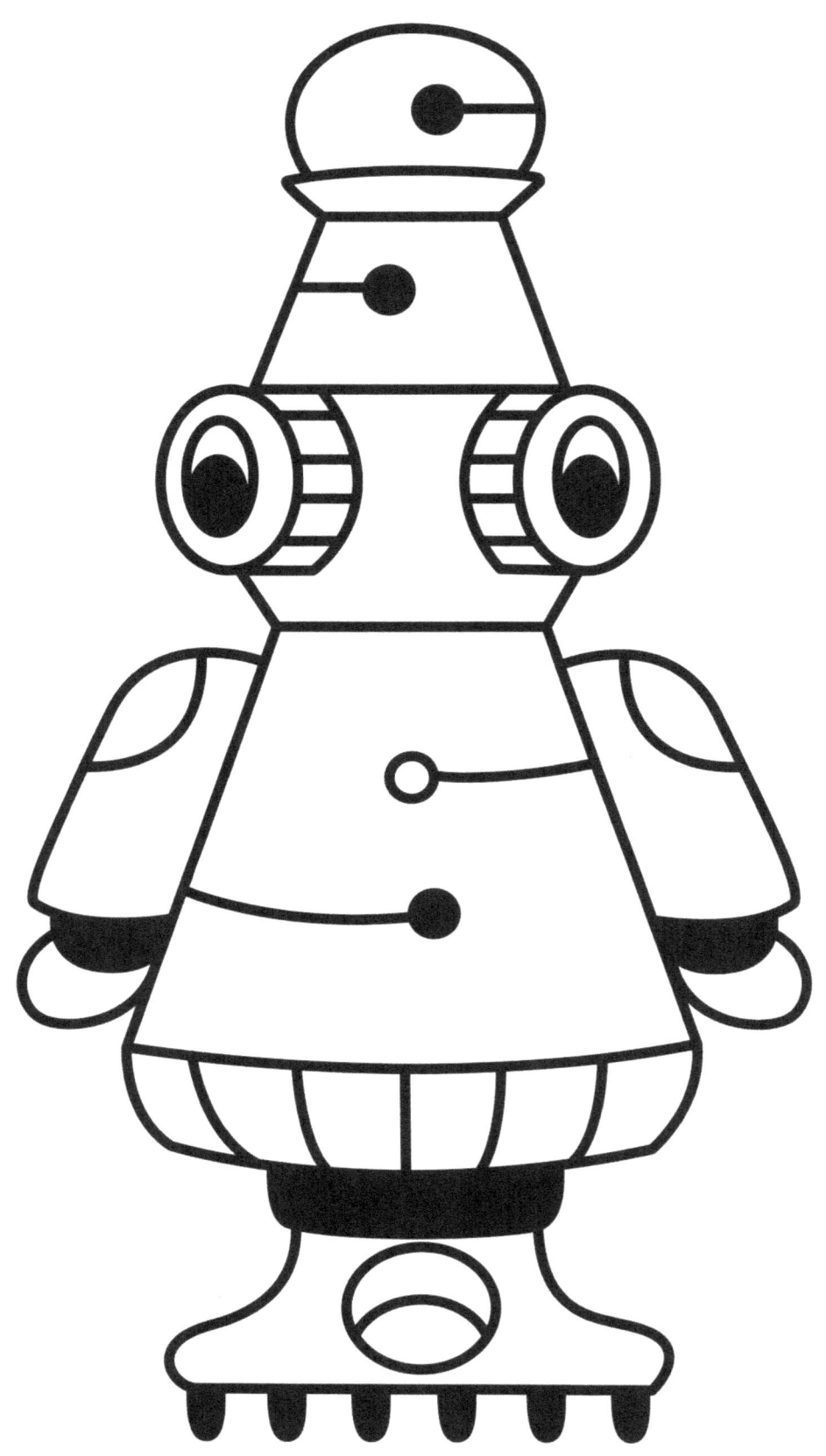

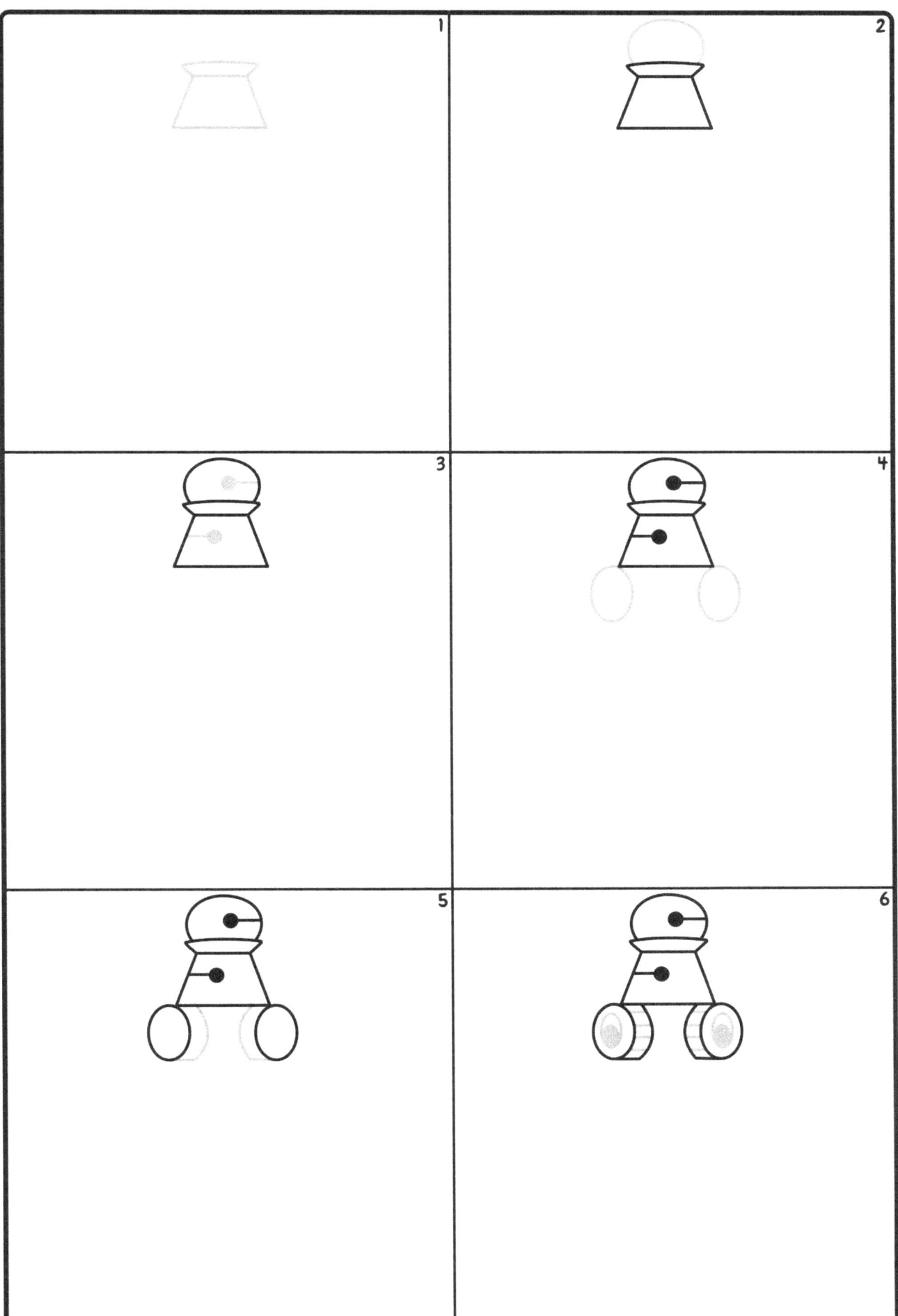

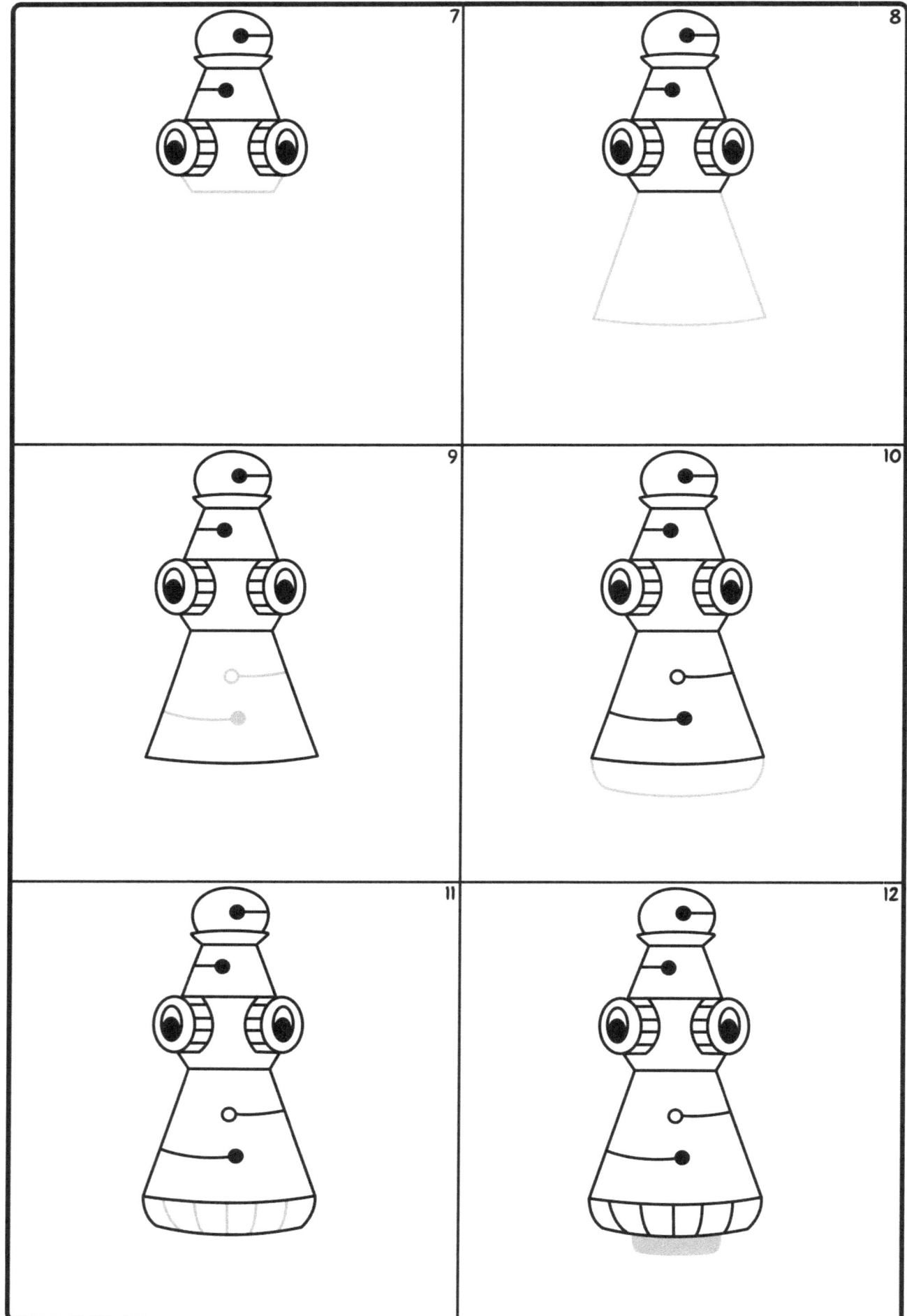

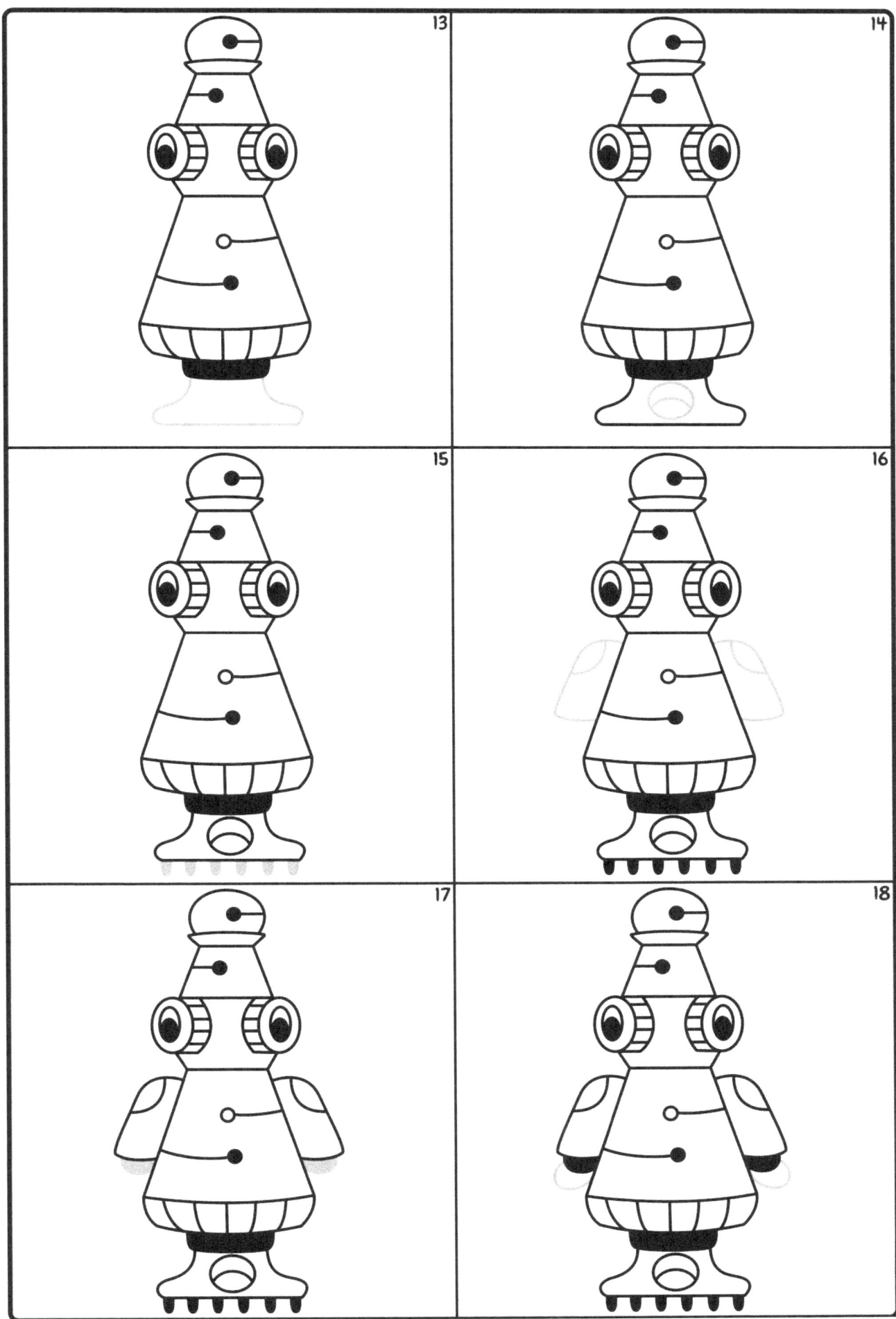

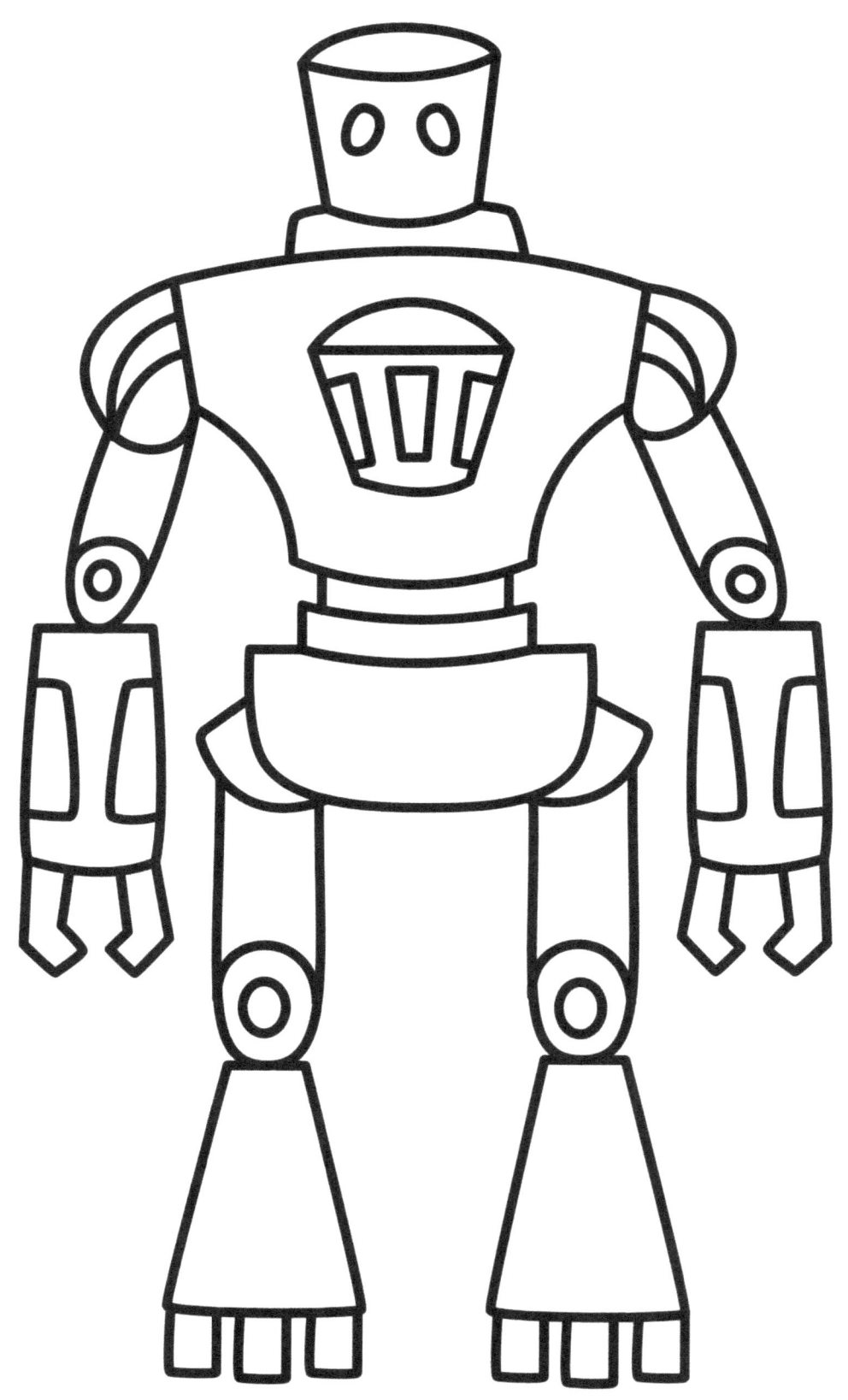

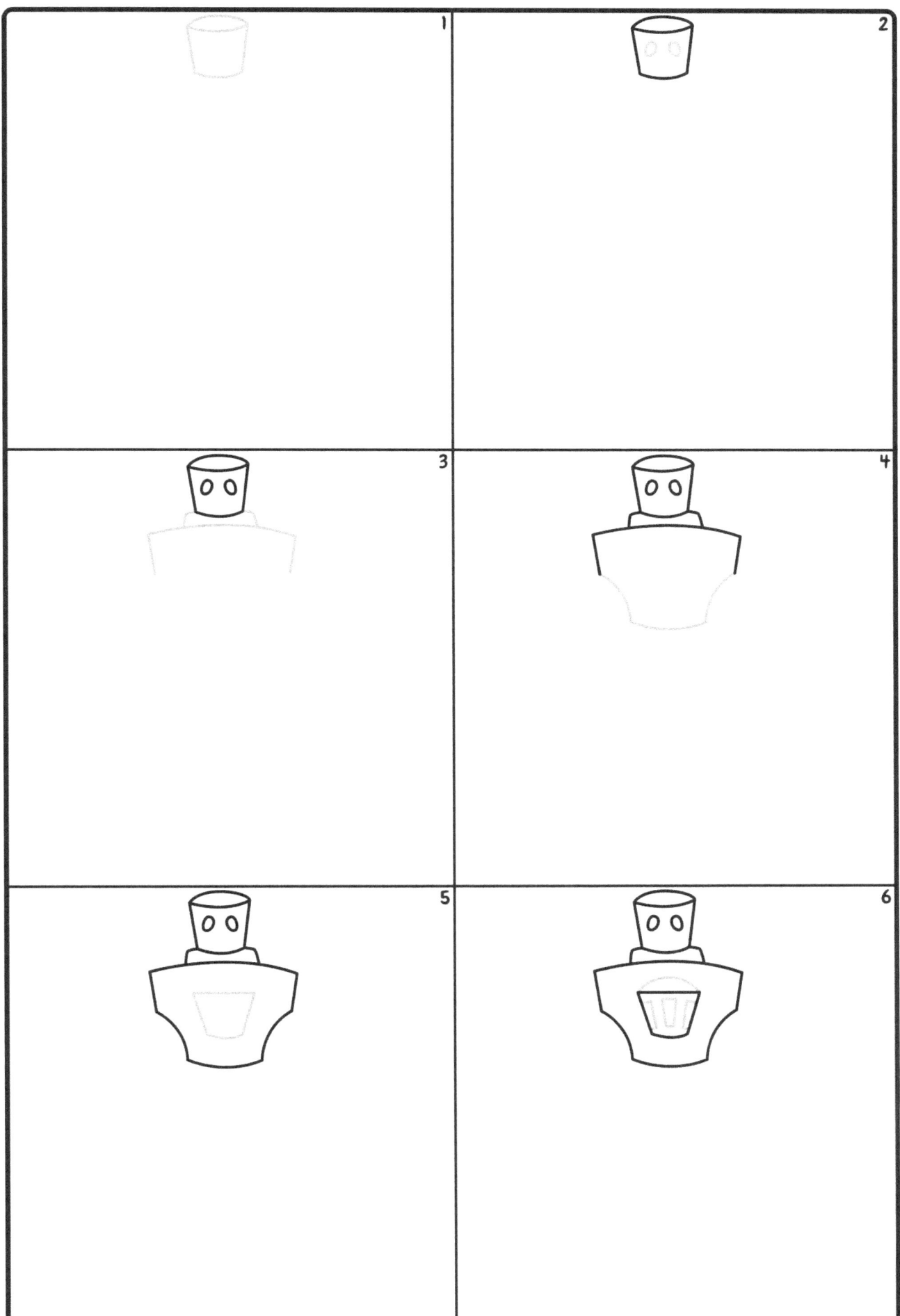

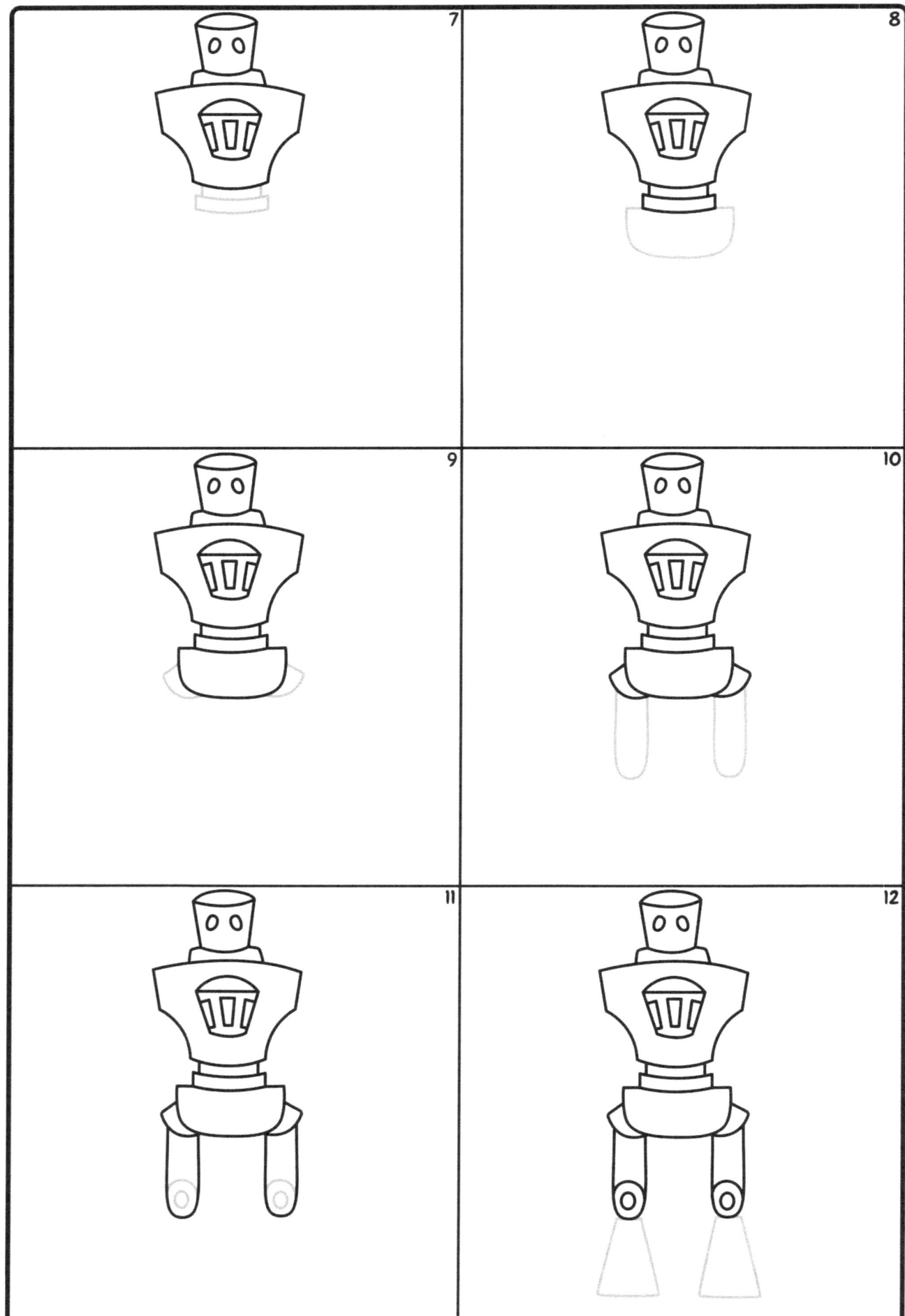

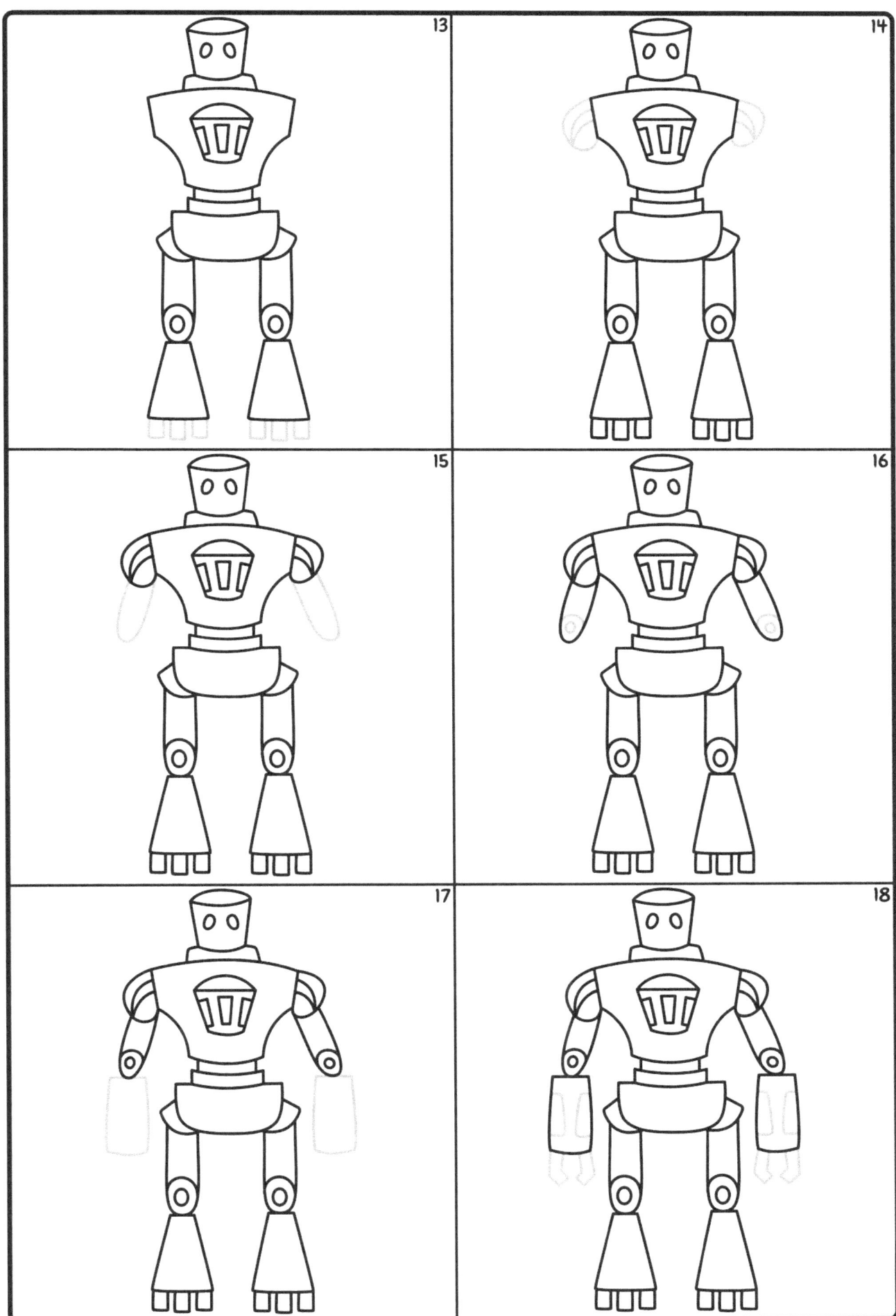

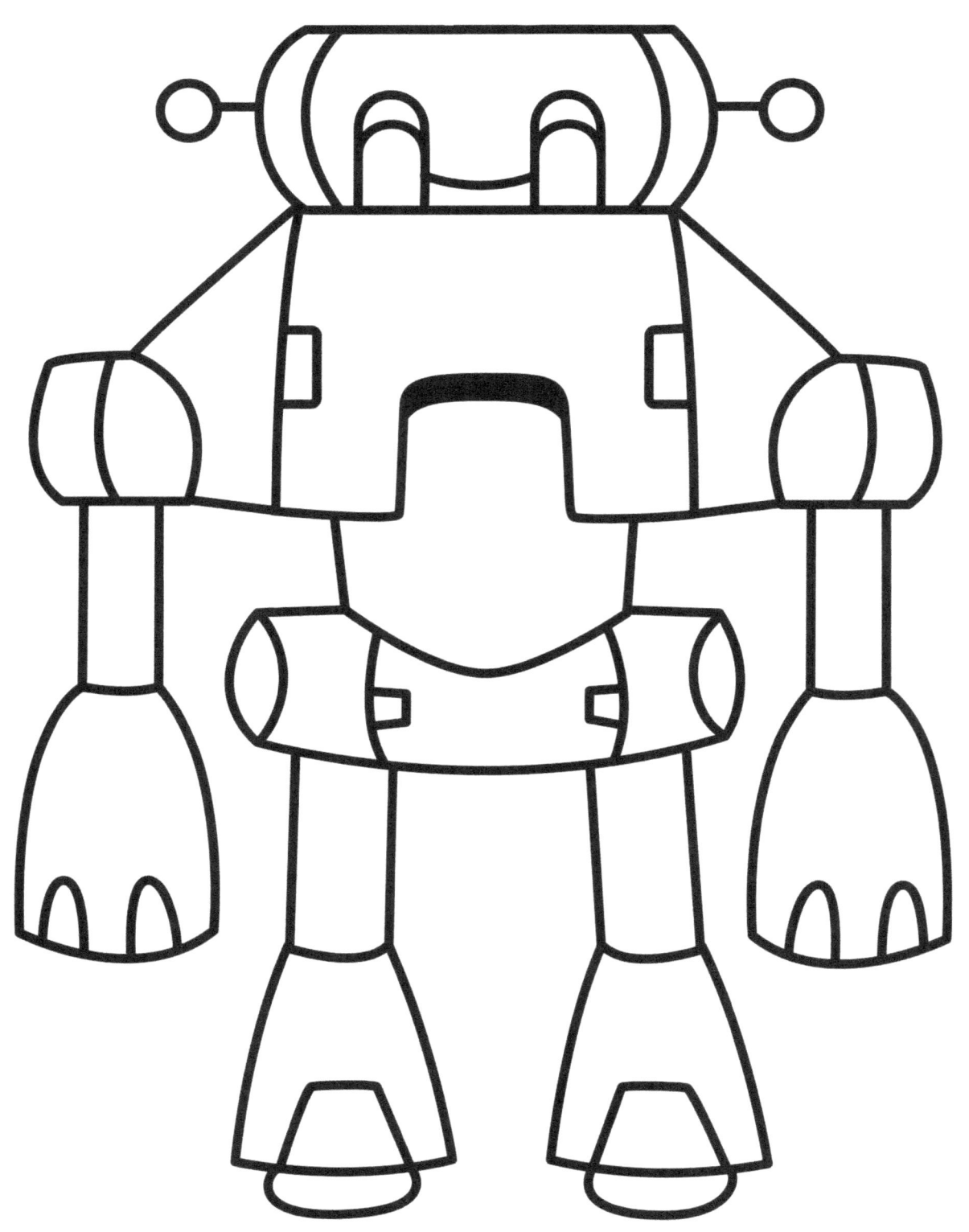

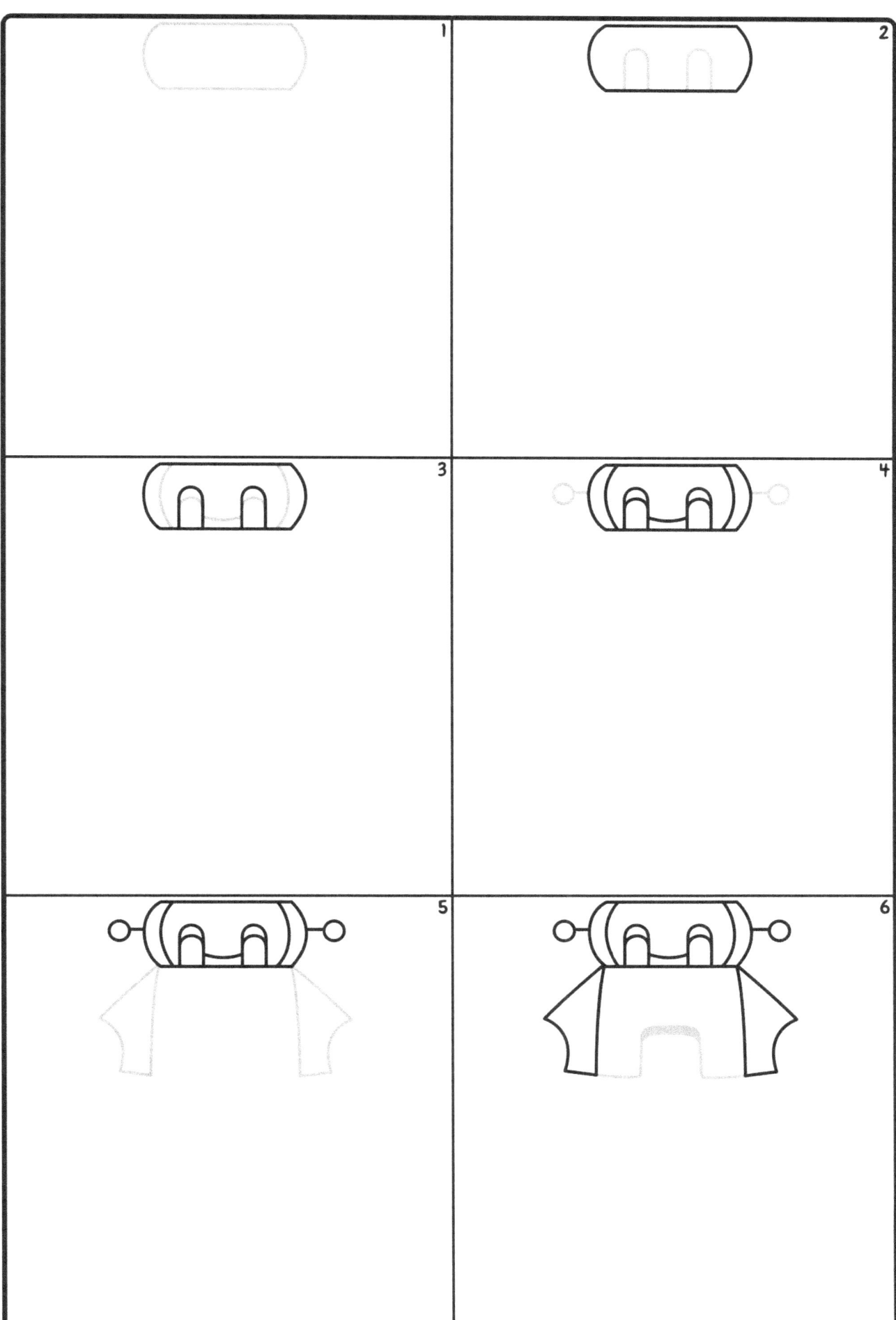

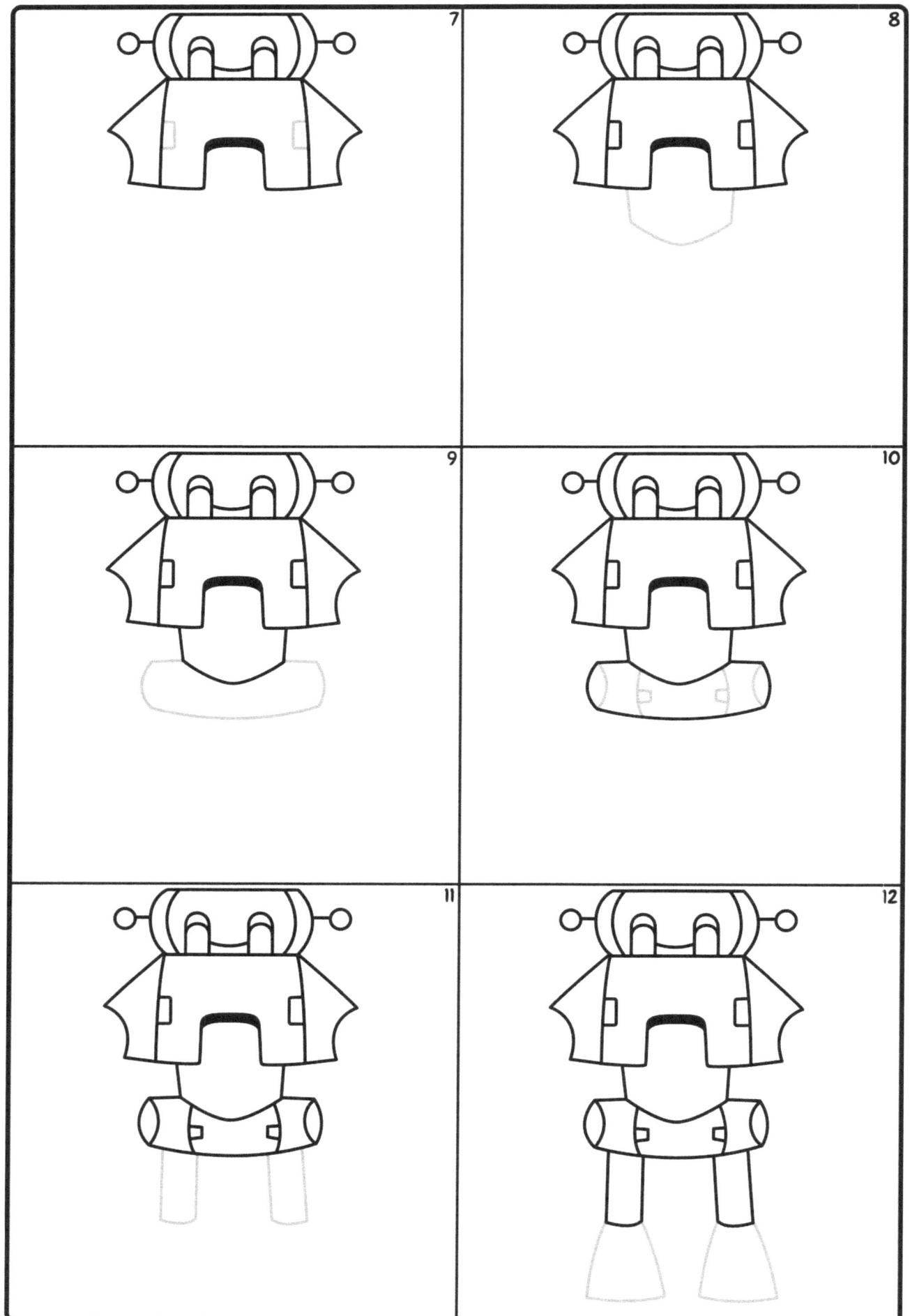

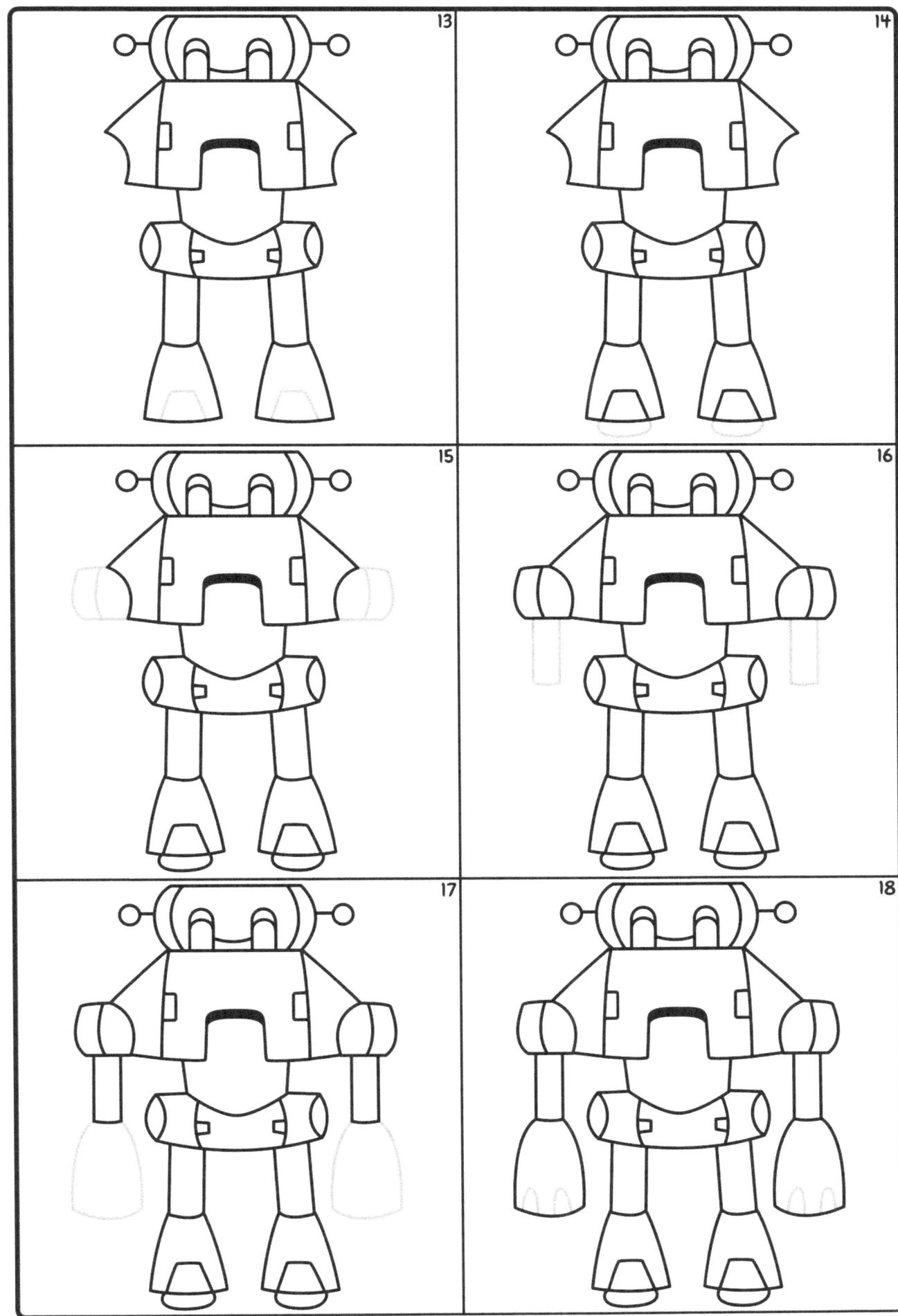

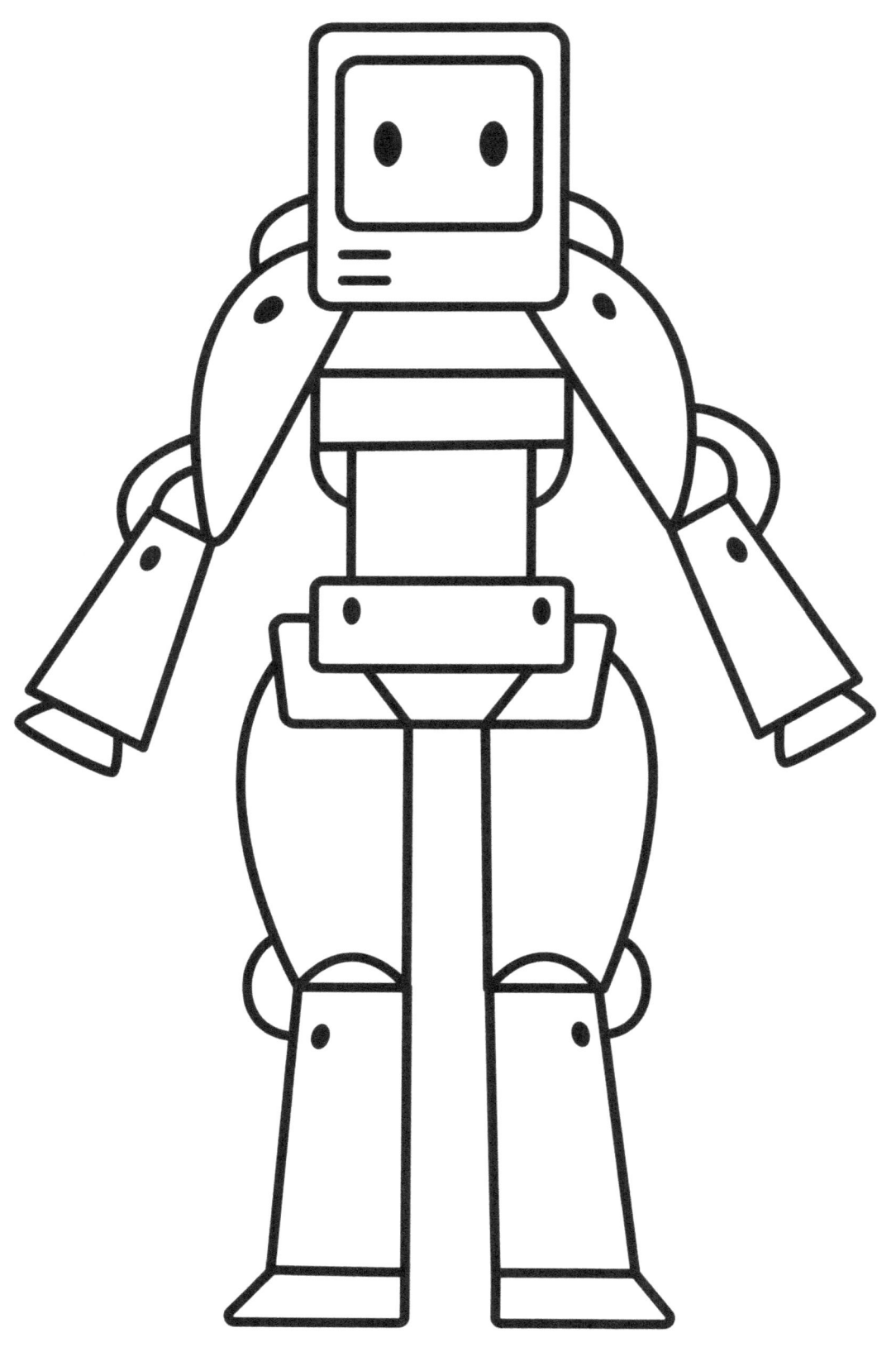

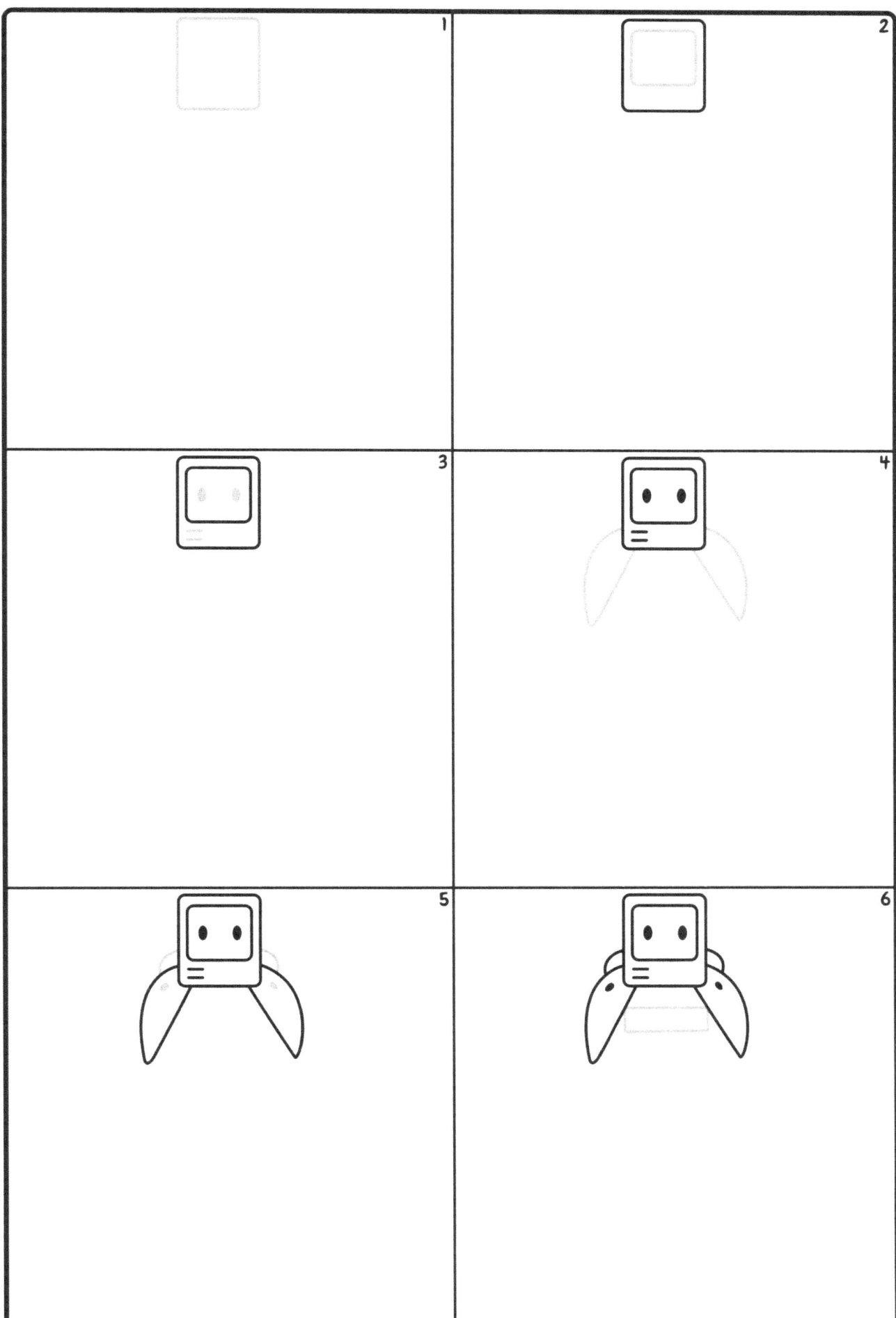

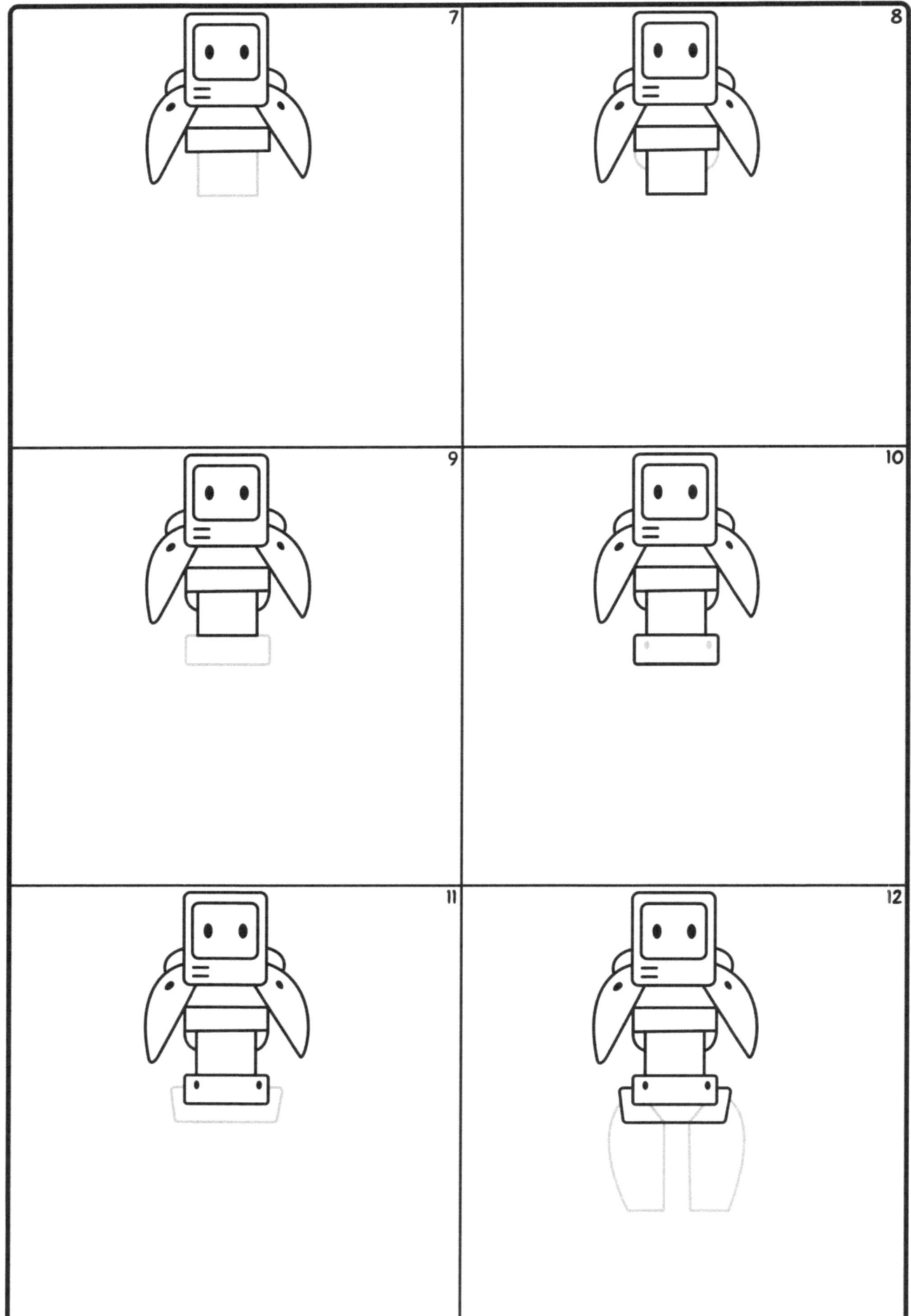

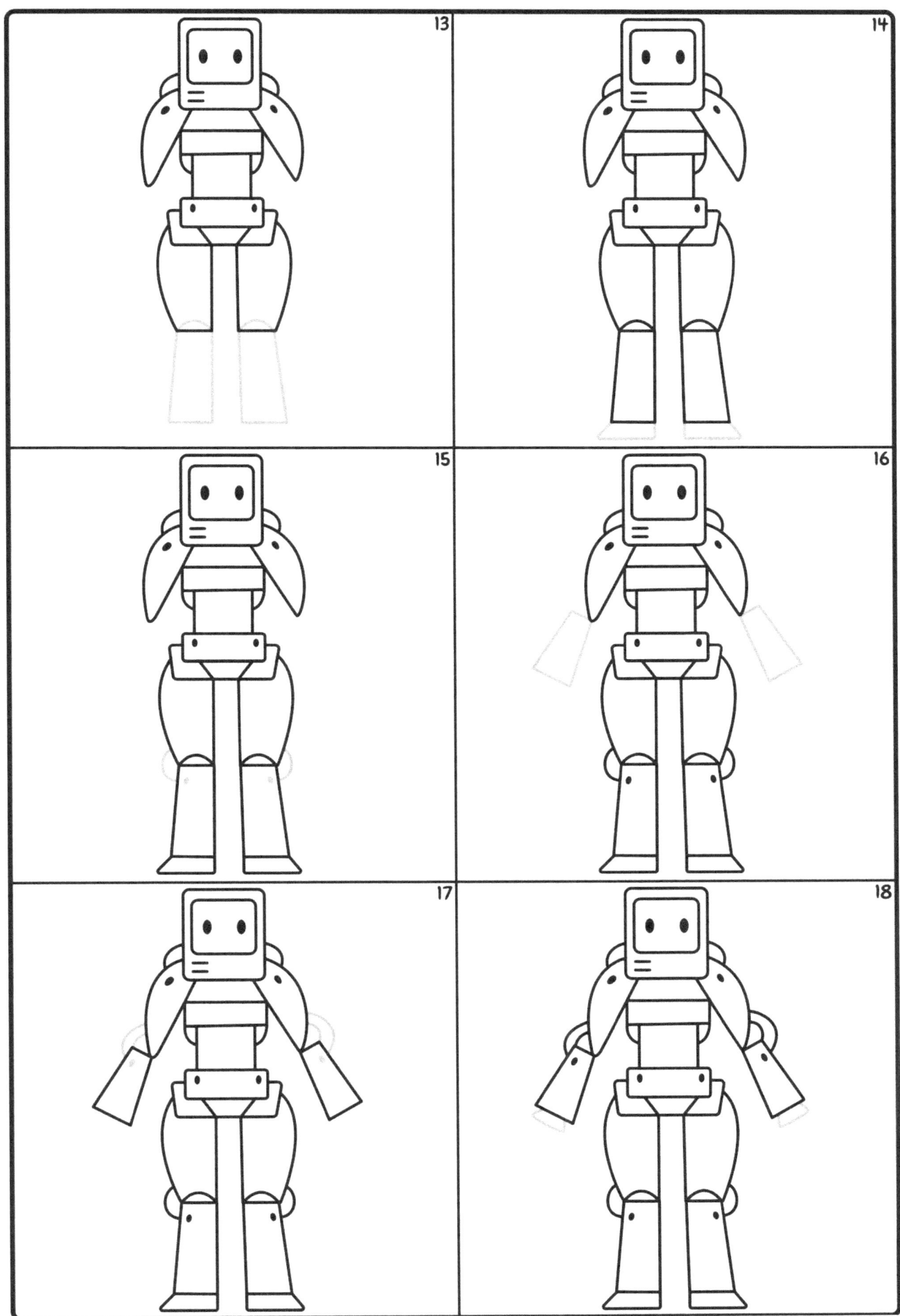

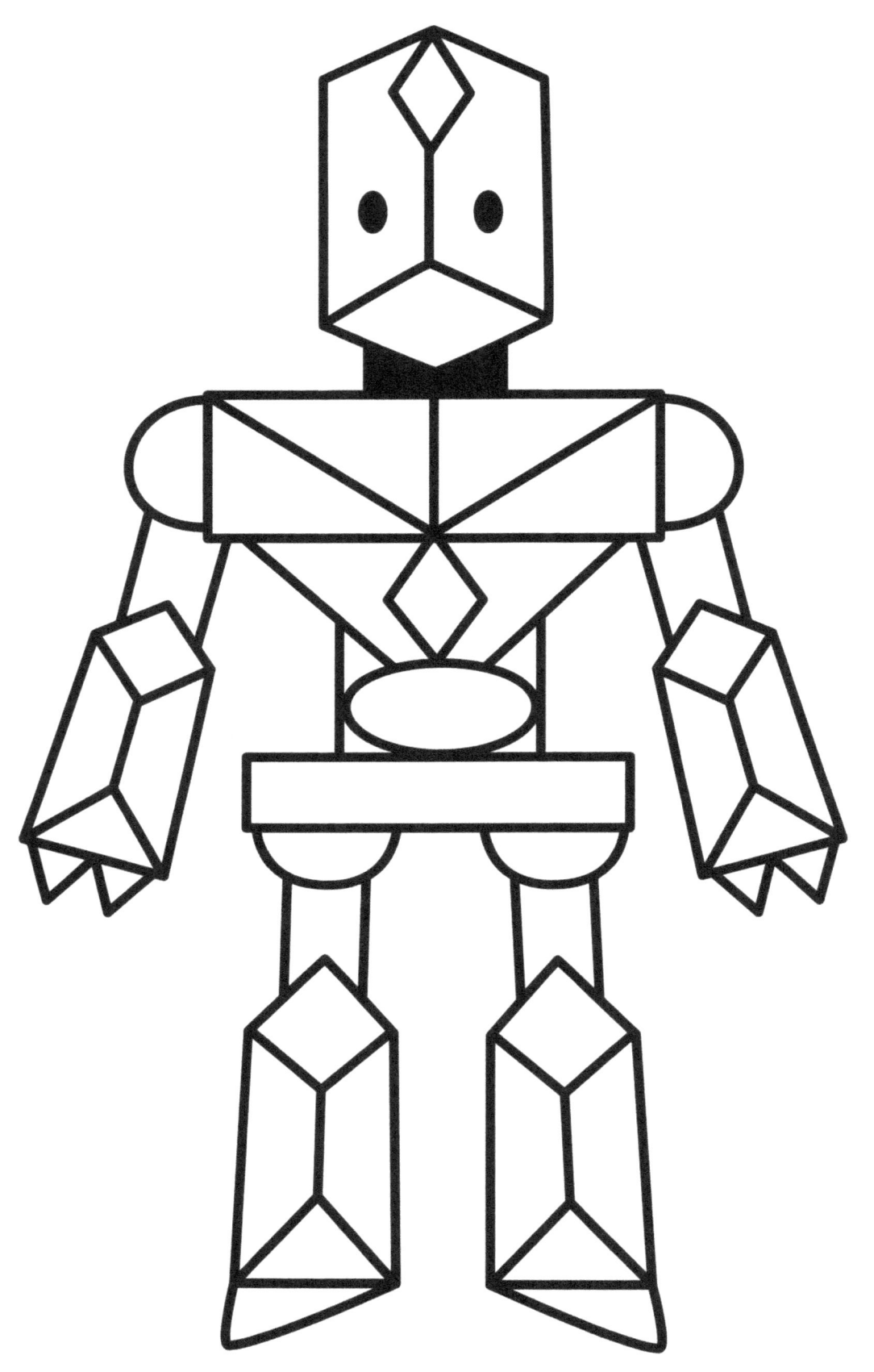

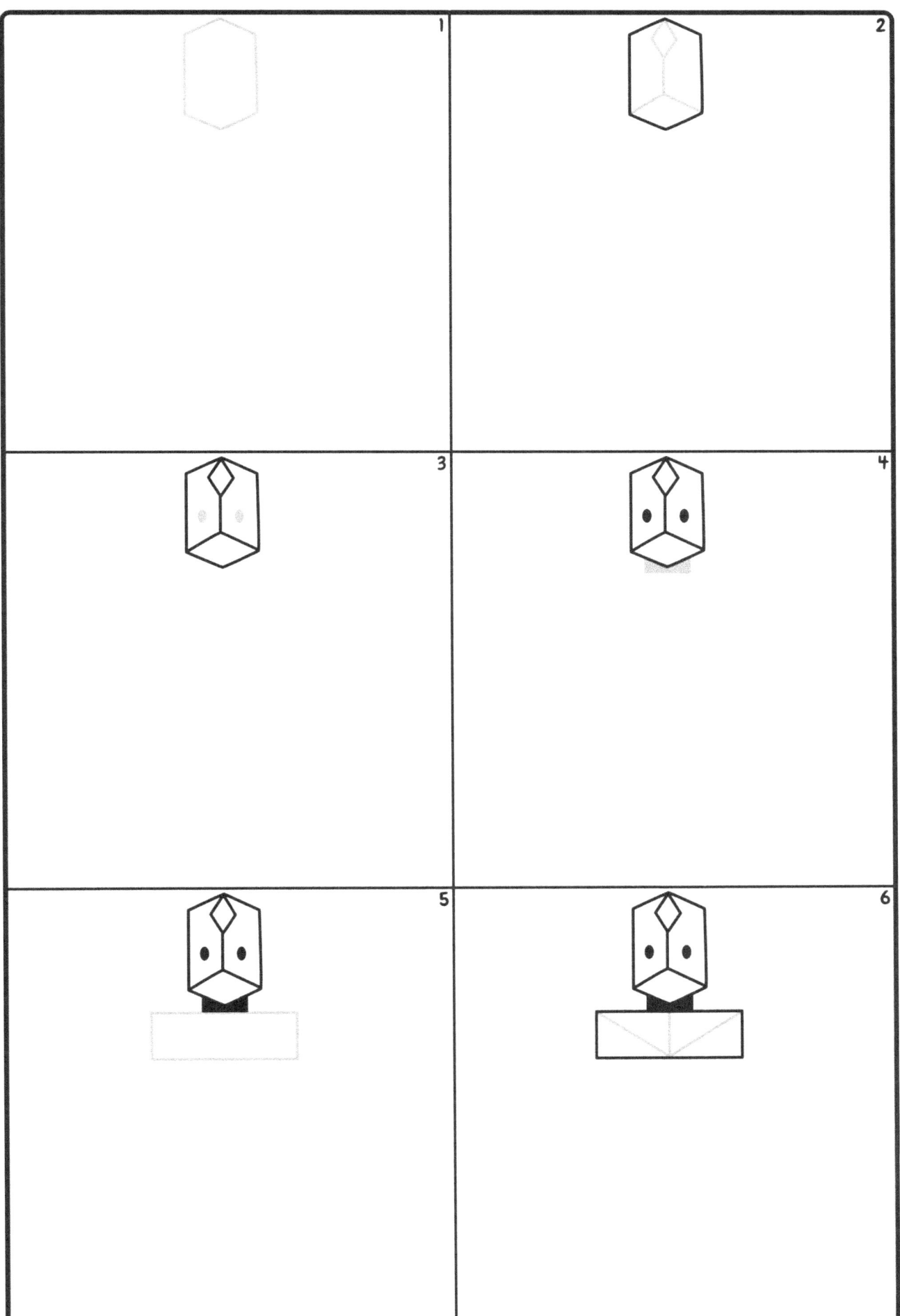

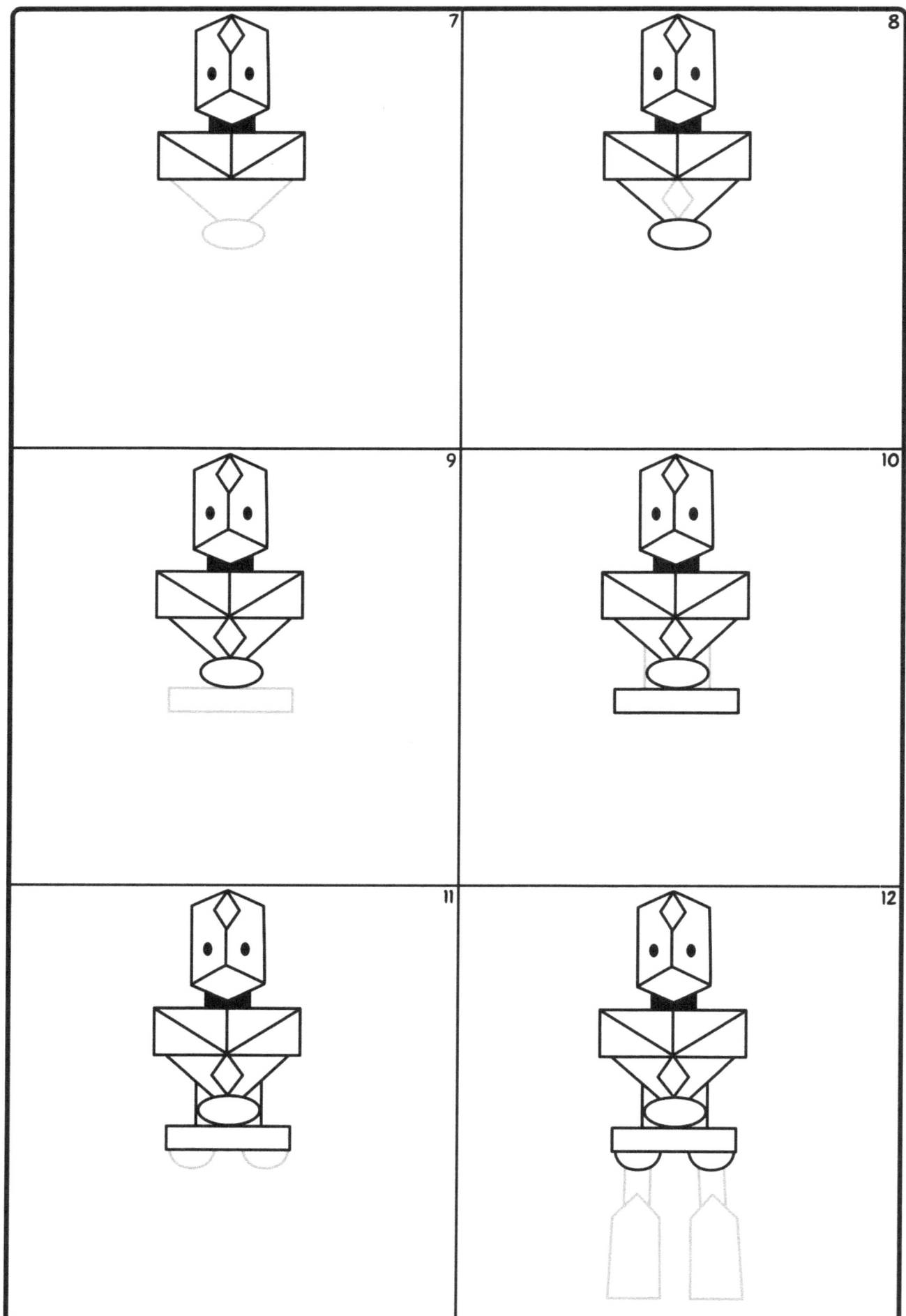

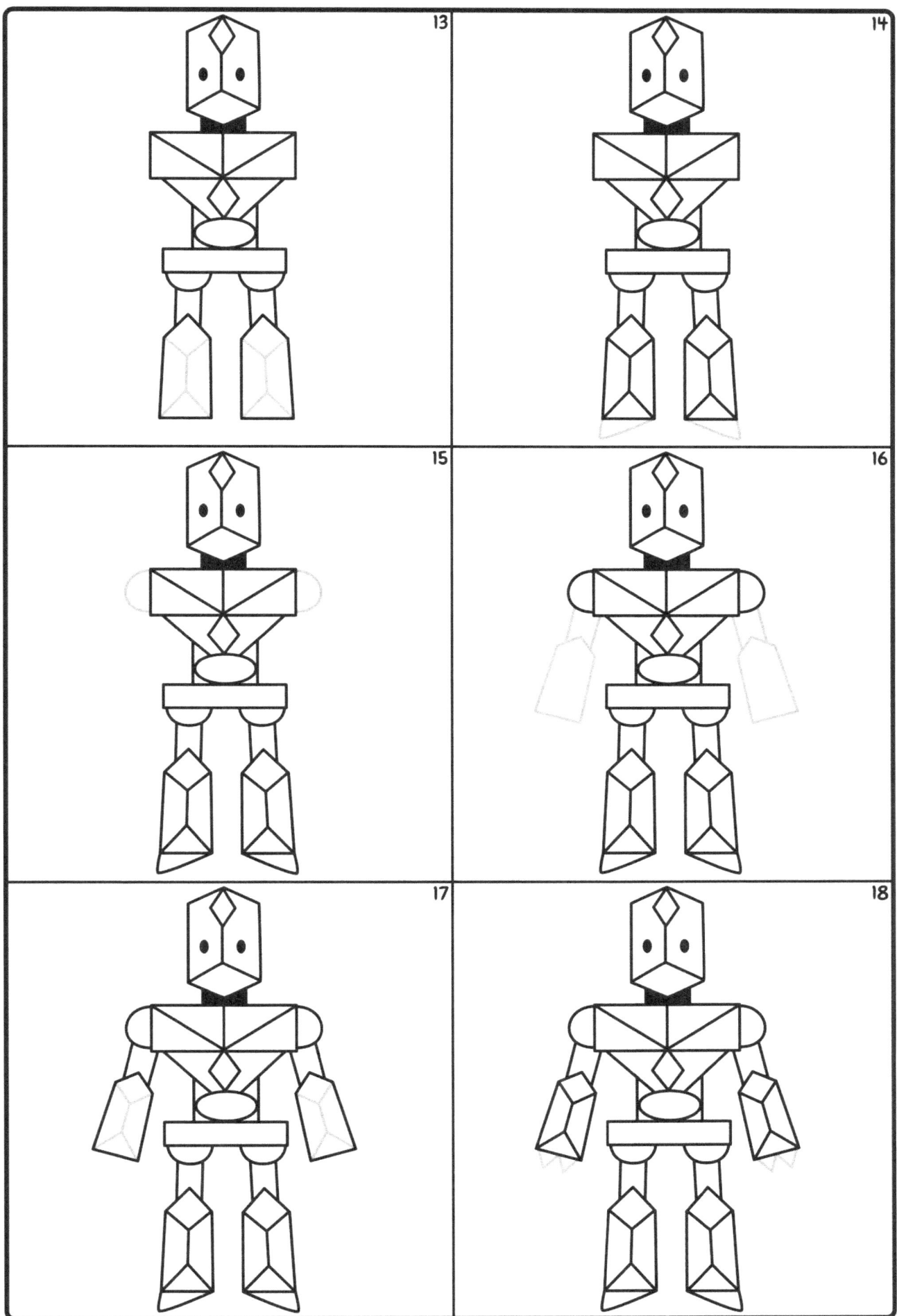

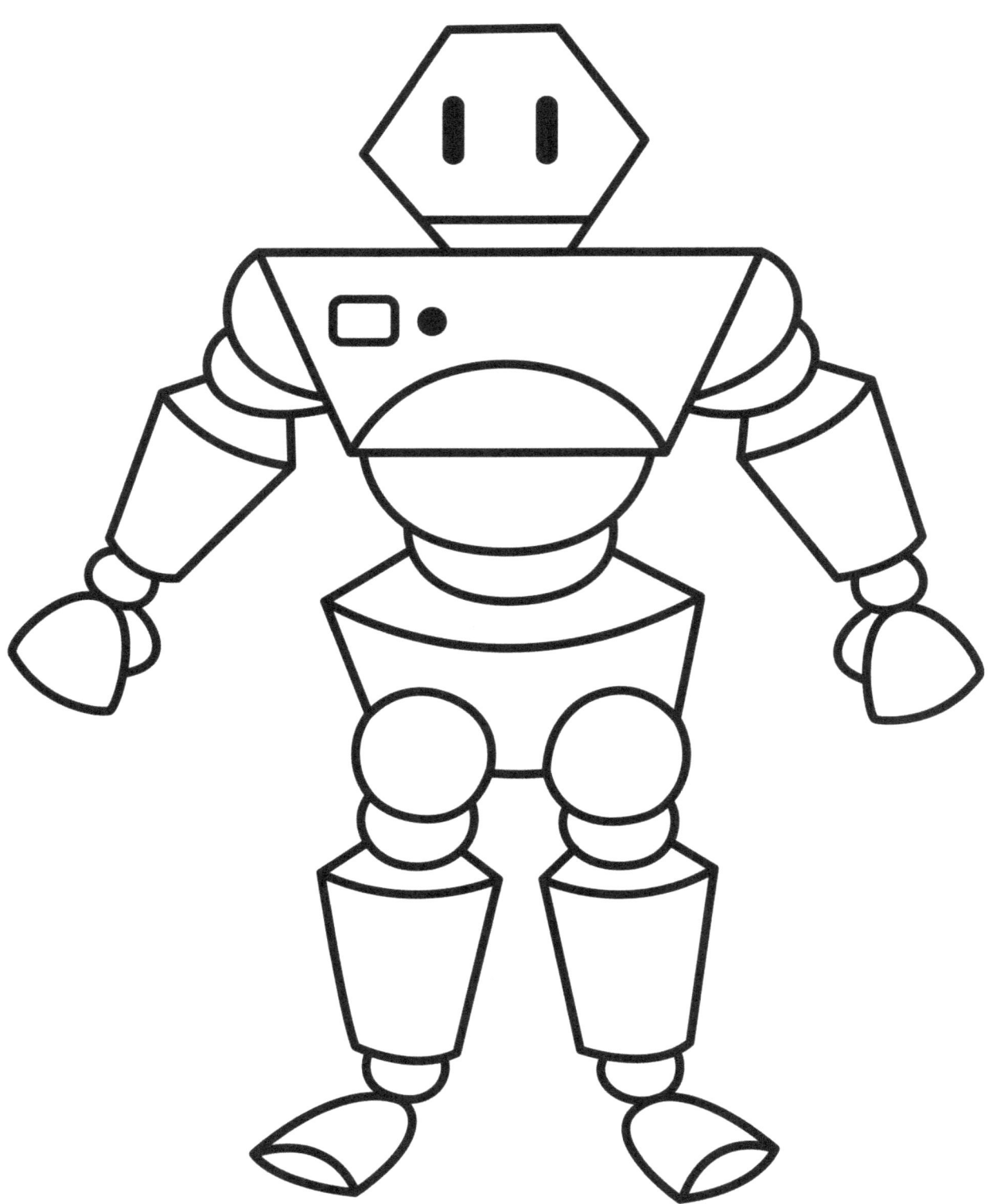

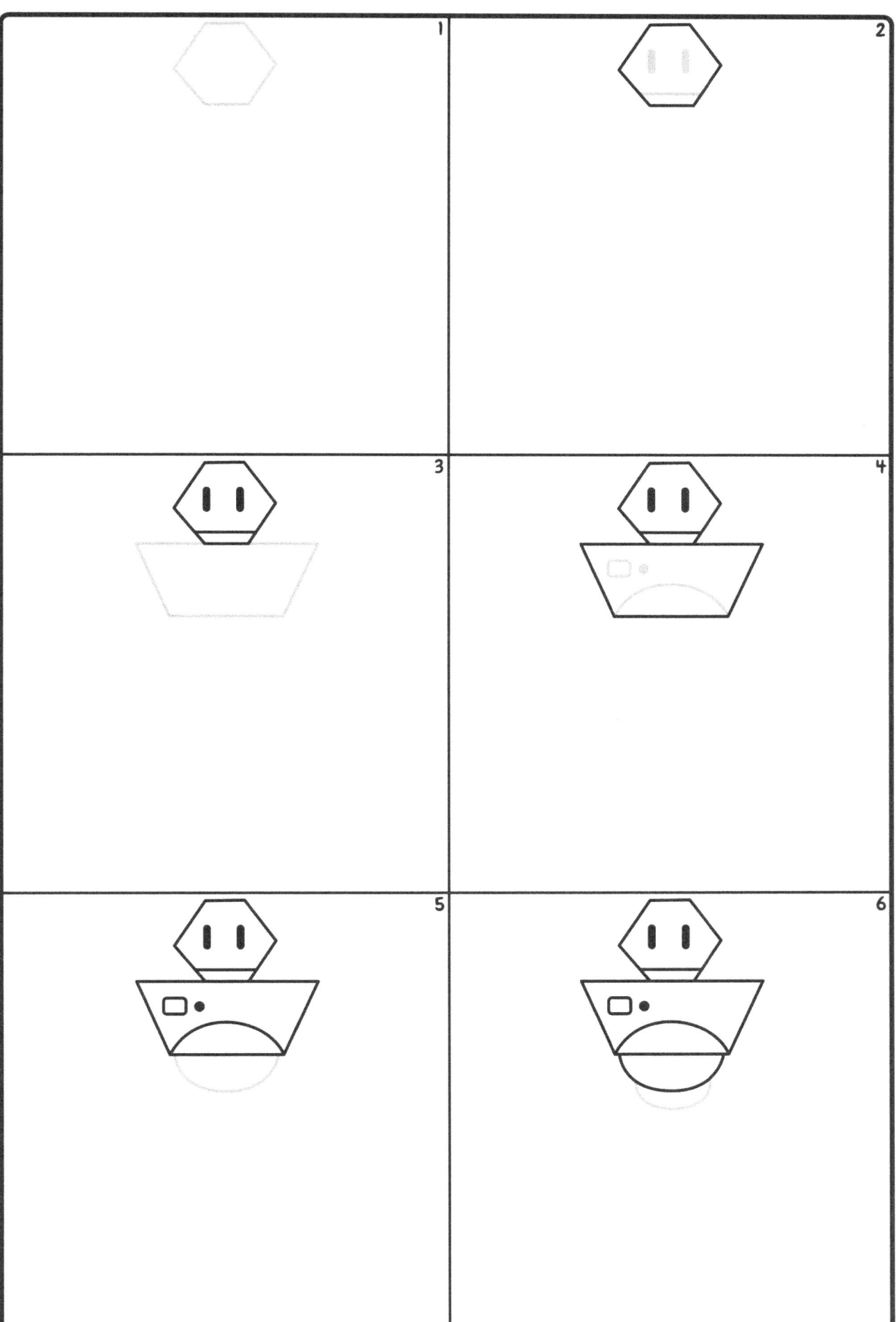

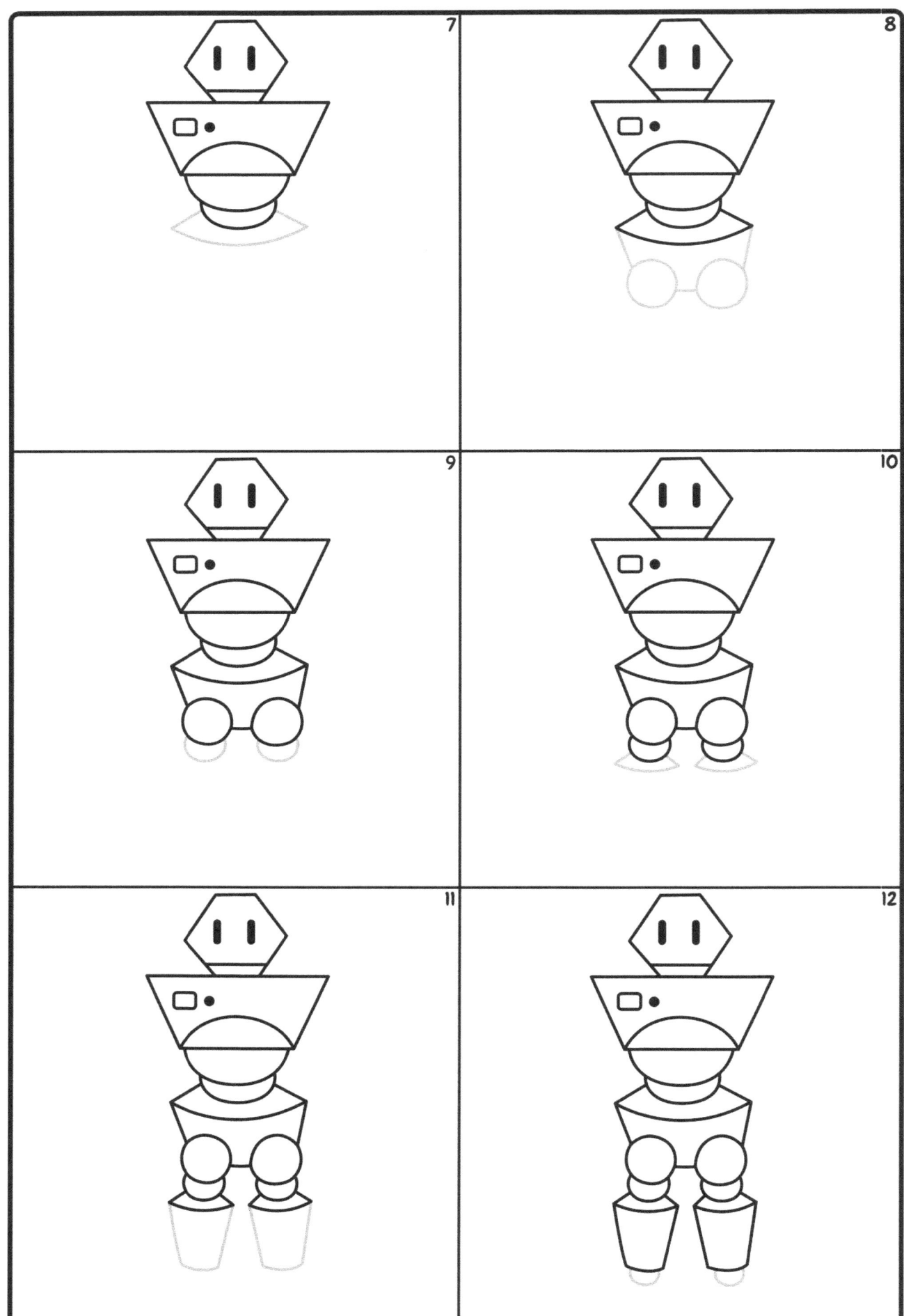

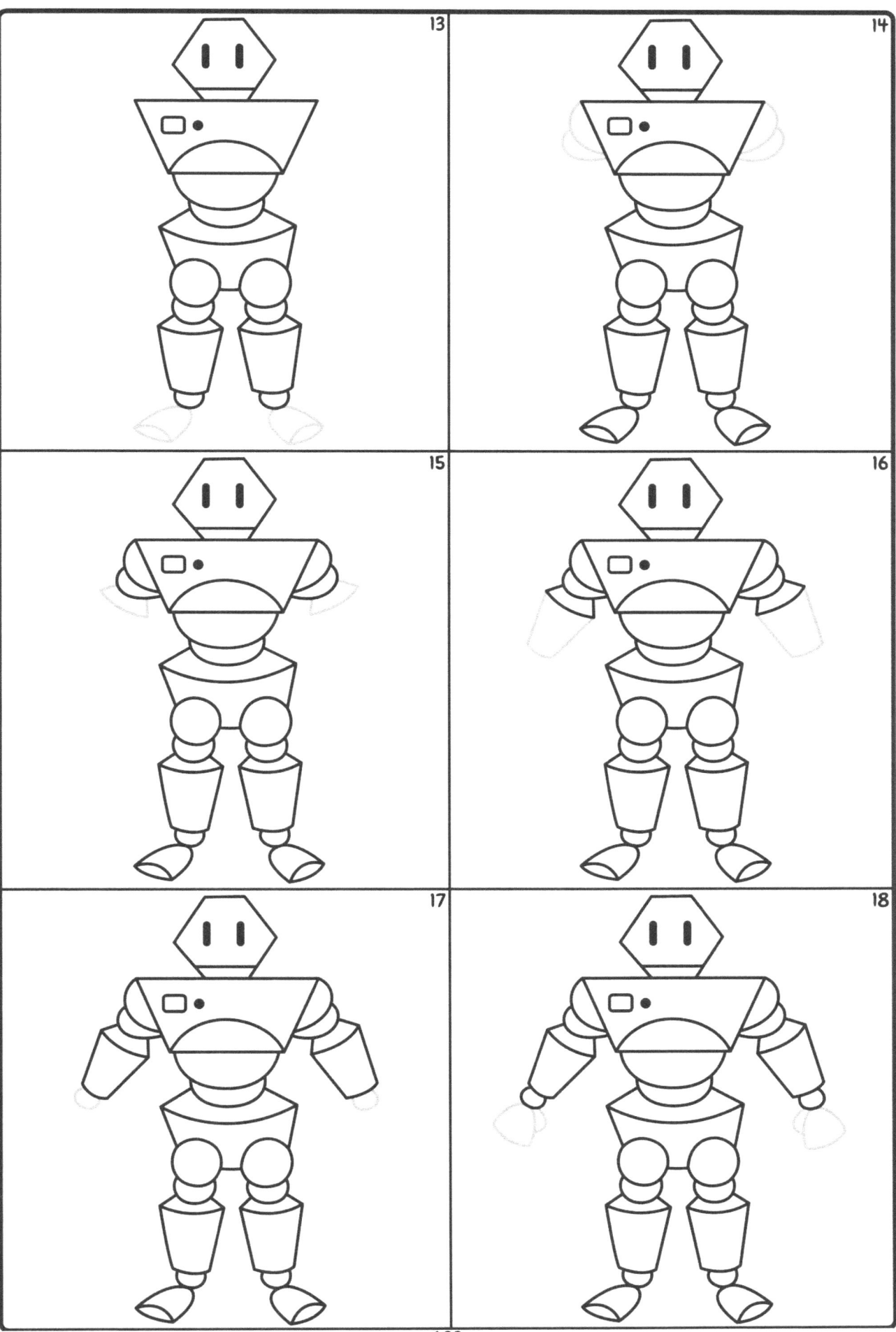

www.ingramcontent.com/pod-product-compliance
Lightning Source LLC
Chambersburg PA
CBHW080503220526
45465CB00006B/2361